TIBET

TIBET

A History Between Dream and Nation State

P. CHRISTIAAN KLIEGER

REAKTION BOOKS

Published by
REAKTION BOOKS LTD
Unit 32, Waterside
44–48 Wharf Road
London N1 7UX, UK
www.reaktionbooks.co.uk

First published 2021
Copyright © P. Christiaan Klieger 2021

Printed and bound in India by Replika Press Pvt. Ltd

A catalogue record for this book is available from the British Library

ISBN 978 1 78914 402 4

Contents

Notes on Transliterations

TIBETAN ORTHOGRAPHY PRESENTS a particularly difficult problem in transliteration to the Roman alphabet. This is primarily because the Tibetan spelling is usually vastly different from how it is now spoken, especially in the standard Lhasa dialect. Since 1959, the system derived by Turrell Wylie has been widely used to capture the exact spelling of most Tibetan words, but not its modern sound. The Wylie system is also problematic in transliterating foreign words continually entering the Tibetan language, such as those from Sanskrit. In order to deal with the Wylie inadequacies, under the leadership of Nathaniel Grove and David Germano, the Tibetan and Himalayan Library at the University of Virginia (THL) has developed an Extended Wylie Tibetan System (EWTS) that provides for the use of the standard Latin keyboard for a more comprehensive facility to transliterate Tibetan. An equal consideration is that the lay reader should have some idea how the Tibetan words sound. Germano and Nicolas Tournadre have similarly provided the THL Simplified Tibetan Phonetic Transliteration (2003), which is useful here.

In the People's Republic of China ZYPY, or Tibetan pinyin, is used to transliterate Tibetan into a Roman alphabet similar to that used in standard Chinese pinyin. However, it generally does not capture the sound of modern Tibetan language accurately and is not often used in the scholarly world outside of China.

In this work, I use a modified THL phonetic rendering for terms and proper names, followed by the Wylie transliteration in parentheses for the more significant proper names and terms. Some well-known names are rendered as these individuals have been generally known in the Western press.

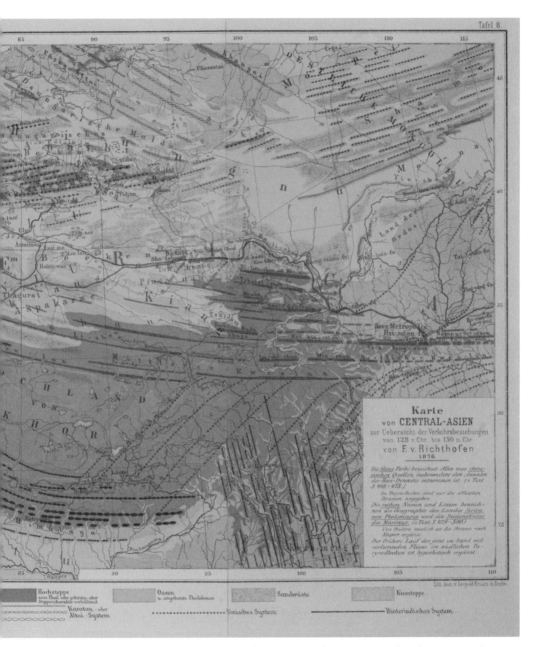

Ferdinand von Richthofen, 'Map of Central Asia for Overview of Trade Routes and Movements from 128 BC to 150 AD', 1876.

Introduction

The history of Tibet has long fascinated the world, along with the present controversy about its future: will it ever be (again) an independent nation or will it remain part of China? Is the transnational Tibetan movement – a 'Tibet without Tibet' – a viable expression of self-determination? How will the succession of the ageing and revered Dalai Lama affect Tibet and the world? Will China's leadership continue to be intransigent on the 'Tibetan question'? These are some of the questions to be examined in this work, questions of ideals, legitimacy and nationalism in the still-evolving Tibetan state.

As this book takes a look into the future of Tibet, it also must deal with the past. Tibet is an idea, or several ideas that people have articulated throughout time. These views have formed the Tibetan state throughout history and will inform the future. Considering that ideas of Tibet have been around for 2,500 years and the success of Tibetan refugee settlements abroad, Tibetans can be considered a most persistent people.

There are two themes involved in the problematics of the Tibetan state: first, interpretation of the Tibetan state and its status vis-à-vis its neighbours is grounded in widely divergent historiographic paradigms. China, India and the West all tend to look at Tibet according to their own perspectives, which seem at times radically different to indigenous ones. The Chinese perspective has been particularly intractable. The modern Chinese state views Tibet as having been an integral part of China for centuries, beginning as early as Tibet's affiliation with the Mongol Empire that had also conquered China proper. However, this is the language of the victors. As noted by Christine Sleeter, 'researchers from dominant social groups have a long history of producing "knowledge" about oppressed groups that legitimates their subordination.'[1]

The paradigmatic dissonance is the heart of the 'Tibet question' on the world stage. The process of self-determination among Tibetan peoples is as active now as it was in the past. It is the mechanism that creates the Tibetan nation. As an active affiliation, nationalism does not always rely upon historic facts in creating a nexus with which a people may identify. The nation-building process often happens through the agency of the imagination; it is not necessarily dependent upon historical precedent, the judgments of international law or the Chinese central government. 'Real' Tibet is somewhere between the dream and the cold reality of the nation state as defined by nineteenth-century European state formation.

'Tibet' has been a concept for the Tibetans for at least 2,500 years. To describe the Tibetan state solely as either a remote polity on the margins of empire (common in Western historiography) or a local administration of an outer province (most 'official' Chinese state histories) is to fail to do justice to its indigenous statecraft. Tibetan nationalism is real, although often difficult to chart. The essential part of the current deadlocked issue is that modern Tibetans often lack a shared sense of political community with the Chinese state.

Summarizing Tibetan chronology from its first flickers of coalescence as a state to the modern era is also a difficult task. But the main premise of this book is that Tibet was a fully independent state for much of its existence. It was a great empire from the seventh to ninth centuries; in 1249 it became a territory of the Mongol Empire of Genghis Khan, a realm that annexed China itself in 1279. Tibet reclaimed its independence from the Mongols in 1349, and from China in 1368. Despite Ming propaganda stating otherwise, Tibet functioned as a completely independent entity until the mid-Qing dynasty (mid-eighteenth century), when the Manchus began to exert their direct influence in Tibetan affairs through the appointment of resident high commissioners (*amban*) and mandating the use of a golden urn to decide the identities of succeeding high lamas. By 1840, the Qing dynasty was weakening its grip, and Tibet began to resume its independent course. Except for a brief period of occupation by provincial Sichuan troops in the last years of the Manchu imperium (1908–11) when the Thirteenth Dalai Lama sought exile in India, the Tibetan government exercised effective control over Tibet as a free state. It extended recognition with newly independent Mongolia in 1914. Tibet remained an independent polity until Communist China invaded in 1950. Since that time, Tibetan nationalism has been maintained primarily by over 100,000 refugees living abroad and by homeland Tibetans who risk their livelihoods and lives by perceived 'splitist' actions.

This book examines the history of Tibet, with a particular interest in deeply enduring political and religious structures, such as rule by reincarnation and the so-called priest–patron relationship between religious prelates and secular supporters. These structures of the *longue durée* can illustrate a framework upon which the concept of an ideal Tibetan state has been formulated throughout time. They are the foundation of a unique national idea that has endured for many centuries, one that continues to provide support for Tibetan national identity in the refugee diaspora and in the occupied homeland itself. These ideals are the primary foil against the goals of assimilation promulgated by the modern Chinese state.

The Tibet issue is not a geopolitical triviality: the question of whether the People's Republic of China has the right to annex and rule Tibet underpins the legitimacy of the Central Committee of the Communist Party's mandate to rule China itself. Each successive dynasty of China was traditionally judged as holding the 'Mandate of Heaven' through its demonstrated ability to expand the previous dynasty's territory. In the modern period, the People's Republic of China invaded neighbours such as Tibet to demonstrate its legitimacy over the Nationalists who never had control over the region.

For over two millennia Tibet has been developing a unique, complex, multifaceted culture. Beginning in the Neolithic and extending through the Iron Age and the first developments of state-level society, the people of the high-altitude plateau are neither Indian, nor Chinese, nor Mongolian, nor Persian, but have their own culture and ethnicity – although they have been influenced by all these neighbours and have, in turn, influenced them.

ONE

Bedrock

What was Tibet like two or three thousand years ago? It was surely a highly animated landscape. Spirits were ubiquitous – in the mountains, lakes, rocks and trees. Animistic Tibet was similar to ancient Shinto-constructed Japan or troll-encrusted Norway. Tibet was one of the myriads of pre-modern societies whose numinal experiences were intimately bound with the forces of nature: the sun on your back, the thunder ringing in your ears. Everything seemed to possess consciousness and natural phenomena were rudimentarily anthropomorphic. In this world of animation, people could be gods, gods could live in your teapot, and the dish could run away with the spoon. With deities and demons at every corner, ancient Tibetans were preoccupied with their propitiation or avoidance. The names of hundreds of spirits have come down to the present day, passing through two major introductions of an 'a-theist' Buddhism and several episodes of cultural persecution, a testament to the tenacity of the otherworldly in ancient Tibetan life. This is the mystic foundation of Tibet, a characteristic interpreted by sensitive, violet-perfumed Western Orientalists centuries later but basic to many foundation myths of the unique Tibetan landscape.

Many Western Orientalists are struck by a landscape that suggests an 'overwhelming sense of awe engendered by a wild, desolate, unimaginably strange place'.[1] Tibet could be Mars. Propitiating the gods of the crossroads by adding a rock to the cairn or doing the daily circumambulation (*bskor pa*) of sacred places may be as mundane to local inhabitants as visiting the neighbourhood food store in curlers may be to others. Nevertheless, numina and phenomena are close here. This preconception is important in imagining Tibet during the foundation of the state.

The bare, high deserts of innermost Asia did not always look so foreboding as they do now, however. In fact, until as recently as three or four thousand years ago, Tibet was much wetter and greener. From about 40,000 years ago to the last glacier maximum 20,000 years ago, a huge savanna-like wooded hunting ground existed between the Tibetan plateau and southern Siberia.[2] It was here the classic 'Mongoloid' physical type developed: humans adapted to the extreme cold, wind and high altitude. As the glaciers reached their maximum development, hunters were squeezed from this region down to the headlands of the great rivers of Asia – the Yellow River to the east, to the Brahmaputra in the south and the Indus in the west. As the glaciers melted at the end of the Pleistocene, about 11,000 years ago, this region of Central Asia, earth's 'Third Pole', again became more liveable, and Mongoloid-featured people repopulated the steppes and plateau of Tibet.

From this time to just a few thousand years ago, much of the Tibetan upland was warmer and lightly forested with juniper and pine, well watered by the receding glaciers. Tibet was an open high-altitude savanna, and its grassy plains supported abundant wildlife, including vast herds of yak, sheep, antelope, deer, bear and other large mammals. The last of the great megafauna of the Pleistocene, including the mammoth and woolly rhinoceros, had retreated to the most remote sections of the Arctic. Tibet's many freshwater lakes supported abundant fish and waterfowl. Big game hunting gave way to nomadic pastoralism as people of the Changthang, the vast northern prairie, took to herding species such as yak and sheep. In more sheltered river valleys, agriculture developed and more permanent communities appeared. In these small villages, the Neolithic gave way to the smelting of copper and bronze, and finally to iron.

The Tibetan tableland is the source of nearly all the major rivers of Asia. Most of these rivers have their origin deep within the upland itself, not along its mountainous flanks. As such, the rivers have cut extremely deep valleys over the millennia as the tectonic plate of Asia is lifted high by the colliding Indian plate. In western Tibet, the great rivers such as the Indus and Brahmaputra (Yar klung gtsang po) find their sources, near one another and near the fabled Mt Kailash, the centre of the Hindu and Buddhist earthly world.

Along the Indus Valley at the western edge of the Tibetan plateau, one of the first great civilizations of the world developed around 3300 BCE. This Bronze Age culture included the sophisticated cities of Harrappa and Mohenjo-Daro. Most likely some of the early Tibetan settlements in the upper parts of the Indus drainage were influenced by these great civilizations.

Around 1700 BCE, the Indus Valley civilizations began a slow decline. A possible natural reason for this disappearance was climate change, which also affected the Middle East and the broadly forested areas of central Tibet. The Indus Valley climate grew significantly cooler and drier from about 1800 BCE – linked to a general weakening of the monsoon pattern. Rainclouds today rarely survive the ascent of the Himalayan ranges. About this time, the Ghaggar-Hakra river system disappeared. There is also evidence that the Sutlej River was diverted from the Gangetic Plain to the Indus to the west, where it continues to be a primary tributary.[3] A tectonic event, such as a sudden seismic uplift, may have been responsible for this major change of course. It also appears that for a time the Sutlej was a major source of the Ghaggar-Hakra system. The current intermittent Ghaggar-Hakra river complex seems to have been possibly the ancient Sarasvati River mentioned in the Vedas, the primary texts of Hinduism. The change of course from the Ghaggar-Hakra to the Indus by the Sutlej was most likely a major factor in the desertification of the region now known as Cholistan and the Thar Desert.

As the Indus Valley civilizations declined, a new society was established in the highlands of western Tibet along the Sutlej River. From about the first millennium BCE to the seventh century CE an Iron Age civilization existed here. From its source in Lake Rakshastal (Lag ngar mtsho) near Gang ti se (Mt Kailash) in western Tibet, the Sutlej is the longest of the Indus tributaries. Its course is also known as the Kinnaur Valley, and the river flows through modern Himachal Pradesh and the Punjab. The upper reaches were known as the Garuda Valley by the ancient Zhang Zhung people, who established a great empire here, creating a capital at Kyunglung (khyung lung dngul mkhar). The city's palatial ruins still exist near the modern village of Moincêr (Smon tser). This civilization left records, many of which were incorporated into the chronologies of the pre-Buddhist Bonpo practitioners that have come down to the present day. Most likely the Zhang Zhung language, of the western

The Kyunglung palatial ruins near the modern village of Moincêr (Smon tser), 2017.

Tibeto-Burman group, was an ancestor of modern Kinnauri presently spoken in upper Himachal Pradesh. The early Iron Age can also be referred to as the protohistorical period in western Tibet. Towards the end of the period, the culture had developed writing, but most examples of these have been lost. Nevertheless, many records were translated and recorded in the early Bonpo chronicles.

Zhang Zhung

It is always subjective to state which ancient civilizations were the foundations of a modern one because the processes of adaptation, acculturation and assimilation are complex, non-lineal and non-deterministic. In fact, it is a strong characteristic of Tibetan historiography to gather threads from the distant past and weave them together into a synthetic, coherent whole in attempts to explain the present. The Tibetan *tertön* (*gter ston*) tradition of discovering ancient religious texts that had been hidden away until the 'proper time' of revelation is a good example. The presentation of Khampa (Khams) guerrillas' personal stories fifty to sixty years after the insurgency in eastern Tibet is a recent secular example, as discussed in Carole McGranahan's insightful *Arrested Histories*.[4] In fact, the official history of the Tibetan state by the government of the current Dalai Lama claims legitimacy by positing that the state of Tibet was prophesied by Lord Buddha himself 2,500 years ago. The current *dharmarāja* (*chos rgyal*) of Tibet (the Fourteenth Dalai Lama) reigns in an unbroken religious and secular continuity with those early Buddhist states. Therefore, to get a solid idea of the concept of the Tibetan state, it is important to look at these various legitimizing threads.

Zhang Zhung is one of the pillars of the Tibetan state. The Zhang Zhung polity of western and northern Tibet was melded into the accreting Tibetan Empire of the eastern Yarlung state along the Upper Bramaputra River (*yar klung gtsang po*) between the seventh and eighth centuries CE. Yet the official narratives of the successor state refer to the former in terms of subjugation with deterministic conclusions: the Buddhist faith is triumphant; the old religion is subjugated to the new, the old animalistic deities bonded to serve the Bodhidharma. It is clearly a history written by the victors. Archaeologist John Bellezza has commented on this particular form of Tibetan revisionism: 'The characteristic mixing of intangible and substantive elements in Tibetan accounts has given rise to a genre of literature best described as "quasi-historical". Many of the texts used in [my] study were written centuries after the events recorded are supposed to have transpired, lending a legendary coloring to them.'[5]

Yet the Zhang Zhung culture is the bedrock of the Tibetan nation and its identity. From the Zhang Zhung come much of the shamanistic underpinnings of Tibetan religion, and the cult of the local deities, which although largely tamed by the great master Padmasambhava in the eighth century, still causes tensions among the Tibetan community. The Zhang Zhung civilization was the major source of the original 'Bon' religion, and much of the written history and oral accounts of Zhang Zhung are obtained through more modern Bonpo sources. Most scholars agree that the Bon proper is relatively new (eleventh century CE) and was stimulated by the co-development of the first wave of Buddhism in Tibet. The Bon *tertön*, however, have claimed a greater antiquity for their religion. As such, I refer to the pre-Buddhist religious stratum as 'foundational Bon'.

From the Zhang Zhung comes the connection with the sacred peak of Kailash, at one time shared with the founders of the Vedic religion

The sacred peak of
Mount Kailash.

Detail from *Pilgrimage
to Mount Kailash*,
18th-century thangka
painting, depicting the
central stupa housing
Chakrasamvara before
the triple-peaked
Mount Kailash.

in India in remote antiquity. The sacred mountain of the foundational Bonpo is *gyung drung* (Sanskrit *swastika*). Here also comes the cult of Shambhala, which in later days greatly influenced 'pure land' concepts of a pure Buddha realm and the meditative constructions contained within the great Kālachakra Tantra, introduced to the later Dge lugs pa school by the Jonang sect of Buddhism. In Zhang Zhung records, Shambhala is sometimes identified as the Sutlej Valley, with its capital of Kyunglung.

Zhang Zhung, as recorded by the Bon records, presents a feeling of great antiquity – typical when the razor-sharp reality of the historical record gives way to the fuzzy memory of remembered tales and oral transmissions. The founder of the Bon, Ston pa Gshen rab mi bo che (Gshen rab), is thought to have lived 18,000 years ago but probably was no earlier than the early Iron Age. The origin story traces Shenrab back to a land called *'ol-mo lung-ring* in Stag gzig, where the real Kailash is considered located, directly northwest of the modern Tibet Autonomous

Tsakli (initiation card) of the ancient Bon religion, featur-ing a gYung drung symbol (left-facing swastika).

Long stone grid
necropolis, one of
the most distinctive
and extensive types
of funerary sites in
far western Tibet
and the Changtang.
Talus-blanketed
Red House (Khang-
dmar rdza-shag),
East complex (4700
m). The west half
of the array of long
stones and temple-
tomb are pictured.
A tomb integrated
into the site has
been radiocarbon
dated to *c.* 10th to
8th century BCE,
possibly indicating
the foundation date
of this long stone
grid necropolis.

Region. From here the teachings were introduced into Zhang Zhung.[6]
Stag gzig is associated with modern Iran and Tajikistan.

Another strong characteristic of the mythological world of Zhang
Zhung and the foundational Bonpo is a continuum between gods,
humans and animals, not specific categories as espoused by Buddhism.[7]
Spirit mediums in Tibet are still referred to as *lha pa,* 'the medium of
God'.[8] The traditional practice of shamanism is strongly associated with
the arc of inner Asia, from the foothills of the Himalaya to the Korean
peninsula. It is also a traditional practice in many circumpolar regions
and, archaically, into North America.

The Zhang Zhungpa moved into a land that was already occupied
by people. John Bellezza suggests that the Mon people occupied upper
Tibet previously and migrated southwards and eastwards with the

coming of the Zhang Zhung people. Currently the Monpa live in the Tawang region of Arunachal Pradesh, India, a former tributary state of Tibet, and other closely related people live eastwards to upper Burma and into Yunnan, China. Although the term Monpa is somewhat of a catch-all exonym, the movement of other eastern Tibeto-Burman speakers from the northern plateau southwards through the river valleys towards Southeast Asia is supported through their own oral histories.[9]

One would like to have an indisputable vision of Zhang Zhung culture, but the evidence is tantalizingly incomplete. Thanks to Bellezza's pioneering work, however, we have evidence that the Zhang Zhungpa built monumental stoneworks throughout the west and north of the Tibetan plateau. However, it is notoriously difficult to define ethnicity, Zhang Zhung or otherwise, based on material culture, especially relying

solely on surviving archaeological features.[10] Houses, temples, tombs
and column monuments (*rdo rings*) found by Bellezza are mostly stoneworks. Hypothetical structures made of more perishable materials, such
as woollen tents, wood frameworks and beaten earth, may simply not be
presently preserved in the archaeological records. Residential patterns
on the Changtang show somewhat of a preference for sites on islands
in many of the lakes and former lakes of the plateau. Abandoned fields
are also present, indicative of the desertification of the region in the
last few millennia. The relic plots reflect a period of a more intensive
cultivation of resources and, by implication, a sophisticated, complex
society in the distant past.

The records of Zhang Zhung culture interpreted through Bon
chronicles cannot fail to be coloured by the Tibetans who first wrote
them down many centuries after the annexation of Zhang Zhung to the
Tibetan Empire – the *tertön* effect. However, repetition of theme, especially across several sources, is usually a good indication of the existence
of an ancient cultural trait. One repetition that appears is the status of
Zhang Zhung priests, divine kings and other religious practitioners.
More like superheroes than later Buddhist adepts, foundational Bon
practitioners were characterized by their abilities to tame wild animals
or incorporate the attributes of animals within the human dimension.
Priests with great magical abilities could allegedly turn themselves into
birds.[11] We also get a powerful image of Zhang Zhung elites through their
distinctive costumes: unbound hair, white turbans, the use of vulture
feathers, turquoise ornaments, and the prestige of wearing the *gshen*, a
robe (*thul pa*) trimmed in the fur of three ferocious cats: tiger, leopard
and clouded leopard.[12] These symbolic vestments have come down to
the present day among the Khampa.[13]

Yarlung and the Tibetan Empire

Another pillar supporting the development of the Tibetan state is the
south-central kingdom established in the Yarlung Valley off the Yarlung
Tsangpo River. The fledgling polity was ruled by nomadic clans who
swept off the Changtang and ventured into the warmer southern agricultural region along the Tsangpo. It was a dominant cultural pattern seen
throughout Inner and East Asia, as mounted nomadic groups, through

Kampa *dzong*, Tibetan hamlet north of Sikkim, 1904,
photograph by John C. White.

their mobility, had a technological edge over the settled agricultural peasants. In Bod yul, as this kingdom was now called, the ruling classes built fortified castles or *dzong* on strategically located escarpments and hills overlooking the agricultural fields along the broad river valleys of southern Tibet. One of the first was Yarlung castle, home of the *tsenpo* (*btsan po*), the emperor. Like Zhang Zhung, the Yarlung kingdom of Tibet subscribed to the Bon religion, and was a land infiltrated by numerous spirits, gods and demons. Many aspects of the two states seem quite similar. The major difference is that the warmer Yarlung Tsangpo Valley was more intensively agricultural. Surplus was acquired through grain as well as through herds. Pastoralism was dominant in the colder Changtang and the western plateau kingdom of Zhang Zhung.

The Tibetan records of the Yarlung kings begin with the 'neck-enthroned king',[14] Nyatri Tsenpo (gNya' khri btsan po). He is probably contemporary with some of the earlier Zhang Zhung rulers, having lived according to legend about the second century BCE. According to the Bon chroniclers, Zhang Zhung was then divided into outer, inner and central regions. Outer Zhang Zhung consisted of central Tibet (modern Ü and Tsang) and the Kham and Amdo regions. The kingdom of Bod apparently separated from Zhang Zhung at some point.[15] The

Nyatri Tsenpo, detail from a 19th-century thangka painting.

history of the Bon credits the founding of the Tibetan Bod dynasty from
an Indian prince of the Pāndava family. Like Buddhism itself and many
things sacred, the Yarlung kings were believed to have descended from
heaven, a feature strongly associated with Zhang Zhung and Bonpo
ideology. Nyatri had been a leader in the war between the Pāndavas and
Kurus noted in the epic *Mahābharata*.[16] Having been defeated, he fled
to Tibet disguised as a woman. Nyatri was unusual: he had turquoise
eyebrows, pointed teeth, webbed fingers and eyes that closed like those

of a bird. Nyatri sought teachings from the great *gshen*, or priest, Namkha Nangwai Dogchen (Nam mkha snang ba'i mdog can), upon which the religion spread during the reigns of the 'seven kings from the sky'.[17]

When Nyatri assumed the throne miraculous weapons appeared:

The smallest Wal egg
Hatched breaking itself against the waves of the lake,
And from the outer shell of the egg
There formed the boiling 'Moon Face'
From the yolk that spilled onto the ground
There formed the substances for the boiling-over Wal liquid;
From the intermediate membrane of the egg
There formed the 'nine Wal weapons'
The sword that kills by itself,
The hammer that beats by itself . . .[18]

The Bon bird imagery is powerful in this passage; the primordial lake is Mapam (Manasarovar), which lies at the foot of Kailash. The king also received two protector deities, Klu mched bdun and Lha glang rwa dkar (Seven Naga Siblings and Divine Ox with White Horns).

Nyatri was an anti-hero rather than a conqueror, as the structuralist historian Robert Paul suggests: '[He is] an innocent victim of aggression of others, he passes no inherited guilt along to successors in the royal lineage.'[19] This guiltless tradition is maintained by the self-acting weapons and the protective deities of the founding king, who do the sovereign's bidding with the demons of Tibet, leaving the sacred ruler pure and free from karmic burden. This ancient ideological attitude has affected the concept of Tibetan nationhood for its entire length in recorded history. The state of Tibet is primarily defined as a non-violent one; let others fight the wars and incur its karma. The fundamental structure of the later priest–patron relationship, with the priest being indemnified and the karma falling upon the secular patron, is thus seen to have been established at the very beginning of the state. The current Dalai Lama's emphasis on a non-violent settling of the Tibet issue is a direct descendant of this idea.

overleaf: Gurla Mandhata and Lake Mapam (Manasarovar) near Selung Gompa, 2016.

Nyatri Tsenpo is credited with building the first monumental structure in Bod yul, the castle Yumbublasgang. Prior to this time, it was said that Tibetans lived in caves. The first seven kings were linked to heaven with a sacred cord of light, and upon their death they would ascend with it. Therefore, the first kings do not have tombs. From the Bon text *The Mirror Illuminating the Royal Genealogies*:

> Of these early kings called the 'Seven Tri [thrones] of the Sky'
> (*gnam gyi khri bdun*) it is said that, as soon as the prince was
> able to ride, the father ascended to the sky by means of the 'Mu
> (*dmu*) cord' and disappeared like a rainbow. The 'Seven Tri' had
> their tombs in celestial space: dissolving like rainbows into their
> divine bodies they did not leave mortal remains.[20]

Yumbublasgang castle, 2015.

Each of the heavenly kings appears to reproduce asexually, as the successors are considered identical to the predecessors. Each was a *sprul pa* or incarnation of the Yar lha sham po, the mountain god ancestor of the royal lineage. This is another theme that found resonance with the introduction of Buddhism and its development of rulership by spiritual lineages of Buddhist adepts (*tulku* [*sprul sku*]) centuries later.

The eighth king, Drigum (Gru gum), was the first king born of the flesh. He died in armed combat with a minister, Longam (Lo ngam), who was attempting to usurp the throne. During the dispute the sacred *dmu* cord was permanently severed, and the god-kings were for ever-more earthbound. The later Dalai Lamas, through their great spiritual perfections, were able to regain control over this divine intercourse. It could be said that the Dalai Lamas restored the sacred cord of light that was possessed by the first kings of Tibet by having control over their earthly rebirths from the sacred realm. Such are the powers of other *tulku* as well. Drigum was succeeded by his son Chatri (Bya khri, Bird Throne) around the time of Han dynasty emperor Wu Ti (r. 141–87 BCE),[21] and as the last of the Ptolemaic kings were ruling in Egypt.

Tsenpo Thothori Nyantsen (Tho tho ri gnyan btsan), the 28th king, of the fifth century CE, had a miraculous encounter when a golden stupa, a jewel and a book written in a language no one could read were found on the roof of the Yumbulhakang. It came with a prophecy that the book would be deciphered four generations later. It became known as the *Great Secret* (*gnyan po gsang pa*). It was actually a Buddhist sutra, written in Sanskrit, and it had come from India. It was the first intro-duction of Buddhism into Tibet. So auspicious was this event that it is memorialized as Year One in the Tibetan calendar, as can be seen on recent Tibetan currency and elsewhere.[22]

Four generations from Thothori Nyantsen, Prince Songtsen Gampo (Srong btsan sgam po) was born at Gyama (605 or 617 CE). As was usual in the kingdom of Bod yul, Songtsen ascended the throne, as the 33rd king, at the age of thirteen when his father was assassinated. From his youth, Songtsen knew he had to be a strong leader. He was to become the founder of the Tibetan Empire, the territories of Bod yul now becoming the central pillar of the expanding polity. Centuries later, when Buddhism had been re-established in Tibet, Songtsen was seen as an incarnation of Avalokiteśvara and a *chakravartin* (a turner of the wheel of doctrine)

The Demoness of Tibet, late 19th-century painting, a symbolic depiction of the land of Tibet as a she-demon (*srin mo*) lying on her back, which dates back to Songtsen Gampo and the histories of the Jokhang Temple at Lhasa.

in fulfilment of prophecy. Under his reign, Buddhism was introduced to Tibet and the *Great Secret* was finally translated.

Written Tibetan or Bod yul history, in contrast to Zhang Zhung records, begins with Songtsen. He sent the minister Thonmi Sambhota (thon mi Sam bhot) to India to find a script by which the Tibetan language could be written down. The Brahmi and Gupta scripts seem to have been the prototypes. It is said that Songtsen went into retreat for four years to learn and launch the new but complex writing system. Upon emerging, the king provided Tibet with its first written constitution.

Like many successful leaders, the key to Songtsen's success was several strategic marriages. With the king of Zhang Zhung he exchanged sisters. With a king of the Licchavi in Nepal he allegedly received the 'Bal bza' consort', Bhrikuti Devi, although her historicity is presently disputed.[23] From China he reportedly received Princess Wenshan, the 'Rgya bza' consort', niece of Tang emperor Taizong. Wenshan's actual existence is also in doubt: nevertheless, the two Buddhist consorts symbolically represent the first introduction of Buddhism into Tibet, which is a fact. The Belsa brought with her a statue of the Akshobhya Buddha, while the Gyasa brought an image of Siddhārtha, the Buddha Gautama Śakyamuni, said to have been the only such image carved from life. With his highest-ranking Tibetan wife, Mongsa Tricham of Tolung (Mong bza' khri lcam), Songtsen sired his heir, Gungsong Guntsen (Gung song Gung btsan).[24]

While Songsten maintained the traditional nomadic 'royal progress' around the country with tented encampments, he concentrated on two permanent residences: the ancient Yumbublasgang fortress, which he used for his summer residence, and the town of Rasa ('Goat Land') on the Kyichu River. In the latter, the Gyasa consort had a temple built for her gift, which was called the Ramoche Tsukla khang. The Belsa, also wishing to house her statue in an appropriate temple, was advised to construct her chapel over a lake near the edge of town. Because a large number of goats were conscripted to haul timbers and pilings to fill the lake, the temple was called the Rasa Trulnang Tsukla khang (the 'Goat Land House of Mysteries'). Later the two images were exchanged between temples, and the Rasa Trulnang Tsukla khang was renamed the 'House of the Jowo Image', the Jokhang.[25] The Tsenpo, in recognition of what his capital was becoming, renamed the town Lhasa ('Gods' Land').

King Songtsen Gampo, 18th-century thangka painting.

Having made Lhasa his capital, Songtsen chose the prominence of Red Hill (*dmar po ri*) just to the north of town for his palace, the Tritse Marpo. One thousand years later, the Fifth Dalai Lama would construct his own palace, the Potala, on the ruins of Songtsen's fortress. Two portions of the original palace were incorporated in the new: the Phakpa Lhakhang and the Chogyal Druphuk, a recessed cavern identified as Songtsen Gampo's meditation cave directly underneath the Phakpa chapel.

The spark that turned the small central Tibetan kingdom into an empire seems based in the marriage wishes of Songtsen – many of these marriages were political alliances. First, his sister in Zhang Zhung began relaying information about King Ligmikya. This allowed him to be ambushed and killed. Songtsen promptly annexed the vast western and northern plateau of Zhang Zhung, *c.* 645, expanding Tibet exponentially. Next, he turned his sights to the northeast, where the old Tuyuhun Empire was in decay. It was at this time that he asked for the hand of the Gyasa of the Chinese Tang. However, she had already been promised to Thokiki, king of the Tuyuhun, also known as the 'A-zha in

Potala palace, 2015.

Tibetan, home of the Minyuk people (modern Amdo). The Tuyuhun practised a complex culture of nomadic pastoralism and agriculture but were perhaps most closely associated with the east–west trade: the Silk Route. The Tuyuhun were powerful, independent and cosmopolitan. But being situated between two ascendant stars, the Tang dynasty to the east and Songtsen's Tibet to the west, the Tuyuhun kingdom found itself boxed in. In the late 640s, 200,000 Tibetan troops were sent, destroying the Tuyuhun. The Tsenpo subsequently subdued the Qiang, Pail an, Tang hsiang and other tribes.[26] He captured the city of Songpan (in modern Sichuan), and asked again for the hand of the Tang emperor's niece. He sent his minister, Gar, to the capital at Chang'an to press his suit. This time the Chinese emperor granted the petition, and gave Gar a princess, too. Songtsen also asked to build a great Buddhist temple on Wu Tai Shan in Chinese territory (in modern Shaanxi), which was granted. The king, or his successors, also reputedly built the huge stupa of Boudanath (Bya rung kha shor) in the Kathmandu Valley. It is no coincidence that such monuments, still extant today, show some of the effect of the Tibetan imperial reach.

The Gyasa consort reputedly brought a different level of civilization to the Tibetans, who were apparently quite similar in personal accoutrements to the Zhang Zhungpa. In general, men painted their faces red, wore their hair long and bound it with turbans, and, when appropriate to their status, wore felt robes trimmed with furs. Princess Wengshan is credited with introducing silk robes, tea drinking and other Chinese customs to court, but these details do not appear in Tibetan records.[27]

Songtsen continued his expansion. Soon he had occupied present-day northern Burma, Tawang and Nepal. When his son Gungsong Guntsen reached the age of thirteen, Songtsen abdicated, as was the custom. But Gungsong only reigned for five years. His son dead, Songtsen again resumed the throne.

To the south, another great empire was being constructed in northern India by Harsha. He was a strong ally of the Tang. When Emperor Harsha died and his position was usurped by a warlord, Arjuna, hostile to the Chinese envoys in the country, the Tibetans were called to help. Their army soundly routed the forces of the rebel Arjuna, and Harsha's kingdom came under Tibetan influence as well. Vast sections of northern India thereby became culturally affiliated with Tibet during this time and, to a large extent, still are. Tibet had also encompassed the entire Brahmaputra drainage to the Gulf of Bengal. The Land of Snows thus had seaports and beaches.

While still in his thirties, Songtsen Gampo caught a fever and died, leaving a young grandson, Mangsong Mangtsen (Mang srong mang btsan), as heir under the strong leadership of Gar (Mgar stong btsan) as regent. For many years Gar lived in the 'A-zha as the Tuyuhun were still showing resistance to Tibetan rule. The people of the 'A-zha were eventually subdued. Their distinctive culture and language became another pillar of the emerging Tibetan state, and put the Tibetans closer to controlling the lucrative Silk Route.

The early expansion of the Tibetan Empire was facilitated by the powerful Gar family, who held on to the premiership for several generations, much like the shoguns of Japan. During this time, Tibet annexed the Tarim basin and pushed eastwards.[28] The tenacious Tang empress Wu Zetian had refused to negotiate with the Gars over splitting this region of Central Asia between China and Tibet, which meant that war would again break out. Around 699, Tridu Songtsen (Khri 'dus srong btsan), great-grandson of Songtsen Gampo, led his own army around that of Gar khri 'bring and began to physically remove the Chinese soldiers from Central Asia. Routed, the last of the Gar rulers committed suicide. Tridu Songtsen was succeeded by Trisong Detsen (Khri srong lde btsan), one of the greatest of all Tibetan emperors. The formidable Tibetan army continued to capture cities along the Silk Route.

Tibet defeats China

There is nothing in the arsenal of politically charged statements that are currently hurled between the Ganden Phodrang (the Tibetan government, now in exile) and the Central Communist Party of China that is more inflammatory than the historical circumstances of 764, when the Tang capital, Chang'an, was captured by Tibetan forces. Technically China had become a part of Tibet. But Tibet was not intent on unifying its motherland with the addition of China – it was concerned for the control of the Silk Route. The occupation of Chang'an was brief; the Tibetans installed Prince Kuang wu as emperor, and received a letter guaranteeing annual tribute from the Tang. This event was inscribed on the famous zhol *rdo ring* column still standing in front of the Potala in Lhasa (but now largely inaccessible). While the Tibetan invasion would be the death knell for the Tang dynasty, the Tang annals carry on as if nothing happened. In 783 a peace treaty was negotiated between Tibet and China. It established the border only 160 km (100 mi.) west of Chang'an, at Qingshui. Basically, all land west of the modern Lintan, near Lanzhou, was ceded to Tibet by this treaty.[29]

The large Chinese city of Dunhuang along the Silk Route held out for eleven years of siege. But even Dunhuang eventually surrendered, becoming a part of the Tibetan Empire. Taxes were levied, residents had to adopt Tibetan dress, and Tibetan language was introduced. Meanwhile, the Tibetan armies continued to expand to the west, even reaching the legendary Oxus River, close to the ancient Zhang Zhung homeland in Tazik, in western Central Asia. Arab records note that Tibetans set siege to Samarkand. In a sense, the Tibetan Empire was a precursor of the great Mongol Empire of the twelfth to thirteenth centuries, with nearly the same reach and influence in Asia.

Tibet now had control over trade between east and west, and Lhasa became a wealthy cosmopolitan world capital rather than merely the land of goats it had once been. Arabs, Mongols, Indian Brahmins, Nestorian Christians and Chinese packed the bustling markets and shops as merchants and traders. The government grew wealthy. The empire extended from Yunnan in the east to modern Tajikistan in the west. From Mongolia to the shores of modern Bangladesh, the realm was immense.

Trisong Detsen, having learned his lessons in statecraft well, realized that a more universal religion would be useful in Tibet to help consolidate rule. The ancient Bon religion, although powerful, was highly parochial. Its gods and demons were largely localized. It is difficult to build national solidarity when the god of one mountain was foreign to the householder across the valley. Buddhism was a universalistic religion, one that had shown to be a unifying agency countless times, perhaps most clearly in the expansion of the empire of Aśoka throughout South Asia several centuries before. But the *tsenpo* had to continue to develop the Buddhism that had been originally introduced by his ancestor Songtsen Gampo without alienating the Bonpo *shen* whose own priestcraft maintained the mythology and legitimacy of the sacred kingship. Fortunately, there had developed a system for accommodating local practice within Buddhism in India for several generations, and this would be utilized in Tibet.

The tantric difference

Buddhism had already evolved along various divergent lines by the time tantric practice was developed in India, the two main divisions being the Theravāda and the Mahāyāna. The goal of liberation was the same for the two, but in the Mahāyāna tradition it was felt that its practitioners should postpone their own attainment of nirvana until all other sentient beings had been liberated. This is the bodhisattva vow. In the development of tantra, considered the final major development of Buddhism in India, it was believed that even the Mahāyāna was relatively unproductive during a presumed 'age of degeneration'. Only a radical method of religious liberation would see effective results.

Central to the practice of Buddhism in general is the idea of overcoming the distinctions between subject and object, between form and idea, between external reality and inward thought. Matter and thought are considered illusory: simple manifestations of a clinging to existence characteristic of the world. In tantra, the ego is just an illusion based on ignorance. A practitioner must break down the ego in order to find release, and this is done by breaking the perceived norms of this world. In a sense, tantra is all about fighting fire with fire, a mental homeopathy. Negative energies could be used to transform into positive ones, engendering thoughts of compassion to liberate all sentient beings from the world of suffering.

Buddhist tantra developed strongly in northern India, especially at such learned institutions as Nalanda in Bihar. It was also a strong Buddhist practice in the kingdom of Oddiyana in what is now Swat Valley in Pakistan. Tantric adepts became highly skilled in subduing local deities and enlisting them in the support of the more encompassing Buddhist dharma. This ability to accommodate local practice within a system of more universal appeal was precisely what the Tibetan Empire needed. It had been used most effectively in the Maurya Empire of Aśoka of the third century BCE. The Oddiyana practices established a precedent for the accommodation of Inner Asian shamanism, which is almost always based in the locality, clan or family, with a transnational, caste-free, polycultural ideology. The formula would be used in the future by two of the greatest land-based empires ever, the Mongol Yuan and the Manchu Qing realms, of which Tibet was of course a principal player.

The *tsenpo* Trisong Detsen first sent for the great Buddhist abbot Śantarakshita, who skilfully explained Buddhism to the emperor. Trisong was captivated and commanded that a huge monastery be built in Tibet to help establish Buddhism as a state religion. However, anti-Buddhist sentiment was still strong and the local gods seemed displeased, sending all sorts of calamities upon the country. Śantarakshita was sent back to India. But the *tsenpo* was persistent, and after a few years recalled Śantarakshita, who brought a tantric adept who was an expert in converting local gods and demons to be beneficial to the Bodhidharma. This was the Lotus-born, Padmasambhava from Oddiyana.[30] The path was now cleared for the king to build the great monastery he had been planning. The site was located to the east of Lhasa, along the Yarlung Tsanpo River. It would be called Samye, 'the Inconceivable'.

At the site of Samye, however, angry demons tore down in the morning what had been built the day before. Padmasambhava was able to call forth the offending and offended spirits, and, with a lecture on karma and the path to liberation through Buddhism by the sutra-oriented Śantarakshita, was able to convert these demons. They now became protectors of the Buddhist faith. Centuries later the Fifth Dalai Lama wrote that, among other actions, Padmasambhava consecrated Samye monastery with the Vajrakilaya dance and thread crosses to catch the various spirits and appointed the powerful deity Pehar to be chief of the protectors.[31]

Four *vajrakilaya* (*phurpa*) stupa were built at cardinal points around the complex representing the impalement of Samye to the earth. The sacred precincts now stabilized, Samye would stand as Tibet's first Vajrayāna monastery, whose monks in later times would be known as the 'ancient ones', the Nyingmapa school. It was designed in a mandala shape, based on the monastic centre of Odantapuri in Bihar, not far from the great Buddhist university of Nalanda. When it was finished in 780, Trisong Detsen erected a *rdo ring* on the site pledging eternal support of his dynasty to the establishment. Buddhism had become an instrument of state. His work completed, Padmasambhava was sent back to India, but not until he had written the entire canon of the Nyingmapa.

Unknown artist, *Śantarakshita with Scenes from his Life*, 19th-century painting. The vignettes represent the prologue to the story of Buddhism's arrival in Tibet, which begins in the bottom-right corner, with Śantarakshita travelling to Tibet, and continues at bottom centre as he is greeted by King Trisong Detsen upon his arrival. Later we see Trisong Detsen receiving teachings from Śantarakshita at Lungtsubchen Palace.

But Tibet did not become Vajrayāna overnight. The tantric schools were still somewhat of an innovation, and another development of the Māhayāna. Eastern Asia also influenced Tibet at this time: a type of Zen Buddhism from Korea was introduced at the court of the *tsenpo*. Although the general philosophical arguments were the same, the means of achieving enlightenment differed. The Indian schools generally practised a gradual means towards enlightenment, utilizing the Six Great Perfections, the *pāramitā* (*pha rol tu phyin pa*, 'having gone to the other side'),[32] which consist of actions leading towards perfection. These actions include the practices of generosity, morality, patience, energy, meditation and wisdom.[33] The Zen school, on the other hand, felt these could be dispensed with in a flash of sudden insight, leading directly to enlightenment.

It quickly flared up as a major religious controversy. Trisong Detsen went for advice to the abbot of Samye, who suggested that debate would be a civilized way of settling their differences. The two sides squared off. In the end, the use of analytical insight to discern the ultimate emptiness in all categorizations, practised by the Indian schools, won out over the sudden insight of the Zen practitioners. Thus, in the centuries that followed, the Indian schools of Buddhism were more influential throughout Tibet. Some scholars suggest that the polemic seems too clear cut to be actually historical.[34] It may be yet another example of Tibetan chroniclers retroactively historicizing a general trend. However, most of the growing canon of Tibetan Buddhism was India-based, translated directly from Sanskrit, one of the original sacred languages (with Pāli) for Buddhist exegeses and commentaries. And it is a now well-ensconced practice, especially among Gelugpa monastics, to engage in dialectical debates for sharpening analytical skills, something that is traceable to the eighth-century occasion at Samye.

The translation of nearly the entire Indian Buddhist canon – the Tripatika, commentaries and tantras – into Tibetan was certainly one of the greatest gifts to civilization ever made. No corpus of ancient knowledge was as extensive as this, made ever more precious by the fact in a couple of centuries much of the original Buddhist material in India was destroyed by Islamic iconoclasts. Nalanda library in Bihar burned for months when it was torched by the Turk Bakhtiyar Khilji in 1193.[35] Buddhism was practically extinguished in the land where it was born.

Hundreds of neologisms had to be coined in Tibetan to accommodate the flood of Sanskrit texts.[36] The Tibetan language was thus transformed and standardized at the same time.

Around 800 Trisong Detsen died.[37] In 822 a new treaty was established between Tibet and China. The accord reiterated the boundary between two equal states and they vowed to live in peace with one another. *Rdo ring* were raised in the two capitals, Lhasa and Chang'an, and on the border at Qingshui. The new Tibetan emperor, grandson of Trisong, was Tritsug Detsen (Khri gtsug lde btsan), better known as 'Ralpachen' owing to his long hair. This emperor, the third of the so-called religious kings, was to widely propagate the Buddhist faith, building monasteries everywhere and giving them estates to support themselves. He printed and distributed Buddhist sutra and other religious material. The rapid expansion taxed the treasury, and many officials were concerned. There was also severe fraternal strife in the imperial family, fuelled by increasingly disenfranchised Bonpo priests.

Winds of change

The demise of the Tibetan Empire and end of the inherited monarchy coincided with the triumph of monastic Buddhism. The shift was one of the most momentous in the history of the Tibetan state. For 41 generations Tibet had been ruled by a divine king, the *tsenpo*, whose legitimacy was intimately based in Bonpo ritual and the *shem* who maintained the cult of the heavenly descent. The proximate cause that led to the downfall of the Tibetan monarchy was the disaffection of the elder brother of Ralpachen. Nicknamed Lang Darma (young male ox) because of his pugnacious disposition, the brother had been passed over for the throne. Furthermore, Lang Darma was anti-Buddhist, and deeply resented the gains the monasteries received under the rule of his brother. Lang Darma hatched a plot to usurp the throne. First, he had the king's brother Tsangma sent away. Then he had Ralpachen's chief minister, Bande brangkha dpalkyi yondan, sent into exile at Nyethang over a concocted story about an affair with the queen.[38] At Nyethang, Bande Dangka was assassinated by having a scarf stuffed down his throat. The queen, learning of this false accusation, committed suicide by jumping off the palace walls. Finally, in 836, Ralpachen himself was caught off guard by the assassins while staying at the Shampa palace. His neck was broken.

Lang Darma was placed on the throne by the assassins, who were awarded positions, Be Gyaltore becoming prime minister and Be Taknachen minister of the interior. Ramoche, the Jokhang, Samye monastery and Ralpachen's own temple of Onchang Do were closed. Monks were secularized; Indian pandits were sent home. The destruction of Buddhist institutions continued for years. Finally, in 842, a monk named Lhalung Palgye Dorje had a vision of the protector deity of Tibet, Palden Lhamo, which he interpreted as a message to destroy the oppressor of Buddhism. In one version of the story, Palgye Dorje, finding the king at the entry to the Jokhang in Lhasa examining the *rdo ring* pillar there, shot an arrow at the king. In another chronicle Palden's arrow impaled Lang Darma's neck to the back of his throne.[39] The assassin had disguised himself with a black robe lined with white. His white horse was covered in charcoal. After the assassination, Palgye was able to escape by turning his robe inside out and washing off his horse in the Kyichu River. He hid in a cave for a while, and eventually managed to withdraw to eastern Tibet.

The demise of Lang Darma was a victory for Buddhism but signalled the end of the Tibetan Empire. The royal family immediately fractured. Two of the dead *tsempo*'s queens gave birth to sons: 'Od Sung, who was enthroned at Lhasa, and Yum brtan, who established a line at Yarlung.[40] In the next generation, 'Od Sung's lineage was split again between Tashi Tsekpal at Tsang and Kyide Nyimagon, who ruled western Tibet. For the next four hundred years Tibet would remain fractured. Remarkably, eight hundred years after Lang Darma was pinned to his throne, a descendant of the Yarlung kings would again consolidate the ancient Bod yul kingdom and rule a vastly different Tibet.

Much ado has been made about this historical disjuncture by some structuralist scholars. Paul suggests that in the Lang Darma assassination, the centuries-old primogeniture-preferred patriline of the Yarlung dynasty was for evermore replaced by junior males, here represented by Palgye Dorje and all Buddhist monasticism.[41] Celibacy (or second husbands in fraternal polyandry) is associated with junior males in Tibetan society, while the senior male was expected to become a householder and head of the house. Cultural reproduction in the political world of Tibet, then, succeeded over the biological. This can be seen in the development of rule by religious hierarchs throughout the next millennium, first of the Sakya family, who would pass the lineage down in an uncle–nephew succession, and then most famously in *tulku* lineages, such as that of the Dalai Lama, which short-circuited sexual reproduction entirely.

It was a major transformation of the Tibetan state. Buddhism was in fact overthrowing the Bon religion, and the bureaucrats, rulers and resources of state that supported it. With the Lang Darma assassination, central Tibet broke up into petty kingdoms, and Bon was restored. The outer fringes of the former Tibetan Empire, however, kept the flame of Buddhism alive, and it was from these sectors that the universal dharma would be restored in the centre. From this second introduction of Buddhism, the religion would become a primary agency of state, and Tibet would become a theocracy.

TWO

The Rise of Theocracy

After the fall of the ancient line of Tibetan kings, the great empire broke into a dozen petty kingdoms, much as it had been before the unification of the country by the divinities of the Yarlung dynasty. It took the patronage of the formidable Mongol army to patch the state together in the twelfth century, and it did so through creating a theocracy. The religious rule of Tibet continued the ancient dream of a 'pure' and sacred state; karma-accruing security and military matters would be assumed first by secular Mongol patrons, followed by the Manchus during their Qing Empire.

One of the major memories of the expansive reign of Chögyal Tri Ralpachen of the Yarlung dynasty (*c.* 815–836 CE) was learning the value of the monastic estates to the development of stable institutional growth of the state. In response, the ancient landed hereditary Tibetan nobility began a slow decline. It was not an easy transition. Buddhism had been largely absent from the central provinces of Tibet for about sixty to seventy years following the persecutions of Lang Darma. It was the Dark Ages for Tibet, occurring a few centuries after the fall of the Western Roman Empire. Unlike the pope in the West, however, there was no singular ruler or religion that could rally and precipitate national sentiment, and Tibet descended into a proliferation of independent estates.

With the dissolution of the centralized Tibetan state, systematic repression ended and Buddhism began a slow recovery. Several foreign Buddhist teachers and scholar-monks visited the holy sites on pilgrimage in Tibet, but a large-scale revival of the dharma would have to wait until the appearance of a remarkable adept with the stature of a Padmasambhava (or 'second Buddha'). The Indian sage Atiśa is credited with the second introduction of Buddhism in Tibet. He would create

Folds from a Burmese picture book (parabeik) about the life of the Buddha,
18th century, picturing the Gautama Buddha being followed by group of monks
and greeted by a king.

the Sarma (new) lineages in contrast to the Nyingma or old lineages
introduced by Padmasambhava.

Atiśa

Atiśa Dīpamkara Śrījñāna (980–1054) was born a prince in coastal
Tibet, then a part of the Pala state, a region of the old Tibetan Empire
that is now Bangladesh. His life paralleled that of Gautama Śākyamuni
(*c.* 480–400 BCE). His parents were the king and queen of Bengal. At
only eighteen months old, Atiśa already showed remarkable spiritual
advancement. He became a phenomenal student, receiving teachings
and empowerments from over 150 teachers. The Vajrayāna and Māhayāna
routes to enlightenment were at the height of development in India,
especially at the great centres of Nalanda and Vikramaśila, and Atiśa was
a remarkable teacher who stood out even during these highly spiritual
times. He developed a huge following when he moved to the Śrivijaya
kingdom on Sumatra, which became a major centre of tantric Buddhism,
specifically following the *mantrayāna* path of 'skilful means'. One of
Atiśa's teachers in Sumatra was the renowned tantric adept Serlingpa

(Gser gling pa, Sanskrit Dharmarakṣita). Atiśa received invitations to teach all over the Buddhist world, but was particularly interested in visiting Tibet and assessing the condition of the Bodhidharma in that land. His sponsor was the king of Guge in western Tibet, Lha Lama Yeshe Öd (Lha Bla Ma ye she 'od, *c.* 959–1040), who had steadfastly remained Buddhist through the dark period generated by the reactionary Lang Darma.

Although initially resolved to spend but three years in Tibet, Atisa discovered the great textual resources that still existed in Tibetan monastic libraries, both in Sanskrit and Tibetan. He would spend the rest of his life in the Land of Snows, developing meditational techniques such as *lojong* (*blo sbyong* or mind training) and *tonglen* (*gtong len*), the taking of suffering from sentient beings and returning compassion that is still part of most monastic curricula.[1] Atiśa's most renowned commentary is *A Lamp for the Path of Enlightenment* (*Byang chub lam gyi sgron ma*, Sanskrit *Bodhipathapradīpa*). Atiśa, with his extremely broad knowledge of tantra, sought the rather ironic accommodation of its sexually orientated practices with monastic celibacy and monastic discipline. With the apparent unification of opposites, these philosophical gymnastics became a tantric practice for Atiśa and his followers.

Atiśa's main disciple was Dromtön ('Brom ston pa rgyal bi 'byung gnas), who had been foretold of his destiny by a vision of the goddess Tara. He was considered the 45th incarnation of Avalokiteśvara, the future First Dalai Lama being the 51st. Dromtön founded the Reting (Rwa sgreng) monastery in central Tibet, which was dedicated to his teacher's professions. Dromtön called their group the Kadampa (*bka*, the teachings of Buddha, and *gdams*, the transmitted teachings of Buddha). Tsongkhapa (1357–1419), the native Tibetan founder of the Gelugpa sect and its Ganden monastery, was heavily influenced by the monasticism, tantric adeptness and compassion of the Kadampa school, which he saw as placing emphasis on the Mahāyāna principle of universal compassion, and based his reforms largely upon its teachings. Tsongkhapa furthered the accommodation of tantra and sutra and perfected the practice of monastic discipline (Sanskrit: *vinaya*). Tsongkhapa's major influence from Atiśa, though, was the development of Atiśa's *Path*, which has come down to the present as the *lamrim* teachings. The Kadampa itself eventually was subsumed within the emergent Gelugpa order and their development of a government institution, the Ganden Phodrang. But the prestige of the Reting lineage, with its direct ties with Atiśa, the main teacher of the second introduction of Buddhism, did not falter until nearly the end of the Tibetan state (*c.* 1950).

The incarnation body

A major innovation occurred between the ninth and thirteenth centuries, the development of the idea of the *tulku* (*sprul sku*). This is a Buddhist teacher who, in conjunction with their bodhisattva vows and through their perfected spiritual abilities, decides to reincarnate in a new body. It is a distinctive Tibetan formation – not even Indian Vajrayāna had developed this idea, and it is directly descended from the concept of the old divine Yarlung and Zhang Zhung kings taking human form to rule the state.

From the beginning, Buddhist teaching was an oral tradition, 'Thus I have heard' (Pāli: *Evaṃ me suttaṃ*).[2] It was passed to the student from the teacher, who received from his teacher in an unbroken line to the Buddha himself. The oral lineage was the original transmission of the Bodhidharma and is still a vital component of Tibetan Buddhism. However, 1,000 years of divine Tibetan kings left a legacy that would be incorporated into a revived Tibetan Buddhism. Although the body of the kings now reproduced biologically, their divine aspect, originally represented by the *dmu* cord of light, passed on through the generations by a sort of divine animation directly from heaven. This is the process known as *sprul pa*, which became the root of the neologism *sprul sku*, 'emanation body' or *tulku* (a reincarnate custodian of a specific lineage of teachings in Tibetan Buddhism). Although derived from a native source, the phenomenon of corporeal epiphany eventually became identified with the Mahāyāna concept of *nirmanakāya*, the earthly component of a Buddha in the Trikāya, 'three bodies' theory. The historical Buddha Siddhartha Gautama is an example of an incarnate emanation of a transcendent Buddha. But it took over three hundred years before a Buddhist *tulku* succeeded to substantial political power in the Tibetan kingdoms.

The real revolution came when the first *tulku* began to claim the religious estates of their predecessors. The estates were the source of

Düsum Khyenpa, the first Karmapa, 19th-century thangka painting.

economic and political wealth for the new monastics, as they had been
for the biologically reproducing nobility. The first claim to an estate by
an incarnation was achieved when the Second Karmapa, Karma Pakshi,
succeeded as an emanation of Düsum Khyenpa (Dus gsum mkhyen pa,
1110–1193). He was also recognized as an incarnation of the bodhisattva
Avalokiteśvara. Düsum Khyenpa, the founder of the Karma Kagyu sect,

was very accomplished. He was one of the few thought to have achieved enlightenment in his own lifetime. As such, it was believed he could channel his stream of mind consciousness at his passing to a being of his choice. He thus became the young boy Kyil le tsak to, who became Karma Pakshi, the Second Karmapa. This boy was extremely precocious, being able to absorb profound texts in one reading. Nevertheless, he was given all the graduated empowerments as a normative course of study for any monk.[3] It became a standard practice for all succeeding *tulku*: despite the level of their previous body's accomplishments, each new incarnation would receive the formal lineage empowerments. This maintained the original oral apostolic succession to the Buddha himself.

The spiritual accomplishments of Karma Pakshi attracted attention far beyond the old borders of Tibet. He caught the notice of none other than the grandson of Genghis, the Great Khan of the Mongols. This was the famous Kublai, who would add China to the vast empire started by his grandfather. Genghis of the Borjigin clan is the founder of the idea of the Mongol state, similar to the early Tibetan emperors establishing the principle of the Tibetan state.

Kublai established his winter capital at the old Jurchen capital of Zhongdu and renamed it Khanbaliq (Dadu), now known as Beijing. The khan had learned the important lesson that by promoting a universal religion he would receive the support of many ethnic groups within a multicultural empire. By rising above regional particularisms, which, as in old Bon Tibet, were prevalent throughout the Mongol lineages, Kublai could consolidate his vast empire. But Karma Pakshi refused to move permanently to his court, instead spending time with Great Khan Möngke, brother of Kublai. This irritated Kublai greatly, who sent a huge army of 37,000 soldiers after Karma Pakshi. In retaliation, the Karmapa performed a great miracle, freezing the army in place. Impressed, Kublai dismissed Taoist teachings throughout the empire.

While the Kagyu were innovating the concept of *tulku* succession, the Sakya tradition, founded by Khön Konchok Gyalpo ('Khon dkon mchog rgyal po, 1034–1102) southwest of Lhasa, had developed a modified biological succession of Buddhist lineage holders. The Khön family, like the imperial Yarlung family, considered itself descended from heaven, from the 'Gods of the Realm of Clear Light'.[4] The family had been a strong supporter of the Nyingma school for centuries. Before launching the Sakya religious establishment in the eleventh century, the Khön dynasty was centred in Tsang. In an accommodation with the celibacy ideal of Buddhism, the Sakya hierarchs passed the religious succession down from uncle to nephew, at least initially. This is an example of the great transformation that was brought about with the assassination of Lang Darma: the removal of succession from the senior, biologically reproducing males to the juniors who were often celibate (other lineages of Sakya practitioners, including the current throne-holder, reproduce biologically). It is notable that the record of the celestial descent of the Khön family occurred about the same time as that of the Yarlungs: about a millennium before the first introduction of Buddhism. The Sakya reference to heavenly origin is indicative of the persistent strength of the notion of *sprul pa* in Tibetan culture. And in accommodation with the Buddhist theory of *trikāya* emanations, the founder of the Sakya lineage, Sachen Kunga Nyingpo (Sa chen kun dga' snying po, 1092–1158), was considered a reflection of Avalokiteśvara.

Godan Khan, another grandson of Genghis, was administrator of a large portion of the empire. He had planned on invading Tibet. Kunga Gyaltsen (Kun dga' rgyal mtshan, 1182–1251), the Sakya Pandita, was made ambassador representing the Tibetan interests with his nephew and heir, Phagpa Lodro Gyaltsen ('Phags pa blo gros rgyal mtshan). Remaining at the court of Godan, Kunga Gyaltsen had the opportunity to cure the khan of an illness, which ingratiated him to the Mongol ruler. The Sakya embassy converted Godan and many of the Mongol leadership to Buddhism. Following Buddhist precepts, the Sakyas convinced the Mongols to practise compassion and refrain from killing. Instead of invading Tibet, Godan bestowed upon Sakya Pandita the thirteen myriarchies (*khri skor*) that constituted the centre of the country. The Sakyas remained at court at Lanchou, now in modern Gansu. In 1251 Sakya Pandita died and was succeeded by Phagpa. This was followed in 1253 by the death of Godan, who was succeeded by his cousin Kublai as leader of the eastern part of the vast empire. Most likely due to the snub he had received from the head of the Kagyu lineage, Kublai invited the young Phagpa to instruct him in Buddhist teachings.

The Sakya hierarch was quite aware that Kublai was forming a client relationship (or 'priest–patron', *mchod yon*) with the Sakya hierarchs, who now controlled central Tibet. Consistent with the ancient guru–student relationship of India, Phagpa insisted that Kublai assume a subordinate position when taking teachings and initiations. As interpreted by the Sakya Trichen hierarch today:

> Kublai invited the nineteen-year-old Chögyal Phagpa to his court and was much impressed with the young monk's learning, displayed in his intelligent answers to a number of difficult questions. Kublai then asked for religious instructions; but the young Sakya lama told him that before he could receive such teachings, Kublai would have to prostrate himself before Phagpa as his religious teacher whenever they met and to place him before or above, whenever they travelled or sat. Kublai replied that he could not do so in public, as it would involve a loss of prestige and therefore weaken his lama when receiving teachings and an equal seat when dealing with matters concerning the government.[5]

This ordering characteristic of the priest–patron relationship has formed a major impasse in Sino–Tibetan relations for centuries. While even a great khan might be able to prostrate before a surrogate Buddha, it could be a problem for a Confucian emperor ruling China, where all revolved around the Son of Heaven. The same impasse characterizes the totalitarian Communist China – Buddhism must be an agency of the state, not independent of its control.

Indeed, Kublai succeeded as Great Khan at the death of Möngke in 1259. Following further teachings, Phagpa was given a relic of the Buddha and invested with supreme authority over the three regions of Tibet (*chol kha gsum*), as befitting a descendant of Avalokiteśvara. When Kublai assumed leadership of the empire, Phagpa was given the title of Tishri or 'Imperial Preceptor' (Ch. Dishi, 帝師), Phagpa conducted the enthronement ceremony of the new khan. It is said that the priest–patron relationship between the Mongol khan and the Tibetan lama was later referred to as akin to 'the sun and the moon in the sky',[6] a common Tibetan idiom suggesting a binary pair but with a difference of scale; the light symbolism refers to the Buddhist notion of enlightenment (*sangs rgyas*).

Thangka painting of Chögyal Phagpa, 17th century, which also depicts Kublai Khan (centre left), and Drogon Chagna, Phagpa's brother (far left).

Phagpa returned to Tibet in 1265 and set about appointing a principal minister (*dpon chen*) and thirteen *tripon* (throne holders) for the thirteen myriarchies. Tibet was now unified, with its capital at the town of Sakya. All was under the administration of Phagpa; thus, a theocracy had been formed. Phagpa returned to the Mongol court three years later, presenting the khan with a script he had devised. It was named in his honour.

Some Tibetan sources, including mid-twentieth-century Tibetan finance minister Shakabpa, suggest the priest–patron relationship is unique and cannot be defined by Western political theory.[7] This relativist viewpoint is probably constructed as an opposition to modern Chinese claims of historical Tibetan subordination, either nationalist or communist. Priest–patron relationships occur elsewhere, of course, the relationship between the papacy and the Holy Roman Emperors being perhaps the most notable example. Here the Empire ideally served as the 'sword of Christendom'.

It is perhaps more reasonable to suggest that the developing relationship between Tibet and the Mongol Empire was that of a client state to a dominant power. There are formal obligations between these states that cannot be abrogated by the centre. Nor can the imperial preceptor ignore his responsibilities to the secular emperor and the people of the empire. Subordination of one to the other was unnecessary, as the authority of each ruler stemmed from different arenas, in this case secular and religious. Tibet during the Mongol Empire was basically the estate of the Sakya lama, which kept the Sakya imperial preceptors in a manner befitting their status in the empire. It was neither an incomprehensible situation nor one of subordination.

Finally defeating the Southern Sung, Kublai did become emperor of China in 1271, naming his lineage the Yuan dynasty, the first 'barbarian' state to rule all of China. Kublai consolidated the last Sung resistance by 1280, the year that Phagpa died. Official Nationalist and Communist histories of China view Tibet as having been annexed to China when Kublai became emperor of China, but this is hardly valid historically. The logic is equivalent to suggesting that Canada is technically part of the United States because many of the lower colonies (presently USA) and upper British North America were once ruled by the same power (Great Britain). Furthermore, Kublai's China was merely a province of the Mongol Empire; Tibet was closer to a colony, a client state, which maintained its native leader in a high degree of sovereignty.[8]

In 1280 Sakya authority in Tibet passed to Phagpa's brother's son, Dharmapala, continuing the uncle–nephew succession. But the unique Mongol confederation that had created the world's most extensive land-based empire began a sharp decline with the death of Kublai, which occurred in 1294. The last years of Kublai's reign saw vastly expensive attempts at expansion, towards Japan and Southeast Asia. While only marginally successful in Vietnam, the attempted invasions of Japan ended in total defeat of the Mongol forces.

The earliest Western visitor to Tibet appeared during this time. Friar Odoric visited the court of the Great Khan in Khanbaliq, crossing Tibet. He described the wall of Lhasa (now gone): 'Their principal city is surrounded with fair and beautiful walls, being built of white and black stones, which are disposed chequerwise one by another, and curiously put together. Likewise all the highways in this country are exceedingly well paved.'[9]

Seven more Yuan emperors would succeed Kublai, but by the mid-fourteenth century matters were looking bleak for the Mongol rulers. Famine, fatigue and general disappointment were rampant among the people.[10] Rebellion broke out in the Han south, first by the so-called Red Turban Revolt, and then by the founder of the Ming dynasty, Zhu Yuanzhang.[11] Zhu, a peasant, rose through the ranks of leadership in the Red Turbans. He established himself first at Nanjing, where he proclaimed a strong Confucian-influenced rule, the Great Ming. Zhu's good administration won a growing number of adherents, as the ineffective control by the Yuan was replaced by local warlords. Khanbaliq, the imperial capital, fell to Zhu in 1368.

The Sakya domination over Tibet continued to decline. In 1305 Danyi Zangpo Pal (Bdag nyid bzang po dpal, 1262–1322) assumed the throne of Sakya. Far from being a celibate monk, he had seven wives. Four of his sons established their own palaces and dynasties.[12] The Sakya leadership would rotate between these four families from this time forward, but actual power would be shifted to administrators and heads of the myriarchies.

The remnants of the once invincible Yuan withdrew behind the Great Wall to their old summer capital of Shangdu (Xanadu). They were

Niccolò and Maffeo Polo, father and uncle of the young Marco Polo, at the court
of Kublai Khan in 1271. Miniature from *Le livre des voyages de Marco Polo*,
15th century, Bibliothèque de l'Arsenal, Paris (MS-5219, fol. 17v).

pushed out of this site also as Ming forces destroyed the city. The Yuan
retreated to Inner Mongolia, where they suffered another great defeat at
Yingchang. The emperor of the 'northern' Yuan, Toghur Temür, a great-
great-great-grandson of Kublai, died in 1370. He had been a student of
the Karmapas, and had even been recognized as an incarnation of the
Kagyu Tai Situ lineage.[13] The retreating Mongols eventually settled in
Karakorum under the rule of Toghur's son Biligtü Khan. All along, the
still illustrious Borjigin family continued to claim the thrones of the
great khanate and China, even in 1380 when distant Karakorum was
also destroyed by the Ming. But the family persisted, forming a Northern
Yuan state, which existed rather precariously between the Ming Empire
and Central Asia until the 1630s.

For the next two generations, various Mongol armies formed and
terminated alliances. During this period, however, Tibetan Buddhism
continued to expand in Mongolia. With the rise of the latter-day Jurchen
under Nurhaci, the Chakhar Mongols, headed by a Borjigin, finally

Chen Yuandu, *Blessed Odoric Preaching in Chin*a, 1928, painting on silk.

presented the seal of the Yuan dynasty to the new power, now called the Manchus. Under Nurhaci's son Hong Taiji, many of the Mongol tribes would unite again as bannermen, and with the new rising star would help to stimulate the unity of Tibet as well as what would become Mongolia and Manchuria.

The Sakya realm was, of course, neither a unique innovation nor the first theocratic state in the world. Divine kings had ruled for thousands of years in Egypt, Japan and elsewhere. But theocratic dominion over large states by monastic institutions was exceptional in the course of world history.

Western scholars to the mid-twentieth century often compared the theocracy of Tibet with the Roman papacy. There is indeed much that is structurally similar between the two polities. Comparison is useful, as the current political debate as to the nature of the old Tibetan state is often based in legal precedent and metaphor. In fact, the promotion of Tibetan uniqueness is most likely an Orientalist presumption, part of the 'inscrutable East', a position that even taints the writings of native historians.[14]

Civil war

Having such a strong military backing, the Sakya state under Mongol patronage achieved the reunification of the Tibetan state. Not having to spend heavily to maintain border security, Tibet under the Sakyas continued to develop its Buddhist institutions. The great library of Sakya, with one of the most extensive collections of Buddhist works anywhere, was a notable beneficiary of the accumulated intellectual wealth of the Tibetan state. It was all short-lived.

Despite the benefits that the priest–patron relationship had for Tibet during the Mongol Empire, there was a drawback. The relationship, being bound under sacred conventions, had rights and obligations that could not be easily dismissed. The Sakya remained loyal to the Borjigin clan who ruled the empire, not to the empire, nor its successors, nor China. The guru–student bond was, and remains, essentially a personal rather than institutional relationship. When the star of the short-lived Yuan dynasty began to fade, so too did the political influence of the Sakya establishment. The Khön family remained preceptors to the

Borjigin clan as they went into exile and formed the Northern Yuan dynasty. But the glory days of the Sakyapa ruling the Thirteen Myriarchies and the three regions of Tibet were over. Within this changing climate, the Fourth Karmapa, Rolpe Dorje (Rol pa'i rdo rje), finally accepted the last Yuan emperor's invitation to visit his court and give teachings and empowerments.

Between 1346 and 1354, towards the end of the Yuan dynasty, the noble house of Pagmodru (Phag mo grupa) toppled the Sakya, and established a rule of parts of central Tibet from Neudong. Tai Situ Changchub Gyaltsen (Ta'i si tu byang chub rgyal mtshan), a monk, was the scion of this regional dynasty. He emerged as a cultural hero of the Tibetan nation, having overcome intrigue, imprisonment, torture and treachery. Although Sakya forces were rallied, they were not able to overcome Changchub's leadership. He began to 'de-Mongolize' parts of Tibet under his control, assuming the Tibetan title Desi (*sde srid*) and reorganizing the Thirteen Myriarchies of the previous Yuan-Sakya rulers into districts ruled from fortresses (*dzong*). He abolished Mongolian law, replacing it with the old Tibetan legal code.[15] The use of traditional Tibetan dress, instead of Mongol court style, was restored.

The subsequent rule of the Phagmodrupa dynasty lasted in force until 1435. From 1435 to 1481, the power of the Phagmodrupa declined as they were eclipsed by the Rinpungpa (Rin spungs pa) family, who patronized the Karma Kagyu school. Their power base was western Tibet and Guge. They were followed by the three kings who ruled Tsang from 1566 to 1641. The Tsangpa were founded by Karma Tsetan, former governor of Shigatse (gzhis ka rtse) under the Rinpungpa.

Tibet and the Ming dynasty

The relationship between China and Tibet during the succeeding Ming dynasty (1368–1644) was weak. The Ming court did indeed bestow titles upon secular and ecclesiastic nobility in Tibet, which is now interpreted by some scholars as accepting submission to Chinese rule. However, many of the recipients of these honours were not the highest authorities of the land. Many scholars, especially in the People's Republic of China, insist that China has maintained sovereignty over Tibet since the Yuan dynasty, even though there were long periods when the Ming rulers had virtually no relations with important Tibetan leaders, much less direct control over the affairs of the entire region. Tibet's relationship was to the Mongol Empire, not its Chinese province. Thus it seems illogical that title to Tibetan sovereignty automatically passed to China after the fall of the Yuan. Since the Tibetan state was no longer unified, there was never a direct relationship between a Ming emperor and a single Tibetan leader. Rather, the Ming at times patronized individual Tibetan schools and regional leaders.

The Karmapa of the Kagyupa was one such hierarch who was courted by the Ming. In imitation of the Yuan priest–patron relationships, the Ming emperor Yong Le (r. 1402–24) struggled to build a similar secular and religious alliance with Deshin Shekpa (De bzhin gshegs pa, 1384–1415), the Fifth Karmapa, but was largely unsuccessful.

Tibet did engage with Ming China in trade, largely exchanging horses for tea bricks. Tibetans had developed a strong thirst for the astringent leaf, which they churned with butter, hot water, soda and salt into a kind of soup that fortified them on the high and dry Tibetan plateau.

Even though the Pagmodrupa (c. 1354–early 1600s) and Rinpungpa (1435–1565) reigns and the Karmapa lineage were not successful in the creation and maintenance of a unified Tibetan state, they nevertheless provided some of the ideas and resources for the catalytic spark that would eventually lead to one.

Onion Valley man

Since the fall of the monarchy of the Yarlung kings, the principle of hereditary succession had begun to slip out of favour. In its place, Tibet was developing into a meritocracy – the career of Changchub Gyaltsen from Phagmodrupa is a good example. Much attention and power would be given to those who showed exceptional religious insight. It was a tradition that originated with Padmasambhava, who because of his miraculous supernatural abilities was given carte blanche in the transformation of Tibet. Atiśa, the great teacher from India in the eleventh century, brought a fresh wave of Buddhist teachings into a Tibet ready for a major revitalization. And in the late fourteenth century, a native-born lama of extraordinary abilities would establish a new order that would provide the ideological foundation for the re-establishment of a powerful, expansive Tibetan state. This was the phenomenal scholar from Onion Valley, Tsongkhapa.

Tibetan Buddhism had been maturing since the traditional source of Buddhist authenticity, India, had seen the destruction of the great monasteries and universities of Buddhist scholarship. Tibet was now a major source of Buddhist teachings in its own right, and was renowned throughout Asia. The idea that Tibet was now the sole possessor of the complete teachings of Lord Buddha was becoming a factor in the formation of national identity and a sense of Tibet's uniqueness.

While Rolpe Dorje, the Fourth Karmpa, was being feted in Nanjing by the Ming emperor, a toddler monk was already making a name for himself throughout Tibet. The precocious child from Tsong Valley near Koko Nor (mtsho sngon po), Amdo, was presented to the Karmapa on his return to Tibet from Nanjing around 1362.[16] He was given the religious name Kunga Nyingpo (Kun dga' snying po). The little boy was given an intensive course in tantra from a Sakya lama and sent to central Tibet for further education. Now a young man, tall, with prominent ears and a big nose, Kunga was a restless soul. Not content with studying in one monastery and one tradition, Tsongkhapa would devour teachings from the Kagyupa and Sakyapa, Jonangp and Nyingmapa, as well as master a full course in medicine. His restlessness was partially satisfied by his interest in philosophical debate, which took him on tours throughout Tibet. On his travels he finally met his match with the rebel Sakya scholar Rendawa (Red mda' ba). Tsongkhapa's interpretation of Mādhyamaka, the Middle Way, was radical and compelling. Tsongkhapa easily passed all his exams in the Sakya curriculum, and now as a master began to write exegeses and commentaries. He soon attracted disciples, who of course emulated Tsongkhapa's maverick style. Much of their practice consisted of a 'back to basics' aesthetic. The original Vinaya of Buddhist monasticism was to be taken seriously, and imposed strict heterosexual celibacy upon the monks, among other proscriptions. The band took to wearing patched robes, an old reference to the poverty of original Buddhism. And to be instantly distinctive, they changed their hats from the usual red to yellow and became known by this millinery alteration.

Tsongkhapa continued to master tantra, deity yoga (lha'i rnal 'byor) and meditative insight (lhag mthong). On his travels he met another master lama, Umapa, who initiated him into a special Mañjuśrī practice. Tsongkhapa began to experience many visions of the bodhisattva, eventually being able to communicate directly and miraculously with Mañjuśrī. In his wanderings, Tsongkhapa visited the tiny monastery of Lhodrag, a Nyingmapa site that was one of the few that still maintained the lineage of Atiśa and the Kadampa school. He met up with his lama Rendawa at Reting, the original seat of Atiśa in Tibet. It was here that he wrote his masterpiece, the *Great Exposition of the Stages of the Path* (*Lam rim chen mo*). This combined the graduated path of the Kadampa with his own interpretation of the Mādhyamaka. He also wrote an interpretation of mantra.[17] With Tsongkhapa's success as a Buddhist teacher came patronage. The Ming emperor Yong Le sent an invitation to visit. Tsongkhapa responded by sending a disciple instead, Jamchen Choje, who was successful in receiving imperial patronage. The great master also became a favourite of the Phagmodrupa.

Restless, Tsongkhapa wanted to create something new. With financial success, he and his followers were able to establish a new monastery near Lhasa, which was called the 'Joyful' (Ganden, Dga' ldan). With the establishment of Ganden monastery by Tsongkhapa in 1409, followed by Drepung and Sera, all in the Lhasa Valley, the old capital of Tibet was being revitalized. In 1409 Tsongkhapa established the Great Prayer Festival at Lhasa (Monlam, smon lam), a month-long religious celebration following New Year. During Monlam, monks literally took over the city, and the event attracted tens of thousands of pilgrims each year for centuries until banned by the People's Republic of China in 1959. Power had shifted away from Sakya to the new sect's bases in Tsang and Ü. In 1419 the great lama died. He was mummified and embedded within a *chorten*.

While Tsongkhapa himself had never been too interested in forming a new religious order, his disciples were. Jamyang Choje ('Jam dbyangs chos rje, 1379–1449) and Jamchen Choje (Byams chen chos rje, 1354–1435) were particularly evangelistic, founding Drepung ('Bras spungs, 'Rice Mound', 1416) and Sera (Se ra, 'Wild Rose', 1419) monasteries, respectively. With Ganden, the establishments eventually became the largest monasteries in the world, holding over 15,000 monks.

A major disciple of Tsongkhapa was Gedun Truppa (Dge 'dun grub pa, 1391–1474). In 1447, having been successful in receiving rich patronage, Gedun Truppa founded the 'Hill of Auspiciousness' (Bkra shis lhun po, Tashilhunpo) at Shigatse and became its abbot. He is recognized as the First Dalai Lama, a posthumous award. His reincarnation was discovered in Gedun Gyatso from Tsang, who was the Second Dalai Lama. Gedun Gyatso built a residence at Drepung known as the Ganden Phodrang (Dga' ldan pho brang, 'Palace of Joy'), a name by which the official government of Tibet would be known to modern times.

The rather sudden jump to prominence of the Gandenpa, now rechristened the 'Virtuous Ones' (Dge lugs pa), irritated the Kagyupa, especially in their stronghold of Tsang. A deep sectarian distrust began, as many Kagyupa monasteries were overwhelmed by the yellow hat Gelugpa. In 1543 a boy was born near Lhasa who would be recognized as the reincarnation of Gedun Gyatso. He was given initiation and training at Drepung by Panchen Sonam Dragpa, the Fifteenth Ganden Tripa (holder of the throne of Ganden). Named Sonam Gyatso, the young man eventually became Drepung's abbot, as well as Sera's. Sonam became preceptor to the Phagmodrupa king.

In the mid-sixteenth century the Mongols were still in disarray, torn apart by factional strife. The old laws stated that only descendants of the Great Khan Genghis could succeed to the title. With the weakness of the Northern Yuan, other Mongol leaders of the Borjigin clan were eager to ride again. One such was Borjigin Barsboladiin Altan, Khan of the Tümed and, in time, the Ordos Mongols, and with it the entire 'Right Wing' (Western tribes). Altan Khan first invited Sonam Gyatso to Tumet in 1569, but he refused and sent a disciple instead, who reported back to him about the great opportunity to spread Buddhist teachings throughout Mongolia. In 1573 Altan Khan took some Tibetan Buddhist monks prisoner. Sonam Gyatso finally accepted Altan's insistent invitation in 1577, and travelled the broad distance to Koko Nor. Altan hosted an elaborate reception of Sonam, dressing in symbolic white to indicate his pious attitude towards the Bodhidharma. Clearly, the expected roles of priest and patron were at hand. At this meeting, Sonam proclaimed Altan a reincarnation of Kublai Khan; Altan responded by declaring Sonam the 'Oceanic Lama', that is, Dalai Lama, and applied the title retroactively to Sonam's predecessors, Gedun Truppa and Gedun Gyatso. Sonam conveniently declared that he was the reincarnation of Phagpa, the Sakya lama who was the imperial preceptor for Kublai Khan.

By this means, Buddhism again was declared the state religion for a broad band of Mongol tribes. Altan established a new city, Kokegota, now known as Hohhot in Inner Mongolia, and built its first Mongolian monastery, Thegchen Chonkhor. Altan initiated a monumental programme of translating the entire corpus of Tibetan Buddhism into Mongolian. Sonam succeeded in getting the Mongols to give up animal sacrifice, widow immolation and other bloody practices. Like Kublai, Altan found Buddhism a powerful discipline to help rein in the formidable exuberance of many warlike Mongols and thus achieve control. Eventually, Altan used his united armies to threaten the Ming dynasty in China. He led raids into China in 1529, 1530 and 1542, returning with plunder. In 1550 he crossed the Great Wall and attacked Beijing, setting the suburbs on fire. Altan succeeded in recapturing what remained of Karakorum, the old Yuan summer capital.

Altan Khan died only four years after meeting Sonam Gyatso, but the relationship was continued with Altan's son Sengge Düüreng. In 1584 the Dalai Lama returned to Mongolia and founded the great monastery of Kumbum in the Koko Nor region at the birthplace of Gelugpa founder Tsongkhapa. He also established the monasteries of Lithang and Namgyal, the Dalai Lamas' personal monastery, in eastern Tibet. The Ming emperor Wang Li, ever eager to entertain rising Tibetan lamas, invited Sonam soon afterwards. However, the Dalai Lama died in 1588 at the age of 45.

While Sonam would be succeeded by Altan Khan's great-grandson Yonten, Altan's attempt at reviving Kublai's empire would not succeed. There was a fresh new face in Inner Asian politics, a great innovator named Nurhaci, whose ancestors hunted and fished among the icy streams of northeast Asia. He would pick up the mantle of Kublai, and re-establish imperial patronage of the Tibetan religious state.

THREE

Ganden Phodrang

I n 1616 the Jurchen prince (*beili*) Nurhaci declared a revolution that would define a new political order that would eventually place his descendants, rather than the Ming emperor, at the centre of the universe. Although it created a powerful empire, this revolution would set many East and Central Asian peoples on the road to national ethnogenesis and would ignite Tibetan nationalism.

On a frosty morning, Aisin-Gioro Nurhaci, the humble warrior, had just finished a light breakfast of milk tea, millet congee and pickled cabbage. He walked towards his nobles in the audience chamber of a modest *yamen* (official residence) in the Jianshou citadel of Hetu Ala on the Liaoning Peninsula, now renamed Yenden. Backed by a 15,000-strong army fresh with victories that had amalgamated his Jurchen allies, and already recognized as a khan among the Khalkha Mongols, Nurhaci settled on a low throne placed on a low dais. Flanking the exterior of the *yamen* were two small ponds referred to as the 'eyes of the dragon'. Now he declared his intentions that would shake the foundations of all Asia. Rising from his chair, facing south towards China, he declared himself the 'Bright Khan of the Later Jin Empire' (Man., Genggiyen han amaga aisin gurun).[1] He then motioned to his secretary, who brought a large sheet of paper penned with a set of grievances against the Ming dynasty. It was set on a table before the throne. Nurhaci proclaimed that with the unification of the Jurchen peoples, he would avenge the honour of his father, Giocangga, and grandfather, Taksi, of the Aisin-Gioro lineage, the Golden clan (Ch., Jin). The older Jin dynasty had controlled what is now northern China and Manchuria for nearly two centuries prior to the invasion of Genghis Khan and the establishment of the Yuan dynasty in China. Nurhaci, a descendant of the Jurchen founder Möngke Temür, lifted his carved jade seal on to a vermilion ink pad, and slowly pressed

Qing Dynasty Court Painter, *Aisin-Gioro Nurhaci*, 17th century.

the heavy stone upon the paper. It was a declaration of war against the Wan Li Ming emperor of China, a challenge to its Mandate of Heaven. In the process of avenging his ancestors, Nurhaci would stimulate much of Inner Asia to form an alliance against the crumbling Ming of China. The movement would inspire the formation of a new political entity in the storied land of Tibet, the Ganden Phodrang, the institutional rule of the Dalai Lamas.

A key to understanding the development of the Tibetan state in the last half of the second millennium, and its continued claims for self-determination, is the conventionalizing of the Qing as an empire established by the foreign Manchus, not as a dynasty of China.[2] Much of the initial Qing imperial strategy was borrowed directly from the great empire of Genghis. In the absence of this particular supranational view, Chinese nationalist claims to Mongolia, Tibet and most other non-Chinese parts of the Qing Empire fall flat. China proper became part of the Qing Empire, not the other way around. The logic of modern Chinese nationalism could similarly claim large parts of Russia, the Central Asian Islamic republics and the Middle East, since they too were part of the Mongol Empire. In the latter half of the Qing dynasty, China and the Qing Empire became almost synonymous in official usage, having great implications for Tibet in subsequent years.

Nurhaci was certainly an innovator, but much of his strategy was borrowed from his cultural brothers and the near mythological heritage of their great hero, Genghis Khan. In fact, the Chakhar Mongols had inherited the mantle of the Yuan, and was headed by Genghis's descendants. The Chakhar still patronized the Tibetan Sakya sect from the days of Kublai and Phagpa. Through the Chakhar, Tibetan Buddhism had been introduced to the Jurchen, and the protector bodhisattva Mahākāla (mGon po) became as popular as he had been among the Mongols. The thirteenth-century Yuan preceptor, Phagpa, had cast a sacred image of Mahākāla, a wrathful form of Avalokiteśvara. He offered it atop the holy Wu Tai Shan before presenting it as the major cult image for the great empire of Kublai. In the early seventeenth century, Sarpa Khutuktu

overleaf: Matthäus Merian, after J. Blaeu, *Tartaria sive magni chami imperium,* c. 1638, speculative early map based upon the journals of Marco Polo, extending from Mongolia and Xanadu to the Caspian and the Volga River and to Tibet and the Upper Ganges River.

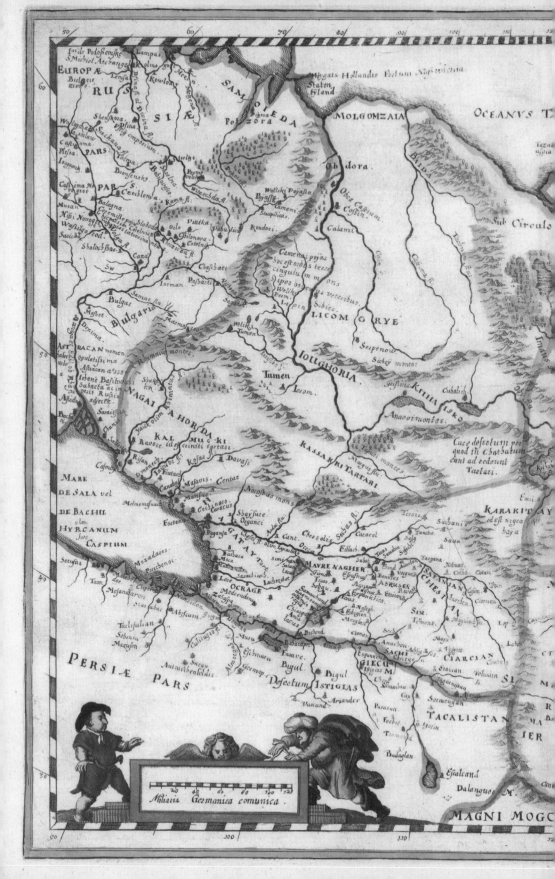

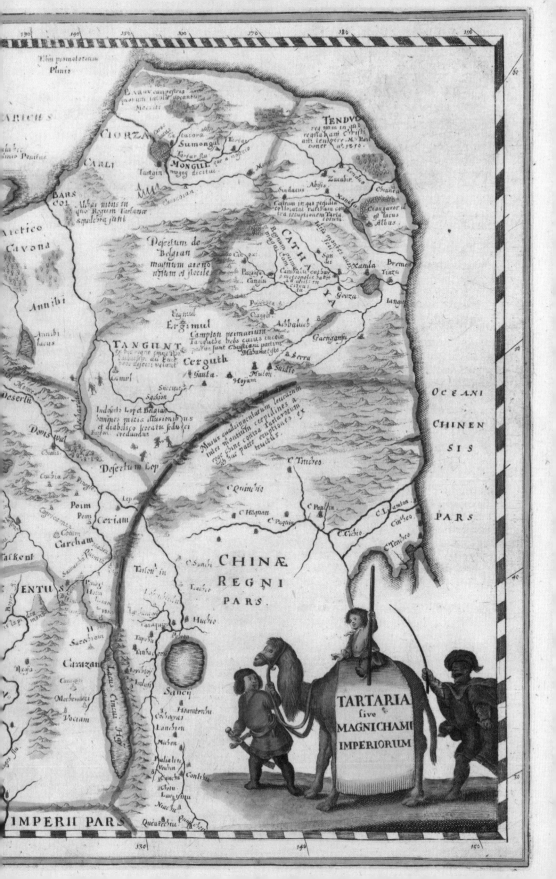

brought the statue to Ligdan Khan as a sign of the latter's continued legitimacy.[3]

Nurhaci received lay initiation into Buddhist practice, and subsequently appointed Olug Darhan Nangso as dharma master of the realm around 1621.[4] That year the Jurchen kingdom overran the Liaoyang Peninsula, and in 1625 the capital was transferred from Hetu Ala to nearby Shenyang and renamed Mukden. Nurhaci invented a new military system that would become characteristic of Manchu prowess. The banner system (Man., *gūsa*) of organization was based on traditional small groups of hunters banded together into 'arrows' (Man., *niru*), which formed a larger, collective hunt. Well into the Qing dynasty, the imperial hunt remained the primary semi-ritualistic military training exercise for high officers and princes of the blood. Importantly, the banner system also provided a mechanism whereby non-Jurchen allies could join the system. Mongols were earnestly recruited into the growing army, forming parallel banners under Jurchen leadership. Tibetan Buddhism provided another nexus by which one could join the ascending alliance, albeit a religious one. The political seduction was one of alliance to avenge various complaints against the Ming. In 1620 the Manchus approached the Khalkha Mongols: 'Our two countries are as one. Let our two families live as one. Let us attack the Ming as one.'[5]

Nurhaci died in 1626 and was succeeded by his son Hong Taiji, who further refined the growing military and civilian bureaucracy. Chinese were also recruited into the banners. At his installation as khan in 1627, Hong Taiji secured the participation of Sakyapa lamas, in imitation of the Yuan dynasty he was usurping.[6] It was clear from the very beginning that Tibetan Buddhism would be the font of Aisin-Gioro legitimacy throughout Northern and Central Asia.

To help forget the loss of empire under the old Jin, Hong Taiji broke with the past and renamed the Jurchen 'Manju'. Commonality of Altaic heritage, shared religious practices (Tibetan Buddhism and shamanism) and mutual political and economic goals (displacement of the troublesome Ming) contributed to the formation of a great alliance. Hong Taiji successfully fought the Chakhar Mongols, who lived between them and Beijing. They had maintained the Northern Yuan dynasty under the Borjigin dynasty of Genghis Khan, were supporters of the Ming, and were diehard patrons of the old Sakya school of Tibetan Buddhism.

Pede Fort or *dzong* on the shores of the sacred Yamdrok Lake, photograph by
Frederick Spencer Chapman, 1936.

In 1635, upon their defeat, the son and widow of Ligdan Khan presented
Hong Taiji with the imperial seal of the Yuan and with it the title Great
Khan. Similarly, the Mergen Lama brought Phagpa's storied cult statue
of Mahākāla to Hong Taiji at Mukden where it was enshrined in a
mandala-shaped temple.[7] It was an acceptance by many Mongols that
the Manchus were in fact the heirs to Genghis and Kublai. Hong Taiji
had become the new *chakravartin*, taking on the mantle of a universal
Buddhist ruler in imitation of Aśoka of third-century BCE India. At
this glorious occasion, Hong Taiji proclaimed the Great Qing Empire
(Man., Daicing gurun) and himself emperor.[8] While it was a multina-
tional project incorporating Mongols, Koreans, Tibetans, Chinese and
even Russians, the Daicing gurun also heralded the formation of a new,
Manchu national homeland in Jurchen territories.[9]

In a manner similar to the incorporation of various Mongol tribes
into the growing Qing state, many Chinese were enlisted into their own
banners. This was a slow process, as the Chinese lacked the cultural affiliation that the Mongols, Tibetans and the Manchus shared. Many of the
Chinese who were overrun by conquering Manchu armies were initially

enslaved. However, the Manchus needed the superior artillery skills of the Chinese against the Ming, and many formerly overrun Chinese communities were upgraded through conscription into the banners.

Gelugpa Tibet entered the Inner Asian alliance of the Daicing gurun through the Mongols of Koko Nor, the Khoshut tribe of the Oirats. They were foes of the eastern Chakhar Mongols and their ancient patronization of the Sakya. The Oirat Khoshuts were converts to the Gelug and thus held the lineage of the Dalai Lamas in high esteem. Previously, the western Mongols, led by Altan Khan of the Tümet, had engaged Sonam Gyatso, the Third Dalai Lama, to guide their people. It was clear to Hong Taiji that in order to receive further support from the western Mongols, he needed to patronize the rising Gelug. The 'Yellow Church' had been established at Mukden by 1639.[10]

The Fourth Dalai Lama, Yonten Gyatso (Yon tan rgya mtsho, 1589–1617), descended from Altan Khan, left for Tibet in 1599, supported by an army of Mongol warriors. He took several years to transit the pastures and plateaus of northern Tibet, stopping at numerous monasteries along the way to give teachings. He was finally enthroned at Drepung and became a student of the future Panchen Lama, Lobsang Chokyi Gyaltsen (bLo bzang chos kyi rgyal mtshan).[11] Finishing his studies in 1614, Yonten Gyatso became abbot of Drepung and Sera. Throughout his reign, he had been viewed with suspicion by many Tibetans, especially the king of Tsang, Karma Phuntsok Namgyal (Karma phun tshogs rnam rgyal, 1587–1620), who ruled from Shigatse. The Gelug responded by snubbing the king and his preceptor, the Sharmapa *tulku* of the Karma Kagyu.[12] The intrigue often forced the Fourth Dalai Lama to go into hiding. He died in 1617 at the young age of 27.

King Karma Phuntsok of Tsang had resented the incursion of the Mongol tribes in the affairs of Tibet, both in the secular and religious domain, and banned the new Dalai incarnation to appear in anyone other than a Tibetan. The central Ü region with its capital of Lhasa was subsequently invaded by the Tsangpa. Many Gelugpa monks were killed at Drepung and elsewhere. Karma Phuntsok captured Lhasa and for the next few years Tibet was reunified. The Tsangpa would be the last hereditary dynasty to rule over large portions of Tibet.

Almost immediately after the Fourth Dalai Lama died, however, Kunga Nyingpo (Kun dga' snying po) was born in Lhoka Chingwar

Taktse (Stag rtse) in Tsang to the ancient royal Zahor family. The family was politically orientated to the Mongols rather than Tsang rulers, and not particularly enamoured of the Kagyupa hierarchs, the Sharmapa and Karmapa, who were being patronized by the Tsangpa. In addition, Kunga's father, Dudul Rabten (Bdud 'dul rab brtan), was most interested in usurping the Tsangpa dynasty and restoring the ancient Zahor to the rule of central Tibet. For this he was arrested in 1618, perhaps not coincidentally at the same time the Gelug and Sonam Chophel recognized his son as the Fifth Dalai Lama. The gauntlet had been thrown.

Little Kunga did his part and showed unmistakable signs of his future vocation, which clearly supported his recognition. He loved to 'play lama', moulding little *torma* (dough effigies) from his breakfast *tsampa* and milk, and ceremoniously offering them on the family altar to his older sister or to the cat. Perhaps more annoying was his ritualistic drum practice with all his mother's pots and pans up and down through the halls of Taktse castle. Sonam Chophel, lord chamberlain of the Fourth Dalai Lama, recognized Kunga as the new incarnation of his master. Fearing King Karma's reaction, he kept the discovery a secret, but eventually the word got out. The family was ordered by the Tsangpa king to reside with him in Samdruptse castle at Shigatse. Instead, the boy's mother, Künga Lhanzi, took the family to her fortress at Yamdrog Tso, the cradle of ancient Tibetan civilization. It was a symbolic as well as strategic move. When matters had settled down, Sonam Chophel took the boy to Drepung where he was ordained a novice with the name Ngawang Lobsang Gyatso (Ngag dbang blo bzang rgya mtsho). In 1622 the child was officially recognized by the First Panchen Lama.[13] King Karma Phuntsok died *c.* 1621, and was succeeded by his son, Karma Tenkyong (Karma bstan skyong).

Throughout Central and Inner Asia the previously moribund Mongol tribes were sorting through their lineages, forming groups and oppositions in response to the shooting star of the newly christened Manchus. In the process, everyone was acutely aware that Tibet would be reunified under the right combination of alliances. Sonam Chophel realized the importance of finding and keeping the various tribes of Mongols as patrons of the Gelug. Fortunately, the lineage from Altan Khan that produced the Fourth Dalai Lama was supplanted by the Gelug-friendly Oirat Khoshut tribe of Koko Nor. Its leader, Gushri

Lobsang Gyatso, the Fifth Dalai Lama, surrounded by scenes depicting his life story from birth to death, 18th-century thangka painting.

Khan, was most interested in enlarging their interests in Tibet. Gushri had allied himself with the Torghud and Dorbeds tribes against the Khalkha and Chahar tribes, who were allied with the old Sakyapa and the king of Tsang. In 1621, just as the Karma Tenkyong of Tsang was enthroned, the Koko Nor Mongols invaded Ü in order to support the Dalai Lama.

The Tsang king Karma Tenkyong was ultimately defeated at the battles of Gyathanggang and Chakpori.[14] The Panchen Lama, wishing a peaceful settlement, was able to negotiate wide concessions with the Tsangpa, winning back many of their Gelugpa monasteries. It was the end of the brief rule of the Tsangpa over all Tibet.

The Gelug had skilfully tiptoed around the rulers of Tsang and their Kagyu chaplains. But both the Yellow Church and Sonam Chophel wanted more, nothing less than domination of all Tibet. With Ngawang Lobsang Gyatso, a scion of the ancient kings of Tibet, now recognized as an incarnation of Avalokiteśvara, the young boy was being groomed to assume combined secular and religious powers not held since the downfall of the Tibetan Empire. And as *chakravartin*, he would be a product of Gelug religious heritage.

In order to accomplish this feat, Ngawang Lobsang Gyatso would have to excel in his studies, which he did with ease, becoming a renowned scholar. He also continued receiving teachings from the Sakya and the Nyingma, who were traditionally associated with his family. In this non-sectarian manner, he made many allies in the multifaceted world of Tibetan Buddhism, a characteristic of the Dalai Lamas ever since.

Having lost Ü, Karma Tenkyong returned to his palace in Shigatse. In 1628 he was visited by Portuguese Jesuit missionaries Estêvão Cacella and João Cabral. The airy apartments of the king were hung with rich silk brocade in this remarkable palace in the dry, dusty hills of Shigatse Valley.[15] With the support of Ligdan (Legs ldan) Khan of the Chakhar, Karma pushed back Gelug advances. But in 1635 the Chakhar were absorbed by the new Manchus under Hong Taiji, further eroding the power of Tsang. Gushri visited the Dalai Lama at Lhasa in 1637, and formally recognized the re-establishment of the priest–patron relationship. The next year, Ngawang Lobsang Gyatso was fully ordained by his teachers, the Panchen Lama Lobsang Chokyi Gyaltsen and Lingme

Shabdrung Konchog Chophel (Gling smad zhabs drung dkon mchog chos 'phel).[16]

In 1641 Gushri Khan was called upon by the Dalai Lama to defeat the king of Beri, the ruler of Kham who was a practitioner of Bon, hostile to the Gelug, and allied with Karma Tenkyong. Beri was summarily defeated and Kham was added to the Gelug realm. Sonam Chophel convinced the Dalai Lama that the country needed to be further unified, but they disagreed about turning Gushri back on his planned invasion of Tsang.[17] It was too late, however, and the Panchen Lama had to be evacuated from Tashilhumpo monastery. It became an all-or-nothing war, and the Great Fifth had to acquiesce to the wishes of Sonam and Gushri. As the Dalai Lama performed rituals for the success of Gushri, the khan's forces pushed the Tsangpa army back to Shigatse, then set siege to Shigatse *dzong* itself. Sonam Chophel finally entered the war with the army of Ü.

On 13 April 1642 Gushri met the Fifth Dalai Lama at Shigatse and placed Ngawang Lobsang Gyatso upon the vacant throne of King Karma Tenkyong. The Dalai Lama proclaimed Gushri nominal king of Tibet. However, Gushri invested the Dalai Lama with the spiritual and secular rule of all Tibet. Sonam Chophel became the chief minister, or *desi*, for the Dalai Lama. This was represented at the enthronement in Shigatse Phobrang with three thrones, the Dalai Lama on the highest.[18] The Dalai Lama named his government after his old palace at Drepung, Ganden Phodrang. It was the beginning of the theocracy that persisted until 1959 and into the exile of the Fourteenth Dalai Lama.

With the defeat of the Chahar, Khalkha, the Tsangpa and other petty kingdoms by Gushri Khan and Hong Taiji of the Manchus, most of Tibet, Mongolia and Manchuria fell solidly into the Gelug camp, evicting both Sakyapa and Kagyupa from their centuries of influence. It was a bitter defeat, and fomented an uprising by the Karmapa adherents later in 1642. A furious Gushri sewed the hapless captive King Karma Tenkyong up in a yak hide and threw him in the Tsangpo River. Many Kagyupa monasteries were forcibly converted to Gelug. The Dalai Lama also made moves to suppress the Jonang school of Buddhism, the old Atiśa group that had supported the Tsangpa.

The Jonang had developed in the eleventh century in Tibet as part of the Sarpa blossoming of Buddhism. It differed slightly from the

Gelug in the conceptualization of emptiness, which the Jonang refer to as *zhentong* (*gzhan stong*, 'empty of other'). But it was responsible for the popularization of the practice of the Kālachakra Tantra (Dus kyi 'khor lo), which was adopted by the Gelug and is still a popular teaching under the current Dalai Lama. Jetsun Taranatha (1575–1634) was perhaps the Jonang's most renowned lama. His reincarnation appeared in Zanabazar (1635–1723), the son of the Tüsheet Khan, ruler of the central Khalkha. In addition to the strong Tsangpa patronage,

Jetsun Taranatha, as depicted in a 17th-century thangka.

Zanabazar was of the imperial Mongol Borjigin lineage and therefore a direct threat to the Dalai Lama, Gushri Khan and the Gelug ascendency. In fact, Zanabazar was declared the First Jebtsundamba Khutuktu, spiritual leader of all Mongolia. In reaction to this challenge, the Dalai Lama simply declared the Jonang heretics, and forcibly converted the monks and nuns within his grasp to the Gelugpa. Even the Jebtsundamba Khutuktu suddenly became Gelug. The suppression of the Jonang would cause tensions between the Mongolian and Tibetan Gelug lineages for generations to come (discussed in Chapter Five), but the immediate challenge was thwarted. And despite the suppression, a small contingent of Jonang practitioners still exists.[19]

In 1644 the troops of Hong Taiji, now led by his half-brother, Dorgon 'the Badger', burst through the Great Wall. Conveniently, the Ming had already fallen to warlord Li Zicheng, a former shepherd from Shaanxi, and his short-lived Shun dynasty. The Ming's Chongzhen emperor committed suicide. On 27 May the Manchu banner army, with their Ming defectors, marched into Beijing and sent Li scampering. Hon Taiji's favoured son, Fulin, was taken to the Altar of Heaven, where on 30 October he performed the sacrifice, officially seizing the Mandate of Heaven. He was then paraded in triumph to the Forbidden City, the victorious bannermen marching to the magnificent Hall of Supreme Harmony. Six-year-old Fulin was lifted on to the Dragon Throne, and a pearl and gold crown was placed upon his head. With Dorgon looking on, the imperial seal was placed upon the rescript announcing to the ancestors that the Son of Heaven had assumed his duties. Under the purple light of the pole star, Aisin-Gioro hala-i Fulin had now become the Shunzhi emperor (r. 1644–61) of China as well. Auspiciously for the Great Qing, their reign over China did not begin with a regicide; they could portray Li Zicheng as a usurper, thus maintaining an appearance of respect for the recently departed Ming and helping to construct a legitimate succession to the Mandate of Heaven.

Shunzhi's mother, a Borjigid descendent of the great Genghis, was a major factor in the choice of the boy as emperor. Thus, through biology, conquest and religious legitimacy, the Manchus were set to rule as heirs to the legendary über-khan and the Mongol Empire, the largest land empire the world has ever seen. For a generation the Manchu fought the remnants of the Ming, but finally they added China to the Qing realm.

Consolidation

In that same year, 1644, the Fifth Dalai Lama selected the site of the palace of Tibet's greatest king, Songtsen Gampo atop Marpo-ri, in Lhasa to construct a combination fortress, chapel and palace. In style it was obviously inspired by Samdruptse Phodrang in Shigatse, though much larger. This true wonder of the world would be known as the Potala, the Sky Harbour of the Buddha, the abode of Avalokiteśvara.

The establishment of Ganden Phodrang and the move to the Potala mark a pronounced structural transformation of the priest–patron system. Not just a mere reproduction of the political and spiritual arrangement of the Yuan–Sakya dyad, it incorporated various symbols of ancient Tibetan glory and independence into the relationship. This included seating the government at the abode of Songtsen Gampo; recognizing the manifestation of the perpetual patron of Tibet, Avalokiteśvara, in the incarnation of the Dalai Lama; and claiming the blood of ancient Tibetan Yarlung kings as surging through the body of Ngawang Lobsang Gyatso.

The attempted structural reproduction of the priest–patron relationship under the Qing resulted in major changes. The power of the old Tibetan hereditary nobility, which had experienced a brief renaissance during the Ming (as was seen in the relative success of the Tsangpa dynasty), and the old system of hereditary succession within the Sakyapa were replaced by ecclesiastic nobility, whose reproduction was not dependent upon messy biology. Rather than risk the continuity of a dynasty by the haphazard recombination of gametes, reproduction by metempsychosis provided much greater control through time.[20] The Gelug pa had learned lessons both from the Kargyu about the power of asexual reproduction via *tulku*, and from the political instabilities of the former Sakya patronage relationships. And, conveniently, the lineage of the Dalai Lamas was one of Avalokiteśvara. By incorporating ancient symbols of national independence, the Ganden Phodrang was in a better position to define itself not as a viceroyalty to a powerful empire, but as an independent state with a legitimizing function. It was part of the early Manchu genius to allow for this type of self-determination. Furthermore, the institution of the Dalai Lama defined by the Great Fifth is made to appear to be continuous with the entire span of Tibetan

According to a Tibetan legend recorded in the *Mani Kabum*, Shakyamuni Buddha gave Avalokiteshvara the task of teaching dharma in that country. But since no humans lived in the 'snowy domain to the north' during Shakyamuni's time, Avalokiteśvara had to first generate people to train in Buddhist doctrine. In the form of a divine monkey, he mated with an ogress (identified as the deity Tara). From this union came the Tibetans.

history, with the Buddha himself prophesying the establishment of the system.[21] The Ganden Phodrang is thus a fulfilment of that prophecy, with Ngawang Lobsang Gyatso as a supreme *terton* revealing it.

Within a generation, Emperor Hong Taiji, Gushri Khan, Tibetan regent Sonam Chophel and Ngawang Lobsang Gyatso unified and reorientated much of Central and Inner Asia. This was followed by the incorporation of China into the Qing Empire. The dynasty was thus formed as a political amalgamation of various Tungusic, Han, Mongol and Tibetan factions. While much symbolism had been borrowed from that golden past, each of these four men was also an immensely talented innovator who left Asia with some institutions that are still extant. Legitimizing one another, they were adept at convincing others to join them.

So strong was the ideal of the northern alliance that one could speculate that the conquest of China might have been a secondary goal. It would suggest that Nurhaci and Hong Taiji, like Genghis and Kublai before, were not primarily interested in the unification of China, as modern Chinese nationalism suggests. They were simply charismatic leaders who shared the same dream with those they inspired.

It was not a surprise when in 1648 an invitation was received by the Dalai Lama from the Shunzi emperor. Ngawang Lobsang Gyatso initially demurred, but finally accepted in 1652. The Dalai Lama recognized in this invitation a 1578 prophecy of his predecessor Sonam Gyatso, which stated that descendants of Altan Khan would rule Mongolia and China eighty years hence.[22]

Accompanied for a portion of the way by the Panchen Lama, Gushri Khan, Sonam Chophel, the entire cabinet and 3,000 others, the Dalai Lama left at springtime for the 4,000 km (2,500 mi.) journey to Beijing. The stately movement of this court, with its myriads of guards, retainers, servants, camels, horses and yaks, was nearly identical to the great processions of the Mongol and Manchu courts. In the centre of the Tibetan encampment was the yellow pavilion of the Dalai Lama, covered with awnings of white with blue appliqué. At Koko Nor, the old meeting ground of Mongols and Tibetans, a grand reception was held. The Dalai Lama also visited the birthplace of the Gelug founder, Tsongkapa, at nearby Kumbum monastery, now built up as a formidable Gelug place of pilgrimage.

The Fifth Dalai Lama meeting Emperor Shunzhi, mural in the Norbulingka.

At Xining, after about eight months on the road, the Dalai Lama reduced his entourage to about three hundred, at the request of the hard-pressed imperial court. He was hosted by the Manchus from there onwards.[23] The emperor accepted the Dalai Lama's request to meet outside the Great Wall, but Shunzhi's wish would be thwarted. Manchu and Chinese officials differed as to appropriate protocol. The imperial preceptor of a great khan would be greeted as an equal; however, under the Chinese Confucian system, all had to be subordinate to a Son of Heaven, which Shunzhi had become. Manchu officials were sensitive to the need to appear to cultivate Confucian sensibilities. Citing inauspicious astrological signs, the Chinese bureaucrats thought they had won the day. But a compromise of sorts seems to have occurred: the Tibetans would be greeted by the teenage emperor near Beijing. Shunzhi sent an imperial prince with 3,000 horsemen and a pirate's booty of gifts to intercept the incoming party. The imperial theatre was designed to impress the Dalai Lama and the people alike, showing that the new Manchu rulers were indeed blessed with the mandate to rule.

The sacred procession finally appeared as an epiphany in the frosty winter of 1653. The Tibetan leadership in its yellow travelling garb, the Manchu nobility in sable-lined robes, and 3,000 mounted bannermen padded eastwards on the snow-muffled road. The procession of the Dalai Lama entered the Tartar City and into the Imperial City. Special ramps had been constructed allowing the Dalai Lama to pass over the numerous walls. It was decided by the court that no mere mortal could look down upon the head of the Holy One. Remarkably the Shunzhi emperor had built an entire complex for his special guest, the Yellow Temple (Xi Huang Si) near the Forbidden City in the Western Park. Shunzhi also constructed the immense White Stupa (Baita) there.

Once the Dalai Lama had settled in, a formal reception party was held at the Nanyuan, the hunting park that Shunzhi was developing as an estate for his court immediately south of the city.[24] The bulk of the Tibetan party, much too large to have entered the confined spaces of Beijing, had encamped here. The reception was staged within new buildings that had been built at the park, and within the scores of tents set up for receiving the various dignitaries.

At the appropriate time in the main hall, Shunzhi descended from his throne to meet the Dalai Lama, walking approximately four

Manchu bow-lengths (about 9 m or 30 ft) towards the Tibetan leader. The emperor took the Dalai Lama by the hand to a large throne where they both sat down. The Fifth Dalai Lama recalled in his autobiography: 'When tea was served, the king asked me to drink first. I replied that this would not be proper. So he suggested we drink at the same time. He showed much respect.'[25] A grand banquet was held for the two rulers, imperial princes and high Qing officials. The two were seated side by side at the Te Shou Palace.[26]

The imperial records (Shilu of 14 January 1653) and the autobiography of the Fifth Dalai Lama differ considerably in their accounts of this reception.[27] Most likely the gathering was held outside of the highly structured, Confucian ceremonial confines of the Forbidden City, in the imperial hunting grounds, a traditional Manchu *habitus*. This was probably done for the convenience of the large party, but it also could be construed as symbolic of an Inner Asian tribal meeting of Mongols, Manchus and Tibetans, an alliance that was responsible for the triumph of the Qing over the Han Ming dynasty. It also could be a place where the wishes of Shunzhi and the Confucian court officials could be balanced. The dynasty was new, the emperor was young – the dynasty had not had time to consolidate its rule and push subordination. The meeting at Nanyuan would clearly be more celebratory than one based in the hierarchical political theatre of the Forbidden City. Meeting outside the Imperial City, in a Manchu hunting estate, solved that problem.

A mural painting prominently displayed in the Potala depicts the Dalai Lama giving the Shunzhi emperor religious teachings. The Tibetan leader is sitting on a throne that appears to be slightly lower than the emperor's, although this easily could be construed as a matter of perspective.

After having spent two months in oppressive Beijing, which was clearly not to his liking, the holy guest asked the emperor for leave. Shunzhi, concerned for the Dalai Lama's health, confided with him that he also was having difficulty adjusting to Beijing's climate.[28] Shunzhi suggested that he might personally escort the Dalai Lama as far as Daigar (now Liangcheng, Inner Mongolia).[29] It also would be a convenient place to meet other Mongol and Manchu leaders and further consolidate Qing authority.

In the second month of 1653 the Dalai Lama had his farewell audience with the emperor. It was held in the Forbidden City, in the Taihe Dien, Hall of Supreme Harmony, the most prestigious audience hall of all. Here the Tibetan leader was weighed down with gold, silver, pearls and silks, and was given fine horses and saddles.

So with the spring thaw, the Tibetan visitors left, escorted by Jirgalang, the emperor's great-uncle, the president of the Board of Rites, and a detachment of Manchu troops who travelled as far as Daigar.[30] Here, a few weeks into the muddy journey, Manchu riders caught up with the Dalai Lama and presented him with a golden seal proclaiming him 'Dalai Lama Dorje Chang' (T. and Mon. glosses: 'Ocean Lama, Holder of the Thunderbolt'). The Chinese version adds 'Most Excellent, Self-existing Buddha, Universal Ruler of the Buddhist Faith'.[31] Since he was already Dalai Lama, he was not very impressed. The attempt by the Qing to appropriate the title and then confer it from *fons honorum* authority is a strategy that Chinese leaders have applied ever since.

Overlooked by later Chinese nationalist historians, titles were actually *exchanged* between the rulers on this occasion. The emperor was given the title 'Namgyi Lha Jamyang Gongma Dakpo Chenpo' (T., Gnam gyi lha 'jam dbyangs gong ma bdag po chen po, 'God of the Sky, Mañjughoṣa [Mañjuśrī] emperor, Great Patron').[32] Only an equal sovereign could give such a title to the emperor, which in effect deified him in the Mahāyāna Buddhist system. In the Chinese system, however, accepting a title from the emperor meant submission.[33] But inasmuch as the Confucian system could bend for the establishment of Manchu rule, the Dalai Lama was treated as closely to an independent sovereign as was possible. The priest–patron dyad had been restored. Immediately upon return to Tibet, the Fifth Dalai Lama had the new relationship codified.

As in the Sakya–Yuan alliance, the theocratic ruler of Tibet would not be sullied by the bloody business of war in defence of the state. The Qing warlord, on the other hand, would be legitimized in his authority through the patronizing of the priest, a meritorious activity in Buddhism. As we have seen, this business of keeping the Tibetan state from incurring the karma of war was a foundational principle.

'National' borders were not an issue. The priest and his estate did not become subordinate to the patron by agreeing to such an arrangement, because as religious preceptor he held the higher karmic authority. Shunzhi and Manchu Regent Dorgon were most acutely interested in obtaining the blessing of the Tibetan hierarch for the matriculation of the Qing in Beijing. Later, however, the priest–patron relationship would be increasingly reinterpreted as subordination with the consolidation of empire, especially under the Kangxi emperor (1661–1722). Such appreciation of subordination did not happen in Tibet: the Ganden Phodrang maintained the essence of the binary priest–patron relationship until the abdication of the Qing in 1912. And, perhaps most importantly, the Dalai Lama had begun to assume the secular role of king as well, being the scion of the Yarlung family as well as the incarnation of the patron deity Avalokiteśvara. The Fifth Dalai Lama soon had an opportunity to communicate his interpretation to the emperor. In 1655–6, just two years after the Dalai Lama's visit to the capital, the Shunzhi Emperor sent an inner-court high official and a Tibetan lama doctor (*amchi*) to lead forty monks to the Qingliang mountain to conduct a forty-day ritual to bless the dynasty and fortify the people (*zhuguo youmin*).[34] Ganden Phodrang moved swiftly to consolidate their powers following the meeting of leaders in Beijing. When the Shunzhi Emperor wrote to the Dalai Lama in 1657 over the inquiry of a Phagmodrupa nobleman to receive his old title, the Dalai Lama wrote back that he was indeed the king now.[35]

The honeymoon between the Qing emperor and the Dalai Lama did not last long, however. The slow erosion of the Mongol–Manchu–Tibetan alliance with the later consolidation of the Qing led to an increasing disparity in the interpretation of the relationship between Tibet and the empire, ultimately leading to the Han nationalist claims of the Chinese republican successors to the Manchu realm.

Much to the chagrin of his Gelug monasteries, the Fifth Dalai Lama remained supportive of most of the other Buddhist orders. He did suppress the Jonang school, but mended fences with the Kagyu. The Dalai Lama was already an ardent student of the Nyingmapa, and he actively supported the newly established Mindroling (Smin grol gling) monastery. Under his rule, the Nechung (Gnas chung) oracle, an ancient Nyingmapa institution, was established in its own monastery adjacent to the great Drepung complex. It became one of the two state oracles.

Sensing the end of his current body, the Fifth Dalai Lama decided to appoint a regent and transfer his political powers. In 1679 he appointed

Sangye Gyatso (Sangs rgyas rgya mtsho) regent, ending the Dalai Lama's unprecedented 43-year rule of the spiritual and secular realms of Tibet. The edict, one of the most important in Tibetan history, is a magnificently illuminated scroll, signed with seals and handprints of the Great Fifth in gold. A copy of the document is enshrined at the entrance of the White Palace in the Potala, to be seen by all approaching an audience with the divine ruler. Robert Barnett draws a parallel between this document and the 2011 retirement of the Fourteenth Dalai Lama in his secular role.[36] In both cases, a young regent would perhaps be able to weather the circa fifteen-year interregnum between incarnations and maintain Tibetan independence from Chinese intervention. As Ngawang Lobsang Gyatso retired, he gave instructions to Regent Sangye Gyatso to keep secret his eventual death, until such time as the reincarnation was found and educated. This was done primarily to keep the expansive Qing from interfering in the most sensitive of all Tibetan matters.

The Great Fifth died in 1682. Sangye Gyatso maintained the ruse of a Dalai Lama in meditative retirement by installing his folded vestments upon the Snow Lion throne. On those rare occasions when His Holiness had to attend in person, an elderly monk in sunglasses was proffered. It was not until 1696 that China realized there was already a new Dalai Lama on the throne. The Qing Kangxi emperor was furious. From then on, the imperial court began to contrive ways to take control over the selection of high lamas, a legacy which is still being fought between China and the Ganden Phodrang.

FOUR

Qing Consolidation

Having spent much of its early years creating military alliances with Mongol tribes and seeking religious legitimization from Tibetan hierarchs, the Qing Empire began an unprecedented march of expansion in the later seventeenth century and throughout the eighteenth century. This was to greatly alter the relationship between the Tibetan theocracy as sanctifiers and the Manchus as pious patrons. The Qing court began a stage of direct rule of the highland nation that lasted as long as the empire itself.

A flight of fancy

The great and powerful Fifth Dalai Lama was succeeded by another precocious young man, Tsangyang Gyatso (Tshangs dbyangs rgya mtsho), who was from Monyul (now in Arunachal Pradesh, India). He was born to a family associated with the Nyingmapa, the oldest form of Buddhism in Tibet. The child was recognized by the longtime *desi*, Sangye Gyatso, in 1688 and sent off for an education. The Panchen Lama administered novice vows to Tsangyang and became his primary tutor. Intelligent and handsome, Tsangyang was an appealing and popular figure, and an excellent student – he was enthroned in the Potala in 1697. When adolescence kicked in, however, Tsangyang preferred carousing with his contemporaries in the *chang* (barley beer) shops of Lhasa, flirting with girls and writing love poetry rather than religious exegeses. He was enamoured with games – archery was his passion.

While Tsangyang's *joie de vivre* may have been appropriate for tantric adepts in the times of Padmasambhava in the eighth century, it garnered a chorus of tut-tuts and harrumphs from the austere lamas of the virtuous order founded by Tsongkhapa. After all, was not the chaste

Tsangyang Gyatso, the Sixth Dalai Lama, 18th-century thangka
painted in the tsal tang style (gold on a dark red background),
which includes his hand- and footprints.

Shol village, right below Potala as photographed from the south, which was frequented by a young Tsangyang Gyatso, photograph by O. M. Norzunoff, 1901.

purity of the Great Fifth Dalai Lama a karmic factor to the demonstrated power and success of the Ganden Phodrang in the reunification of Tibet and the exercise of its independence? The appearance of the worldly Sixth Dalai Lama challenged the essential notion of metempsychosis and succession by *tulku* reincarnation. How could the formidable Great Fifth allow himself to be reincarnated in the profligate Tsangyang Gyatso? Was this innovative mode of succession no better than the roll of the dice of the old hereditary system? Furthermore, Sangye Gyatso's deception of keeping the death of the Fifth Dalai Lama secret for so many years, retaining control of the government, showed another inherent weakness in the *tulku* system.

Tsangyang's obstinacy increased. First, he refused to take full *gelong* (*dge slong*) ordination. In fact, he travelled to Tashilhumpo and renounced even his minor *getsul* (*dge tshul*) vows to the Panchen Lama. He grew his hair long and took to wearing the blue robe of a layman. He pitched tents in the parks of Lhasa where he would entertain women that he and his friend Thargyanas procured. The *desi* sought to murder Thargyanas, but the plot backfired and spoiled the relationship between the Dalai Lama and his administrator.

Meanwhile, back in Beijing, the still young Shunzhi emperor had died of smallpox in 1661. He was succeeded by his son, Hiowan yei (Ch., Aisin Gioro Xuanye), who survived the disease. He was proclaimed the Kangxi emperor (M., Elhe taifin). Kangxi was aided in his minority by Grand Dowager Empress Xiaozhuang, a Borjigit Mongol princess born with the name Bumubutai. She would become one of the most powerful women in Chinese history, and her grandson perhaps the greatest emperor of all. Early on, the pair overthrew an ambitious regent, Oboi, to take direct control over the empire. Kangxi was of brilliant intellect and remarkable stamina. He would serve as one of the world's longest ruling and most successful monarchs. As Tsangyang Gyatso was no Fifth Dalai Lama, Kangxi was no naive Shunzhi. He was fluent in Manchu, Chinese and Mongolian, and expected his court to be the same. Later, he would learn Tibetan. Tibet was thus caught between a weak Dalai Lama and a strong Manchu emperor. Tibet's independence would crumble before the might of an expanding Qing Empire.

Remarkably, Tsangyang Gyatso's tenure as Dalai Lama lasted longer than many had expected. His love poetry was widely circulated, becoming one of the few secular works of literature ever penned in Tibet. Despite his shortcomings as a monk, he was wildly popular with the people. Tibetans, as many people elsewhere do, gravitate to charismatic leaders. He was in many ways a Monpa country boy seduced by the ways of the big city. And the Sixth Dalai Lama was honest about his weaknesses:

> Even if meditated upon,
> The face of my lama comes not to me,
> But again and again comes to me
> The smiling face of my beloved.[1]

However, the wily Tsangyang was found to be difficult to depose; his earnest manner was disarming. In fact, it set a precedent that no earthly power could depose a Dalai Lama. Many tried.

Surrounded by a sea of grumpy old lamas, the energetic Dalai Lama fought back. The *desi* was first to go. But Sangye Gyatso achieved one more great accomplishment: the construction of the golden stupa to house the mummified remains of the Fifth Dalai Lama. The magnificent tomb, studded with jewels, is one of the largest golden monuments anywhere. It was completed in the inner recesses of the Potala just before Sangye was compelled to resign in 1703. Sangye remained active behind the scenes, however.

The disagreement between the *desi* and the Dalai Lama had an unsettling effect on the Mongol overlords. The proud title king of Tibet was still held by the Khosots. It had passed from Gushri Khan to his son Dalai Khan, and to his son Lhazang. Since the time of the establishment of the Ganden Phodrang it had been rather an empty title. But Lhazang was determined to take advantage of the tense Lhasa situation and rule Tibet himself. The court of the Dalai Lama caught wind of this adventure and banished Lhazang to Koko Nor. The Ganden Phodrang then allied itself with the powerful Dzungar Mongols. Previously their leader, Galdan, had received a title from the Fifth Dalai Lama, 'Boshoghtu Khan'. Basking in the light of its alliance with the Dalai Lama, the Dzungars became the effective leaders of the western Mongols, displacing even the Khalkha.

Meanwhile, Lhazang Khan did not exile himself to Koko Nor as requested – in fact, he cobbled together an army for an invasion of Tibet. Lhazang asked the Kangxi emperor for support, which was eagerly granted. The Qing were at war with the Dzungars and believed that an alliance with Lhazang would boost their interest in Tibet as well as help to vanquish the Dzungars. Diplomatic niceties between the opposition and the courts of the Dalai and Panchen lamas, however, resulted in a temporary ceasefire between Tibet and Lhazang. Soon, however, when the Dalai Lama sent Sangye Gyatso back to his estates in Gongkar to prevent him from further meddling in Tibetan affairs, the ex-*desi* was captured by Lhazang's men and executed, perhaps by his warrior wife.[2] Lhazang then proceeded to move into Lhasa and assume control as king of Tibet.

While initially supported by the Sixth Dalai Lama, upon consolidating his power in Lhasa, Lhazang turned on him, ranting about the hierarch's numerous shortcomings. Lhazang browbeat the abbots of the major Gelug monasteries to admit that the 'spirit of enlightenment' had left this Dalai Lama.[3] He finally had the Sixth Dalai Lama arrested in 1706 in a humiliating dressing-down before the royal court. Like a spurned lover, Lhazang had the Dalai Lama's possessions thrown out of the Potala. Tsangyang was to be sent to Beijing to be judged by the emperor, a deal

The golden stupa in the Potala Palace, housing the mummified remains of the Fifth Dalai Lama, constructed by Sangye Gyatso.

Lhazang had struck with Kangxi. On 27 June 1706 the Dalai Lama was deposed by Lhazang.[4]

While the exiled party trudged past Drepung on their way to China, the Dalai Lama was rescued by his own monks. The band was quickly joined by monastic forces from Sera and Ganden. The Nechung Oracle was consulted, who proclaimed that Tsangyang was indeed the true

Dalai Lama. However, fearing bloodshed, the Dalai Lama eventually gave himself up, prophesying his return from the Lithang area near the Chinese border.[5] Just outside of Koko Nor, Tsengyang Gyatso died, apparently from the fatigues of travel and privation – he was just 23. The Kangxi emperor never had a chance to depose him, thus testing whether the Qing ever had the authority to do so. King Lhazang then installed a 27-year-old lama, Ngawang Yeshey Gyatso, as the 'true' Sixth Dalai Lama, without any sort of consultation from the religious community. Many thought he was his own son. Expectedly, Ngawang was rejected by the Gelug hierarchy and the common people alike, who would only call him by the title 'mister' (*Sku zhab*).[6]

Around 1711 reports of a miraculous child surfaced from the Lithang region of Kham. Lhazang Khan sent an investigation party and they were impressed with the boy. The child was removed from Lithang and sent to Koko Nor under Mongol protection. The Manchus also sent a representative; the boy was eventually placed in Kumbum monastery to be educated.

It was inevitable that continued Khoshut rule of Tibet would be challenged by the rising Dzungars. The actual confrontation was precipitated when Tsewang Rapten, the Dzungar khan, offered a

General view of Pelkor Chode monastery in the Gyantse valley, with the Kumbum chorten visible in the centre, photograph by G. Ts. Tsybikoff, *c*. 1900.

marriage alliance between his daughter and a son of Lhazang, Ganden Tenzin. The union was agreed, and the young man travelled to Dzungaria to claim his bride. En route, however, he was captured and killed. Tsewang Rapten promptly invaded Tibet with an army disguised as a bridal escort. Since Lhazang did not know his son had been ambushed, Lhazang allowed the 'escort' to enter deep into Tibet. Once the plot was discovered, it was too late. The Dzungars attacked Lhasa, setting siege to the Potala where Lhazang was in residence. Eventually he emerged, and was killed in hand-to-hand combat. The Dzungars subsequently assumed control of Lhasa and all Tibet.

End of the grand Manchu alliance

By the turn of the eighteenth century, it was clear that the Qing culture of dynastic conquest was being replaced with one of consolidation. In Mongol lands there was a deep spilt between the western and eastern wings. In 1688 the eastern Khalkha Mongols and their leader, the Jetsundampa Zanabazar, were driven by the Dzungars under Galdan Khan into making submission to the Qing dynasty. Dzungar aggression precipitated the first Dzungar war with the Manchus in 1696, and the Manchus chased the Dzungars westward out of Outer Mongolia.

One of the Dzungar leaders, Ilaguksan Khutuktu, was caught by Kangxi's forces, brought to Beijing, and executed by the slow slicing process at the Yellow Temple. To drive home the message, all the Manchu and Mongol princes were forced to be witnesses.[7] Galdan was roundly defeated by the Manchus, whose forces were personally led by the Kangxi emperor. Galdan himself was discovered east of Urga (Ulaan Baator) but disappeared in 1697. It is believed that he poisoned himself.[8] The nemesis of the great Qing emperor was cremated.

But despite losses, the Dzungars continued their unpopular rule of Tibet. One of the first matters of business for the Dzungars in Tibet had been to depose the false Sixth Dalai Lama set up by Lhazang Khan, Yeshe Gyatso. 'Mr Dalai' was arrested and confined to the Chakpori (LChags po ri) medical school across from the Potala. Since the people never supported Yeshe, the Dzungars found it easy to remove him.

The Dzungars, now under the leadership of Galdan's son Tsewang Rabten, already had a candidate for the position of Seventh Dalai Lama.

He was immediately whisked away by Mongol leaders from Koko Nor to Kumbum in Amdo, ostensibly to be educated. This boy had apparently been spontaneously declared through a lama of Lithang monastery channelling the Nechung Oracle. Dzungar rule in Tibet was not popular, for they had been persecuting Nyingma lamas. And because of the open war with the Qing dynasty, they could not arrange for the release of the true Dalai Lama. However, Tibetan officials sent a secret letter to Kumbum, recognizing the boy as the reincarnation of the Sixth Dalai Lama. Since Kumbum and all Amdo were under Manchu control, the emperor soon learned of the acknowledgement. Kangxi immediately seized the opportunity to 'confirm' the new Dalai Lama, and offered to support his expenses for his remaining education at Kumbum.

The unpopularity of the Dzungars empowered strong leaders in western Tibet and Tsang to assume regional control. In the northeast, a large Manchu army under General Erentei advanced to Nagchukha, but was defeated by the Dzungar army along the upper Salween River. Infuriated by his loss, Kangxi dispatched his own son Yunti and an army of 300,000 through Xining to escort the new Dalai Lama to Lhasa and to defeat the Dzungars at the same time. General Yunti spent some time mobilizing the Mongols who had submitted to Manchu rule. The rulers of western Tibet and Tsang were already pelting the Dzungars when, on 24 September 1720, Lhasa was taken by the imperial army. Yunti planned on continuing the invasion to Dzungaria itself, but in 1722 was recalled to Beijing due to his father's death.

With the Manchu invasion, the false Dalai Lama, Yeshe Gyatso, was removed from the Chakpori and taken to China.[9] In his place, Kelsang Gyatso was enthroned as the Seventh Dalai Lama at the Potala – the prophecy of Tsangyang Gyatso that he would return from Lithang had been fulfilled. To help stabilize the situation, the Manchus established a permanent garrison in Lhasa and made changes in the administration. The strong position of *desi* was abolished, to be replaced by a council of ministers, the *kashag* (*bka' shag*). The first senior ministers were Khanchenne (Khang chen nas) and Pholhane (Pho lha nas), the Tibetan warlords of western Tibet and Tsang who had fought the Dzungars.

In 1722 Kangxi was succeeded by Yunti's older brother, who became the Yungzheng emperor. One of his first tasks was to withdraw the Manchu garrison in Lhasa, as forces were needed to quell an uprising among the Khosot Mongols in the Koko Nor region. The Khosots were defeated in 1724, and Amdo was annexed to China, eventually becoming Qinghai province. In addition, half of Kham, including Lithang, was annexed to the province of Sichuan. It was a significant loss of territory that had been ethnically Tibetan since the days of empire.

With the absence of the Manchu garrison, the new *kashag* seemed anything but stable. Soon the senior ministers, Khanchenne and Pholhane, whose bases were in the western provinces, found themselves at odds with the junior ministers, who were more orientated towards Ü. Civil war loomed. The Dalai Lama was sent back to Lithang for his safety, and Pholhane asked for the emperor's support. An army was dispatched. Swiftly a tribunal decided against the junior ministers, and they were executed. The Manchus then re-established their garrison and appointed two high commissioners, *amban*,[10] to represent the emperor in perpetuity. These officials would remain until the fall of the Qing in 1912. The emperor provided vast sums to restore the devastated Potala. The Manchus appointed a new *kashag* and the empty title of king of Tibet was abolished. Although the Manchus were welcomed as heroes in saving the lineage of the Dalai Lamas, it was clear to most that Tibet was no longer independent – it had become a Manchu protectorate, a colony but not a province of the empire. The priest–patron relationship had been abolished.

On the Mongolian front, the Yungzheng emperor continued his father's policies by granting titles to friendly Mongol leaders and incorporating them into the imperial lineage through marriage alliances, symbolically becoming 'Manchu' in the process. The Dzungars of the Oiriats, the Qing's biggest nemesis, were entirely and finally defeated by the Manchus at the Battles of Yili between 1755 and 1757. Soon thereafter Muslim Hui people in the region rose up, but they too were subsequently defeated at the Battle of Qurman in 1759. The Qianlong emperor ordered the genocide of the remaining Dzungars.

With privations and disease, the Dzungar population plummeted to about 20 per cent of what it once was.[11] At that point the Manchus annexed both Dzungaria and the Tarim Basin to the south. It had been the last nomadic empire of Inner Asia. The new region conquered by the Qing was called Xinjiang, although referred to in the West as 'Chinese Tartary' or 'Chinese Turkistan' for decades. Some Dzungars

Unidentified artists, *The Great Victory of Qurman*, 1760,
left and right fragments of painting, ink and colour on silk.

managed to leave for the Caspian Sea region, where they are today referred to as Kalmuks.

The conquest of Dzungaria marked a turning point for the Qing dynasty. The Manchus moved many Turkic groups into the new province, Hui, Uighur and Han, and also sizeable Manchu and Xibe garrisons. Although the Manchu elite tried to avoid assimilation of their highly artificial identity into wider Chinese culture through residence and miscegenation laws, by the mid-eighteenth century the empire was defining itself more as a multi-ethnic state. Xinjiang province was specifically incorporated not into the Qing state but within the 'Dulimbai Gurun', a 'Chinese' empire.[12] The identification of the empire as China would become inherited by the republican Nationalists and Communists in the twentieth century. The Tibetans themselves would soon feel the efforts of Qianlong to bring the 'outer' and 'inner' peoples together.

To commemorate the annexation of Dzungaria, the Qianlong emperor commissioned the painting of a hundred portraits of the most meritorious officers of the campaign. They were installed in the Ziguang Ge, the Hall of Purple Light, built in the Zhongnanhai to impress foreign and tributary visitors of the success in the expansion of the Qing Empire. In following years another 180 portraits were painted from other campaigns. Scenes of the battles themselves were painted by Jesuit monks, including the famed Giuseppe Castiglione, in conjunction with native court painters.[13]

In 1721, under the sponsorship of the new Qianlong emperor, the Seventh Dalai Lama, Kelzang Gyatso (bsKal bzang rgya mtsho), was installed with full secular and religious powers. He immediately appointed a new *kashag* and the regency was ended. The four officials of this new *kashag* structure, which lasted until the end of the Buddhist state, had to act unanimously. Although this eased the tendency to dictatorship that had characterized Tibet since the rule of the Fifth Dalai Lama, it also made any high-level decision practically impossible. This structural indecisiveness was a major factor in the weakness of the Tibetan government, especially during its period of independence in the twentieth century between the death of the Thirteenth Dalai Lama in 1933 and the invasion by China in 1950.

The Seventh Dalai Lama, universally regarded as a scholarly and pious monk, lived to be fifty, dying in 1757. He would be the last to wield effective executive power until the enthronement of the great Thirteenth Dalai Lama in 1879. He would restore much of the ideals of the Ganden Phodrang of the Dalai Lamas, which had been wasted by years of brawling khans, libertine and false Dalai Lamas, and squabbling *desi*. It was also a time where Tibetan and official Qing versions of current history would begin to diverge greatly. The ideals of the priest–patron relationship still framed internal Tibet governance, whereas they were practically set aside by the Qing court and their rule through the resident *ambasa*.

At the demise of the Seventh Dalai Lama, the Tibetan government met and decided to institute a regency until a new incarnation was found, educated and enthroned. This new regency concept ultimately came to dominate the Ganden Phodrang, as for nearly two hundred years most Dalai Lamas would barely reach maturity and assume full powers. The dominance of the interregna also catapulted the Panchen Lamas, traditionally the senior tutors of the Dalai Lamas, into power. A divide and rule strategy was adopted by the Manchu court to keep the Panchen and Tsang province in opposition to the powers of the Dalai and Ü. In 1762 a bright boy was brought to the Potala and installed as the Eighth Dalai Lama. He was given the name Jampal Gyatso ('Jam dpal rgya mtsho) by Lobsang Palden Yeshe, the Sixth Panchen Lama.[14] During his reign the summer palace of the Dalai Lamas was built in 1783. The Norbulinka was established west of Lhasa, out on the Kyichu flood plain. Jampal was dominated by the regent and remained behind the scenes until his death in 1804. The next four Dalai Lamas would die before reaching the age of 22.

During the last half of the eighteenth century, the British were ascendant in India, working through the British East India Company. In 1772 the king of Bhutan had invaded Cooch Behar, old 'South Tibet', along the plains of Bengal and kidnapped its *raja*. The Panchen Lama, being the man of the hour, sent a letter and presents to Bengal's first governor-general, Warren Hastings, in the matter of Bhutan. Impressed, Hastings decided to send an expedition to Shigatse to meet the Panchen, and dispatched the Scotsman George Bogle. While Lhasa attempted to block the passage and China had forbidden any dealings with foreigners, the Panchen prevailed – Bogle and his party received permission to visit Tibet. Panchen Lobsang Palden befriended Bogle during their stay

Giuseppe Castiglione, *The Qianlong Emperor in Ceremonial Armour on Horseback*, *c.* 1754, coloured inks on silk.

at a monastery north of Tashilhunpo. In fact, the two could converse
in Hindi. The Panchen was thus able to negotiate directly with Warren
Hastings, and from the very beginning established a relationship with
British India – a relationship that would eventually be fraught with
mistrust, misunderstandings and betrayal.

The wily Bogle stayed in Tibet until the spring of 1775, fully ingrati-
ating himself in the curious but isolated court of Tsang. As Bogle left,
the Panchen Lama set a request back to Hastings that a *dharamsala*,
or travellers' rest, be established for Tibetan pilgrims along the banks
of the Ganges. Hastings subsequently ordered the construction of a
Tibetan temple and monastery across the Hooghly at Calcutta. This
action helped to reintroduce the practice of Buddhism in its homeland,
which had been suppressed for centuries by iconoclastic Muslim rule.[15]
Through Bogle's and Hastings's favourable impressions of the Panchen
and his government, Britain was able to encourage the idea of trade with
Tibet and create a back-door entrance to closed China. Officials may
have considered colonization. The reputation of the Panchen Lamas as
being assessable and the Dalai Lamas occulted began to develop due to
Hastings's and Bogle's success with the Panchen court.

Pax Manchuria

The long reign of Qianlong (r. 1735–1796/9) was perhaps the high point
of the Qing Empire. Cultivated and sophisticated, he set a style as the
epitome of a Chinese emperor that resonated as far as Enlightenment
Europe and beyond. George Washington's and Thomas Jefferson's wigs,
with *queues à la Chinoise*, are testament to this affectation. With the
far west and Tibet stabilized, Qianlong was able to cultivate the centre.
Unlike his grandfather Kangxi, he was not afraid to promote the traditional arts of China and other regions, an action that macho Manchus
once considered effete. One beneficiary of this imperial universalism
was expressed in Qianlong's deep interest in Tibetan Buddhism.

Qianlong's quest to be considered a universal ruler found precedent
in the model of the great emperor Aśoka (304–232 BCE) of the Maurya
in India.[16] The Maurya were successful because they patronized all religious institutions, not just Buddhist ones. They extracted a code of ethics
from many sects and promoted it as a royal dharma to replace the sword

Lai Afong, *Chinese Meal*, c. 1880, albumen print depicting Chinese men
with queue hairstyles.

as the source of legitimacy. This type of statecraft was utilized in the
Tibetan Empire, and it strongly influenced the Manchu state a thousand
years later.

Qianlong was himself a pious Buddhist but was careful not to appear
to show favouritism. In fact, Pamela Crossley suggests that earlier
Manchu leaders practised Tibetan Buddhism in secret so as not to
alienate Taoist and Confucian components of their empire.[17] Qianlong
was not content with leaving Tibetan Buddhism in Tibet. Rather, he
intended to make Beijing the centre of the faith rather than along the
periphery, as Lhasa was viewed. In fact, Tibet itself was objectified and
idealized.[18] It is entirely reasonable that the foundation of Tibet as a
'Shangri-la' in the West arose not entirely from European Orientalism,
but followed the earlier objectification of Tibet by Manchu rulers such
as Qianlong.

With the practically unlimited resources of the Qing Empire at its
peak, Qianlong initiated the translation of the Tibetan canon into
Mongolian and Manchu and initiated learned commentaries on the
ancient texts. He built Vajrayāna temples in Beijing, Jehol and Mukden.
The great Yonghe Gong was established as a major monastery for

Tibetan Gelugpa monks. Qianlong, who was born in the building, raised its status to an imperial temple by changing the turquoise tiles on its roof to the imperial yellow associated with the emperor. Large numbers of Mongolian and Tibetan monks thereupon established residence here, and it was considered the imperial centre of Vajrayāna administration. Many hierarchs of the religion would be confirmed here.

In 1755, at the summer palace town of Jehol (Chengde) established by Kangxi just beyond the wall near Beijing, Qianlong spared no expense building first the Puning temple. It was modelled after Samye in Tibet. It was followed by a somewhat smaller replica of the Potala itself, the Putuo Zongcheng temple, which was completed in 1771. The Putuo temple complex covers a surface area of some 220,000 sq m (2,400,000 sq ft). It was here that Qianlong received the Panchen Lama in 1780, before the party proceeded on to Beijing. The temples were a clear statement that the Manchus, not the Dzungars or other Mongol tribes, were the supreme patrons of the Yellow Religion. In fact, Qianlong really wanted to locate the central administration of the Gelugpa at Beijing and Jehol so it would always be close to the imperial court, not in far-off Tibet that was a year's travel away.

The 1780 reception of the Panchen at Jehol was to celebrate the emperor's seventieth birthday, and Qianlong, a confident sovereign at

Gateway of Lama temple (Yonghe Gong), Beijing, photograph
by Thomas Child, 1876.

the height of his power, could afford to be most respectful to his august visitor. According to the biography of Lobsang Palden Yeshe written by contemporary Tibetan historian Konchok Jigme Wangpo:

> A reception party comprised of persons of various ranks went to meet [the Panchen Lama] on horseback, forming a very long line. They dismounted and prostrated three times upon his arrival. They offered scarves and told him that they had been sent by the Emperor. After they received blessings, they mounted their horses and took leave. In this way, there was a continual stream of reception parties that came to pay their respects. This continued for a very long time. Then the Panchen Lama proceeded on. Placed at a distance of two arrow shots apart were groups of eight, headed by a captain with a peacock feather in

Puning temple, Chengde, 2012.

his hat. When they came to the top of a pass, they saw the city of Jehol from a distance.

As they reached the base of the hill, many officers came to receive them, aided by high ranking officials such as Erle Phugun, Hosa Tazhin, and Kutsha Gangphing Zhe Jailen. Thousands of monks and lay people joined them. As they proceeded further on, they were received with the Emperor's canopy and musicians playing various instruments such as violins, flutes, and so forth. It was a wonderous beholding, like the coming of a Universal Monarch.

As they reached the Chang Tri gate, the entourage dismounted. To the left and right within the gate were high ranking officers with badges on their caps. They were holding scarves, umbrellas of various colors, and religious items. It was a beautiful and awe-inspiring sight! After passing through many gates, the party finally reached the palace.

Although the Mañjuśrī Emperor [Qianlong] requested that the Panchen Lama not dismount, the latter got down upon seeing the Emperor. At the gate [of the audience hall], he was received by Prince Dugpa Chenpo, two cabinet ministers, and the abbot.

[The Panchen Lama] saw the Emperor surrounded by thousands of his subjects. Here the two, priest and patron, met each other for the first time. The Panchen Lama offered a scarf, a statue made of precious metals, and a pearl rosary to the Mañjuśrī Emperor. The Emperor was extremely pleased, and with all due respect, offered a very long scarf and asked about the Panchen Lama's journey. The Mañjuśrī Emperor said to him, 'It must have been a lot of trouble to travel such a long distance.' To this the Panchen Lama replied, 'Because of your grace, I had no problems on the way. I felt warm in places where it is cold, and cool in places where it is hot.' The Emperor was overjoyed to hear this and said, 'That is very fine.' The Emperor took Lord Lama's hand and led him into his inner apartments. They sat together on an exceptionally large throne, and talked for a long time while facing each other. Changkya Rinpoche offered a scarf to the two, priest and patron. Brother Tinley, the attendant Gangjen abbot, and many other people offered scarves and received them in return. When tea was served, the Emperor requested the Precious Lama to drink, and they drank together at the same time.[19]

Like the reception between Shunzhi and the Fifth Dalai Lama, the reception at Jehol was a Manchu exercise in a Manchu space. The emperor found it more expedient to build political capital with both the Mongols and Tibetans by playing the respectful student. Things changed with the venue – receptions in Beijing were far more Confucian and centrist. After the Jehol festivities, the Panchen Lama and Qianlong indeed removed to Beijing. There the Panchen was housed at the Huangsu, built for the Fifth Dalai Lama. Lobsang Palden had all along feared smallpox, which was practically endemic to large Chinese cities. He did indeed contract the dreaded disease in Beijing, and died in November 1780.

The emperor as bodhisattva

The fabulous, nearly unprecedented reception of the Panchen Lama by Qianlong is evidence of the evolving concept of the emperor as a bodhisattva, and thus an equivalent *tulku* in the Buddhist hierarchy of the Mahāyāna and Vajrayāna. The Manchu emperor was revealed to be Mañjuśrī. The notion was not limited to Inner Asia, as national Mañjuśrī cults were popular as far back as Tang dynasty China. Since the establishment of Wutai Shan in Shanxi, Mañjuśrī was a special protector of the empire. Buddhist leader Amoghavajra (705–774) took the Wutai Shan shrine as evidence that the ruler of China could manifest himself as a *cakravartin* ('wheel-turning king').[20]

Some Mongols had considered the great khan Kublai Mañjuśrī,[21] a notion that was canonized in the Mongol *Kangyur* of 1718–20 and applied to the succeeding Manchus:

The Holy Emperor T'ai-tsung of the Manchus [Hong Taiji], after having become the ruler of the great tribes and states of the autonomous Mongolian princes and having gathered them together as his subjects, became ruler of the government of China. After that, the Holy Shun-chih [Shunzhi] assumed the golden throne, and consoled and gave protection to all of his

peoples. After he invited the Fifth Dalai Lama to Peking . . . for
the benefit of those who desired salvation and for all creatures,
the religion of Buddha came to be spread even more than before.
The emperor, his ministers, and all his subject peoples made a
vast number of offerings and oblations, and showed the most
profound respects [to the religion]. Then Mañjuśrī, the savior
of all living forms [with the] intellect of all the Buddhas, was
transformed into human form, and ascended the Fearless Lion
Throne of gold; and this [was] none other than the sublime
Emperor K'ang-hsi-Mañjuśrī who assisted and brought joy to
the entire vast world, and who, because he was the veritable
Mañjuśrī in his material essence . . . [22]

Confident emperors such as Kangxi and Qianlong had nothing to
lose by welcoming the Tibetan leaders as fellow bodhisattvas, although
such demonstrations may have raised a hoary eyebrow in Beijing among
the Taoist and Confucian officials.

Qianlong is memorialized as Mañjuśrī in several *thangka* paintings
of the time. One of these portraits is prominently pointed out at the
Potala under modern Chinese control, implying that the Tibetans worshipped the emperor. The concept of twin bodhisattvas in Tibet and
the empire, however, reflects the ideal of the Tibetan state from a native,
Vajrayāna point of view: each bodhisattva has a specific realm of activity.
Avalokiteśvara's domain is Tibet, representing the western paradise, the
colour red and the *dhyani* bodhisattva Amithāba; Mañjuśrī's realm is
China, the eastern paradise of Vimala, the realm of Akshobhya, the
colour blue. As both bohisattvas are ideologically equivalent yet separate,
their respective realms are by extension of equal status. The priest–
patron dyad, in this case, is what tied the two spheres of activity together
according to the classical Tibetan standpoint, with a notable exception:
the patron was also a divinity, with the power to legitimate.

The Gurkha wars

Another opportunity for the Manchus to demonstrate their influence
in Tibetan affairs arose during the last part of the eighteenth century.
'Southern Tibet', the region south of the Himalaya that had once been

a part of the Tibetan Empire, had succumbed to colonial pressures of the new power, Great Britain. Cooch Behar, Sikkim, Bhutan, Tawang-Monyul, Ladakh, Lahul and Spiti were all former Tibetan tributaries that had begun to develop their own nationalisms in response to shifting regional powers. Many of these regions had become sanctuaries to non-Gelug sects, such as the Kagyu and Nyingma. Others were Muslim or Hindu regions. Under the leadership of Prithvi Narayan Shah, the Gurkhas of central Nepal were also challenging their neighbours for dominance. Especially coveted was the wealthy Kathmandu Valley, ruled for centuries by the Malla kings, and vital for the lucrative Tibetan–Newari–Moghul Indian trade networks. Prithvi Narayan was finally able to conquer Kathmandu in 1769, making him the first Gurkha king of Nepal.

When in 1780 Lobsang Palden Yeshe, the Sixth Panchen Lama, died in Beijing, his half-brother, the Shamarpa ('Red Hat', Zhwa dmar pa) Mipam Chodrup Gyatso, claimed his inheritance from their common mother and a share of the gifts the emperor had lavished upon the Panchen and his other brother, the Trungpa Rinpoche. Trungpa refused to share with the Shamarpa, and locked up the loot in Tashilhumpo in Shigatse. Undaunted, the Kagyupa Shamarpa, with assistance from his monks, stormed the monastery and took what he thought was his share. The Gelug recaptured the possessions and banished the Shamarpa. Mipam Chodrup left Tibet and became the guest of the new king of Nepal. The Kagyu Shamar had a long relationship with the Malla kings of Kathmandu, and now it was being extended to the new dynasty.

The Shamarpa inheritance led to an armed conflict in 1788, when the Shamarpa conspired with the Nepalese Gurkha army. The Gurkhas had been looking for an excuse to invade Tibet, due in part to an earlier conflict over Sikkim. A crisis over the circulation of inferior Nepalese coins in Tibet precipitated a threat by Prithi Narayan to seize several border districts of Tibet. Futhermore, the king captured the Shamarpa and held him hostage. The Red Hat lama promptly wrote the Dalai Lama informing him of his plight. The Ganden Phodrang was reluctant to devalue the old Nepalese coins, which could cause an economic panic. They also brushed off the Shamarpa's plea as his own business. The Gurkhas subsequently invaded Tibet, taking the districts of Nyanang, Rongshar and Kyirong. The Nepalese army, consisting of

3,000 soldiers, 5,000 porters and four generals, then proceeded to head directly for Shigatse. They were met by Tibetan forces from Tsang and Ü. The *ambasa* in Lhasa immediately informed the Qianlong emperor, who dispatched an army of 2,000 men. Before the imperial forces arrived, however, the Tibetan army pushed back the Gurkhas to their previously held districts. Meanwhile, the Nepalese opened up a second front by attacking Sikkim.

The Gurkhas were ultimately defeated by Tibetan forces. The Manchus never fought – in fact, the Shamarpa was already arranging for negotiations between the Tibetan and Gurkha representatives and a ceasefire was under effect when the Manchus finally arrived. The agreement that was hammered out in 1789 devalued the old coins in circulation, ensured the trade of pure rice and salt, granted Nepalese extraterritoriality rights in Tibet, and imposed a tribute upon Tibet to Kathmandu to assure the withdrawal of Gurkha troops from the districts seized. The Chinese witnessed the agreement, and escorted Gurkha representatives back to Beijing to give respects to the emperor. The Tibetans also sent a delegation to Beijing.

The next year the Tibetan government entered into negotiations with the Gurkha king to reduce the annual tribute. Instead, the Nepalese captured the negotiators and moved them to Nepal. The Gurkhas then invaded Tibet again, this time taking Shigatse itself. Panic broke out in Lhasa, as the capital itself was in range of possible Gurkha occupation. The Dalai Lama, however, reassured the populace that he would not leave, despite the *ambasa*'s insistence. The Tibetan army succeeded in driving the Gurkhas out of Shigatse, then to Kyirong and Nyanang. The Tibetan army of 10,000 men was joined in the spring of 1792 by 13,000 imperial troops. The combined forces beat back the Nepalese army, and through Sikkim entered Nepal itself. The Gurkhas began to sue for peace; the traitorous Shamarpa killed himself. The allied forces arrived within 32 kilometres (20 mi.) of Kathmandu, and demanded the Shamarpa's valuables, retainers and all the booty previously looted from Shigatse. This was granted. Nepal also had to send a tribute envoy to the emperor every five years.

Heads rolled. The two *ambasa* were replaced. The officials that were held prisoner by the Gurkhas were demoted. The Shamarpa's estates were confiscated and his reincarnation was forbidden.[23] In fact, in an act of great defilement, the red crown of the Shamarpas was buried under a public space in Lhasa, subject to the trampling of hundreds of feet daily.[24]

The emperor sent the king of Nepal the title of *wang* and a sable hat with peacock feathers, and similar honours for the uncle-regent of the young king. Qianlong upgraded the position of *amban* at Lhasa and beefed up the Tibet garrison by establishing bases at Shigatse and Dingri.[25] It was the high point of Manchu power in Tibet, used in modern claims of sovereignty over the region by the People's Republic of China. But the imperial forces were called to help Tibet exorcize foreign invasion, not to occupy it, according to Tibetan priest–patron ideology.

The Qing, however, were anxious to consolidate their power in Tibet, and stumbled upon the idea of taking control of the selection process of the high lamas. At the end of the Gurkha war, Qianlong sent a golden urn to be used in drawing lots to select reincarnations of the Dalai, Panchen and Jebtsundampa lamas. One urn was kept in Beijing – the other in Lhasa. The traditional selection of a child reincarnation had been focused on those spiritually closest to the previous incarnation. Tutors, regents and, in the case of the Dalai *tulku*, the Panchen lamas were called upon. Dreams, divinations, images in sacred lakes, instructions from the departed incarnation and oracular prophecy were all weighed by the great lamas in their search for signs of divinity among promising candidates. Occasionally, a child under consideration might correctly identify personal possessions of his predecessor. Once convinced, the lama in charge would proclaim the candidate as the true successor. Through the socialization process, that child would then be educated to fulfil his predecessor's position.

Although the process was ideologically based in cleromancy, it also could be a means to politically control the succession. As with the Fourth Dalai Lama, who was conveniently discovered in the son of Altan Khan, a child's family position, region and other affiliations could seem to weigh politically in the selection. Following the defeat of the Dzungars and the Gurkhas, the Qing court was eager to control the selection of high lamas as a key in their consolidation of Inner Asia. While perhaps they could not directly control the attendant political machinations, they could be seen as the authorizing agency in the selection process. The priest–patron relationship was turned on its head when it became the emperor who claimed to have the exclusive right to legitimize the Dalai, Panchen and Jebtsundampa *tulku.*

Modelled from the drawing of lots in the selection of finalists in the Chinese Civil Service exams, the golden urn was mandated in 1792 in *The 29-article Imperial Decree for Better Governing in Tibet.*[26] The drawing of lots 'allowed' the gods to steer the election. The golden urn also reduced the human temptation to channel the selection for political reasons. The successful application of the golden urn selection process demonstrates another historical discrepancy between Tibetan and Chinese records. According to the Fourteenth Dalai Lama, only the Eleventh Dalai Lama was actually chosen by the golden urn.[27] Other high lamas had been recognized by traditional means – the urn ceremony became a pantomime used only to placate the Qing.

FIVE

Independence

The Oceans of Scriptural Realization, Morality, Complete Learning and Spiritual Activities all nominally ruled Tibet in the nineteenth century. In rapid sequence, Dalai Lama Lungtok Gyatso (Lung rtogs rgya mtsho, 1805–1815) was followed by Tsultrim Gyatso (Tshul khrim rgya mtsho, 1816–1837), Khendrup Gyatso (mKhas grub rgya mtsho, 1838–1856) and Trinley Gyatso ('Phrin las rgya mtsho, 1857–1875). Whether by subterfuge or karmic reckoning, the Ninth to Twelfth Dalai Lamas largely reigned in name only during their minorities, which they barely survived. Instead, Tibet was ruled by their senior tutors, the Panchen Lamas, the regents and the Manchu *ambasa* in the name of the Qing emperor.

The nineteenth century was also a time of retrenchment for the Manchu Empire. The period of expansion and consolidation ended with the death of the Qianlong emperor in 1799. The treasury exhausted, the remaining 112 years of the Qing were largely spent trying to resist aggressive colonization of its territory by Japan, Russia and the Western imperial powers. Internally, the Manchu dream became a nightmare. The last half of the century was led by a vain, insecure woman, Cixi, who clawed her way to the top of a termite-eaten throne, grasping at what power was left to the dynasty, pushing aside legitimate emperors along the way. Tibet would be keen to take advantage of this weakness. The Tibetan regent during the reigns of most of these teenaged Dalai Lamas was Jamphel Tsultrim Tsemonling, a ruler who seemed to become increasingly unpopular as the years rolled on. Boy Dalai Lamas suspiciously followed one another. Visiting Catholic priest Abbé Huc and Father Gabet recorded the temperature of crowds on the streets of Lhasa:

It was said that the first Tale-Lama [Ninth?] had been strangled, the second crushed by the roof of his sleeping apartment, and the third poisoned with his numerous relations, who had come to settle at Lha-Ssa . . . The public voice denounced the Nomekhan [Tsemonling] as the author of all these crimes.[1]

The Panchen Lama, Tenpai Nyima (1781–1854), and the four officers of the *kashag* conspired with Amban Kichan to have Desi Tsemonling arrested. Under threat of torture, the regent admitted having 'used violent means to make the Dalai Lamas transmigrate'.[2] The monks of Sera attempted to rescue Tsemonling, but the regent decided not to pursue the effort. Under orders from the Qing emperor, he was exiled to Sakhalin, a large island off the Pacific Coast in remote Manchuria. For a brief time, the Panchen Lama assumed responsibility for running the Ganden Phodrang. A new regent was found in the young incarnate lama of Reting (Rwa sgreng) monastery, Ngawang Yeshe Tsultrim Gyaltsen. These reforms did not seem to help too much, as the Dalai Lama after the Catholic priests' visit, Trinley Gyatso, died at only eighteen years old.

The Gurkha wars had a profound effect upon the Ganden Phodrang government and the successive monk-led regencies.[3] Tibet decided to close in upon itself and concentrate its political efforts on the stabilization and perpetuation of monastic institutions over all other considerations. The prolonged regencies empowered the various abbots of the great Gelugpa monasteries to assume full control over Tibetan life. It was ruled that no one could enter or leave Tibet without government permission, and that would not be forthcoming. Thus, throughout the nineteenth century, Tibet disappeared from maps of the world, especially those drawn in the West. It is from this era that the romantic view of Tibet as a forbidden Shangri-La developed. Although for centuries the crossroads of Asian caravans, Tibet vanished, becoming a featureless 'white' zone of the unknown and inflaming the passions of countless would-be Victorian explorers.

Tibet's apparent xenophobia was an attempt to maintain the purity of the realm through a foreign policy of resisting outside contact and

overleaf: John Cary, *Map of Central and Eastern Asia, from the Caspian Sea to China*, 1806.

London Printed the J. Cary Eng.

an internal policy of securing the borders. The *raison d'être* of the state – keeping deleterious karmic agents away – was thus maintained.

Tibet's isolation was accomplished in the eastern part of the land not with policy or high mountains, but with the slow rot of the once-great Manchu Qing Empire. Until the last decade of the dynasty, successors to the Qianlong emperor had neither the resources nor the will to interfere with local politics or engage in border disputes with Tibet. A self-imposed isolation fostered self-confidence within the Tibetan government. It could manage its own affairs, but this did nothing to help it cope with the changing vicissitudes of world politics. The new superpower of the world, the British Empire, was viewed with great suspicion, as the Ganden Phodrang had witnessed their aggression and interference in Cooch Behar, Sikkim, Bhutan and Gurkhali Nepal.

Arrival of the Great Thirteenth

In 1876 a bright baby boy was born at Thakpo near Samye. He would take the state of Tibet to full independence, free from the centuries-old intrigues of Manchu and Mongol princes. When he was only ten months old, a nationwide search party arrived at his home. The birthplace of the child had been seen in a vision at the oracular lake of Lhamo Latso (Lha mo bla mtsho) at Chokhorgyal (Chos 'khor rgyal).[4] The baby was too young to undergo the traditional tests, although he already seemed promising as a candidate for the reincarnation of the Twelfth Dalai Lama. The party returned the following year and gave the child the traditional identification tests with articles belonging to the Twelfth Dalai Lama. Although there were three candidates, everyone agreed that the boy from Thakpo was the true incarnation. The Nechung Oracle confirmed the findings and Qianlong's golden urn was not used.

In 1877 the regent Chokyi Gyaltsen Kundeling announced publicly that the new Dalai Lama had been found. He was named Ngawang Thubten Gyatso (Ngag dbang thub bstan rgya mtsho) by the Fifth Panchen Lama, Tenpai Wangchuk (Bstan pai dbang phyug). The Thirteenth Dalai Lama was enthroned in the Potala in 1879. He would break the spell gripping Tibet that had existed since Qianlong – he would survive, rule as a sovereign and declare Tibet independent. Modern

Thubten Gyatso, the Great Thirteenth Dalai Lama.

Tibetan nationalism dates from when the newly born Thirteenth Dalai Lama fought to take his first breath in 1876.[5]

At the same time, British surveyors arrived in Tibet, secretly sent by the Imperial Survey of India. They were led by Indian scholar Sarat Chandra Das, disguised as a Buddhist student. The party was able to visit Lhasa, albeit clandestinely, making geographical measurements along the way. The subterfuge was eventually discovered by the Ganden Phodrang, however, and punishments were meted out to those lamas and officials who had assisted Das. The government became even more suspicious of the motives of the British Raj from this incident. The goodwill that had been built in the past between the Panchen and Hastings of the previous century seemed to have evaporated.

In 1883, when the Dalai Lama was seven years old, the royal family of Sikkim paid a visit. Young Ngawang Thupten became friends with Mahārāja Thuthop Namgyal's (Mthu stobs rnam rgyal) son and heir, Sikyong Namgyal (Srid skyong sprul sku rnam rgyal), recognized as a *tulku* of his late lama uncle. The development of close relationships between the two governments would be an asset in dealing with much of the world beyond. Sikkim would be a strategic ally with the Ganden Phodrang in keeping foreign incursion at bay.

In 1885, according to the 1876 Treaty of Chefoo, the Qing Empire agreed to allow a British expeditionary force to transit Tibet on its way to India. The Tsongdu (national assembly) acted in an emergency session to declare that the Chinese emperor had no authority to agree to such an event and vowed never to allow a British person to enter Tibet. And by demonstrating that they could secure their border, the Tibetan government illustrated that Manchu authority in Tibet was nil. The expedition could not proceed. In compensation to the British, the Qing was forced to recognize British annexation of Upper Burma.[6] As a result of the British asking to build a dak bungalow near the Tibetan border at Dzalep la, Tibet and Sikkim worked together to define their common frontier, and the Tibetan army sent border troops to the region.[7] In fact, a brief battle between British and Tibetan forces occurred at Lungthur in 1888. Sikkim itself was being trampled by the British, who eventually took over the government and imprisoned the royal family. Upon accepting a protectorate under the British Raj, the Mahārāja Thuthop Namgyal was released, returning to Gangtok in 1895.

In 1890, when China recognized British colonialization of Sikkim, Tibetans removed the new boundary pillars. The Anglo-Chinese Trade Agreement of 1893 established a trading mission at Yatung. The Tibetans again refused to abide by the stipulations agreed upon in their absence by China and Britain. The defiance was clearly a statement of self-determination.

A new regent, Demo Trinley Rabgay ('Phrin las rab rgyas), assumed leadership of the Tibetan government in 1886 with the death of Chokyi Gyaltsen Kundeling. In 1888 the Dalai Lama named the Sixth Panchen Lama Thubten Chokyi Nyima. He would grow up to embrace Chinese republican ideals and become a thorn in the Dalai Lama's side. In 1894 a permanent monk official was added to the constituency of the *kashag*, and the de facto qualification of nobility was eliminated for secular *kalons*. The following year, the Dalai Lama assumed his majority and was installed with complete secular and religious authority. At the age of 22, he passed all the highest religious exams, and was swiftly climbing through the critical phase where most of his predecessors had died.

Early in his reign the wary Thirteenth Dalai Lama was able to steer clear of the impediments that befell his immediate predecessors, political and otherwise. It surfaced that the ex-regent, Demo Trinley Rabgay, was disappointed to become jobless with the assumption of full authority by the Dalav Lama. On two occasions the Nechung Oracle foretold that the Dalai Lama's life was in danger. It was discovered that the ex-regent had prepared a set of shoes with black magic mantras in the soles

Thubten Chokyi Nyima, the Ninth Panchen Lama, in Calcutta, 1910.

prescribing the death of the Dalai Lama. These were discovered, and the ex-regent and his accomplices were imprisoned. In jail they nevertheless managed to bribe the *ambasa* to overturn the sentences. The Manchu *ambasa* were blocked by the Tibetan government, giving the impression that at this time they had very little effective power over the Ganden Phodrang.[8] The conspirators were given life imprisonment.

The romantic Manchu dream, with its lusty mounted archers and headstrong women enflaming Inner Asia with the ideal of a new Mongol Empire, was quickly drawing to an end. In Tibet, the truncated reigns of the last four Dalai Lamas were cast out by the overthrow of the regent and the routing of the *ambasa* by Tibetan forces. Herein lies one of the roots of modern Tibetan nationalism. Laurence Waddell, who was stationed in Sikkim in the 1890s and knew officials in the Tibetan government well, writes of the toppling of the regent-*amban* system:

> The present Dalai Lama has been permitted to become an exception to this rule, through the influence of the national party which has risen up in Tibet in veiled revolt against the excessive interference by the Chinese in the government of the country. This national party saved the young Dalai from the tragic fate of his predecessors, and they rescued him and the Government out of Chinese leading-strings by a dramatic coup d'état.[9]

While visiting Samye, the Dalai Lama caught smallpox – he recovered but his face remained pockmarked. The second Nechung prophecy had been fulfilled. The event of the 'enchanted shoes' and the recovery from the disease were indications to the people that Thubten Gyatso was destined to rule, firmly and with vigour. Furthermore, the meddlesome Panchen was still a minor.

The foiled Demo Trinley coup was the norm rather than the exception for the nineteenth-century Tibetan leadership. The succession of regents, the autonomy of the Panchens, the isolation of Lhasa, and the weakening agency of the emperor acting through the *ambasa* diffused executive authority. It made it easy for officials to escape individual responsibility for governmental mistakes and punished those who espoused bureaucratic efficiency and transparency within the Ganden Phodrang. If anything, intrigue and obscuration were the standard. It

Lord and Lady Curzon atop the elephant Lakshman Prasad, 29 December 1902, on the way to Delhi for the Durbar.

seemed as if the stars were now aligned for the emergence of a powerful Dalai Lama. In fact, the Great Thirteenth would go beyond the achievements of the Great Fifth.

Throughout the nineteenth century Britain formalized its colonization of India. Following the Sepoy Mutiny, the British took over direct rule of India, deposing the last Grand Mughul, Bahadur Shah II, in 1857. Queen Victoria was proclaimed Empress of India in 1876. The British Raj had also taken the Darjeeling half of Sikkim, a former Tibetan tributary, and had kept the Namgyal royal family imprisoned. Bhutan, Tawang,

overleaf: General J. T. Walker, *Tibet and the Surrounding Regions*, 1894.

TIBET
AND
THE SURROUNDING REGIONS
Compiled from the latest information

KUM-TAGH SANDS

ALA-SHAN

NAN SHAN RANGE

KOKO-NOR

TSAIDAM

TIBET

KHAM

SAM

The Dalai Lama 'fleeing English domination' on the front of *Le Petit Journal*,
20 November 1904.

Nepal and other Tibetan regions south of the Himalaya also came under
British influence. British policy had emphasized the creation of buffer
regions separating their Asian colonies from the still expanding Russian
Empire to the north. Two wars, in fact, had been fought over Afghanistan.
A buffer state of Tibet would well serve British interests, and those in
the know recognized that Chinese control of Tibet was pretty much a

work of fiction. Russia, it was seen in Whitehall and Calcutta, could easily take advantage of Tibet.

In 1898 London chose a diplomat with strong anti-Russian credentials to be Viceroy of India, George Curzon, Baron Curzon of Kedleston. Curzon had a clear idea of Russia's ambitions in Asia, having seen her acquisition of much of Central Asia and the Pacific Far East. Lord Curzon was not just a paranoid official: he was considered one of the top scholars of Russian and Central Asian political affairs. His perspectives were influential in the development of British foreign policy in the late nineteenth and early twentieth centuries. Since the time of Catherine II and before, Russia had aggressively carved out chunks of Central and East Asia, much of it from the remnants of the old Mongol domination. It brought Russian influence right to the borders of Tibet in the west and north of the plateau. Tibet was obviously in her sights for further adventures, which was perceived in London and Calcutta potentially to cause numerous problems with the defence of the British Raj in India. The regents, *kashag* ministers and *ambasa* played a delicate balancing game for generations keeping powerful neighbours out of Lhasa and away from meddling with the religio-secular government of the Ganden Phodrang. The Qing residents, in fact, convinced the Tibetan government and the great monasteries that the British would destroy Buddhism in Tibet, like the Muslims destroyed Buddhism in India. This was all reinforced with the prevailing attitude that the continuing priest–patron relationship with the Qing emperor was the key to Tibet's salvation. This attitude was soon to change with the blossoming of the Thirteenth Dalai Lama into full maturity.

In an attempt to make contact with the Tibetan government and stave off any Russian overtures, Lord Curzon sent an elegantly worded letter to the Dalai Lama, in fact three letters. All were returned unread with their seals intact. The Ganden Phodrang decided to forego direct contact with their aggressive neighbour, noting the apparently pernicious interference of the British in Nepal, Bhutan, Sikkim and other southern Tibetan kingdoms. Not used to being dismissed, the snub infuriated British officialdom. It is not known if the Dalai Lama knew of this attempted diplomatic contact. Misinformation was also being generated by a Japanese monk, Ekai Kawaguchi, who was studying at Sera monastery. He suggested to British agent Sarat Chandra Das that hundreds of Buriat Mongols were enrolled in Tibetan monasteries, and that the Russian government was shipping small arms and ammunition to the Tibetan government.[10] This further inflamed Lord Curzon, who was finally realizing that the Manchus had no influence in Tibet and, worse, that Tibet might soon be absorbed by the voracious Russian Empire.

First exile

In 1904 the Thirteenth Dalai Lama made the decision to abandon Lhasa instead of being forced to meet the British in the capital, maintaining the imperious snub he had meted out earlier to Viceroy Curzon. In his final testament written just before his death in 1933, Thubten Gyatso recalled his motivation for leaving:

> In the Wood Dragon Year the English armies began to build up on our borders and threaten an invasion. It would have been simple enough for me to have placated them by submitting to their demands, but such a course of action could easily have resulted in danger to our independence and sovereignty. Therefore, in spite of the difficult and hazardous journey I left for Mongolia and Manchu China, the two countries with whom the Great Fifth Dalai Lama had established Patron/Priest arrangements, and with whom Tibet shared relations of mutual respect and support.[11]

Significantly, the Dalai Lama took with him his closest friend, teacher and debate partner, the Buriyat Mongol monk Agvan Lobsang Dorjiev, a Russian subject who would solicit the support of the tsar for the Tibetan cause. Of course, one of the main reasons the British invaded Tibet was to prevent Russia from meddling in Tibetan affairs. Husky Dorjiev was a teacher of the Dalai Lama, an expert in Buddhist dialectical debate and 22 years the senior of his pupil. He had been educated at Drepung, and his worldly ways would become a window on the world for the 28-year-old Dalai Lama.

The Russian Empire was heir to large segments of the former Mongol Empire, notably the Buriyat region around Lake Baikal, northwest of

Ulan Ude, home of Agvan Dorjiev. Tsarevich Nicholas's 1890–91 tour to the Far East with the Orientalist Prince Esper Ukhtomsky, Russia's building of the Trans-Siberian railway, and its annexations in Manchuria (for example, 1860) gave the India Office at Whitehall severe headaches. It was also well known that the young Nicholas was interested in Tibetan exotica and spiritualism in general, and these times were rich with Western mystic Orientalism, as characters such as Helena Blavatsky and Alexandra David-Neel conjured up the most fantastic stories (Rasputin would come later). In this climate, and despite strong objections by the Russian Orthodox Church, Dorjiev managed to raise funds and eventually build a Tibetan Buddhist temple in St Petersburg. Through Prince Ukhtomsky, a practising Buddhist, Dorjiev was presented to Nicholas II, now emperor. When the tsar began telegraphing the Dalai Lama messages of appreciation for helping to pacify the Mongolian Russians, the British were unnerved.

In the first years of the twentieth century, Manchuria was being divided up between Japan and Russia, and the Manchus in Beijing could do little. Korea was lost to Japan. With the Qing dynasty so weak, it seemed logical that Britain would see a possible Russian interest in both Mongolia and Tibet. And Tibet created a mythology about the great Russian Empire. It seems to have been a possibility in the Tibetan worldview that Russia was seen as a Shambhala,[12] and that Tsar Nicholas II himself was a bodhisattva. Shambhala, as we recall, was a Pure Land realm closely associated with the Kālachakra Tantra, one of the chief practices of the Dalai Lama lineage. Shambhala, mythologically located northwest of the Tibetan plateau, was also considered the origin of the very ancient Zhang Zhung culture, a pillar of the concept of the Tibetan nation.

Since the Russian emperor was now the overlord of many of the Mongol tribes, he was a likely candidate to be the new patron of Tibet to the Gelugpa. Perhaps even all of Russia would convert to Buddhism the way the Mongols did under Genghis and the Manchus did under Nurhaci. It certainly seemed reasonable to develop a new priest–patron alliance in the light of British aggression and Chinese inaction. A future saint, Nicholas II was a pious Orthodox Christian with a strong appreciation of the mystical and miraculous. It is not a stretch to think that he, the Little Father of all his peoples and God's representative on earth, accepted his deification by his Buddhist subjects with humility and with relish. The tsar's spiritual nature, as well as the influence of Prince Ukhtomsky, were certainly recorded by Dorjiev and communicated to the Dalai Lama. The two close friends, Agvan Dorjiev and Thubten Gyatso, noting the atrocious behaviour of the British towards their allies in Sikkim, the ineffectiveness of Qing protection of Tibet, and the collusion of Britain and the Manchu Empire to maintain the judicial fiction of China's sovereignty over Tibet, were developing a policy that would wrench Tibet and Mongolia away from the Manchus. They would seek support for this natural progression under the patronage of the Russian tsar.

For the players of the 'Great Game', the loss of face was worse than any sort of battlefield or territorial loss. This was as much a reality for the Qing as it was for Russia and Great Britain. For Lord Curzon, the aloofness of Tibet to the great superpower was unacceptable. Perhaps the Dalai Lama might reconsider should British troops appear at the foot of the Potala. Lord Curzon began to discuss the martial possibility with his old army buddy Frank Younghusband. Both shared a conviction that the British Empire had a holy mission to bring modern civilization and order into all corners of the world. Unfortunately, Queen Victoria had died in 1901, and the Boer War had been a misadventure: imperceptibly the British Empire had already started to decline. Still, in the minds of imperial careerists like Curzon and Younghusband, the sun seemed that it would never set. The military incursion of British forces into Tibet would be one of the defining moments, however, that showed the vulnerability of the once unstoppable empire.

Lord Curzon finally received permission from London to send a force to Khampa *dzong*, just over the Tibetan border. Younghusband was asked to lead and eagerly accepted, envisioning pushing his troops all the way to Lhasa to force the Dalai Lama to negotiate. With five hundred soldiers, Younghusband crossed the Sikkim–Tibetan border and arrived at Khampa *dzong* in July 1903. The Tibetans sent a party consisting of an *amban*, a senior member of the Ganden Phodrang and a general with the message that no negotiations would happen until the British retreated back to Sikkim. The troops reluctantly returned, but the colonel was undaunted. He sent a barrage of hyper-inflated accounts of Tibetan mischief to Curzon, trying to inflame British

Drawing of
Captain Francis E.
Younghusband in
*Illustrated London
News*, 17 May 1890.

passions into making a further advance into Tibetan territory. It worked. In November, Younghusband was given the order to return and advance to Gyantse (Rgyal rtse), where it was believed there existed an armoury well stocked with Russian-made ammunition. This time he was fortified with 5,000 troops,[13] mostly Gurkhas and Sikhs, and 10,000 Sepoy porters. Camp followers included a motley crew, some of whom became the first 'Tibetologists' through their exclusive books on travels through Tibet. The Ganden Phodrang sent a 1,500-strong army to meet the British, and the Tsongdu replaced the pacifist *kashag* with hawkish ministers. Outside of the village of Guru, the two forces met. The antiquated Tibetan army was mowed down by the automatic weapons of the British, and those Tibetans who simply walked away were shot in the back. The testosterone-fuelled British proceeded on to Gyantse, blowing up the Tibetan-stocked arsenal at the *dzong* and securing the city. Although now the Dalai Lama was attempting to initiate peace talks through the future king Tongsa Penlop Ugyen Wangchuk (Krong gsar dpon slob o rgyan dbang phyug) of Bhutan, Younghusband was determined to forge on to Lhasa. At the pass of Karo la they encountered

The 7th Fusiliers entering the gate to Lhasa, photograph by Lt William Pyt Bennett.

Tibetan resistance, and three hundred more Tibetan soldiers lost their lives. On 29 July Younghusband received a letter from the Dalai Lama asking him to remain at the Tsangpo crossing and negotiate at that spot. Younghusband ignored the message, crossed the river and aimed for Lhasa. Messengers reported back to the Dalai Lama, who took immediate action.

Appointing the Ganden Trichen Lobsang Gyaltsen Lamoshar (Blo bzang rgyal mtsan la mo shar) as regent, the Dalai Lama left his seals in Lhasa and disappeared northwards with his debate coach-cum-ambassador Dorjiev and the Nechung Oracle – a small party of eight, which grew larger at each stop, a testimony to the fame the reincarnation had accrued over the centuries. The holy protector rode swiftly across the frozen tundra of the Changthang, dotted with salt lakes shimmering in the heat. The long-vanished Tethys Sea where plesiosaurs once swam was the stage for this political drama, now a flat sea of barren land separating North Asia from the island continent of India. The tangible head of the Buddhist faith eyed the attentive wild yaks that rose and disappeared as black dots on a frosty brown steppe. Clear blue skies stretched to the far horizon. Nomads fell to their knees as the god of compassion thundered quickly by in a streak of gold and crimson. Pikas nibbled at blue poppies while listening attentively to the distant jingling of reins and silver gear of the retreating entourage. North–south caravans were rare in this land crossed by the ancient trade routes between China and the West. As Beijing got word of the Dalai Lama's flight, they immediately issued an edict deposing him.[14] It had no effect upon the Ganden Phodrang.

Back in Lhasa, rutting Younghusband and his ebullient men paraded themselves in front of the Potala. But the Dalai Lama had vanished, leaving the tottering old Ganden Trichen to negotiate. The colonel had to choke back the bile accompanying the discovery that not one Russian man, rifle or bullet was to be found anywhere. It had all been a misadventure, save for the fact that British pride had been redeemed, at least in Younghusband's head. The Ganden Trichen quickly signed the agreement with the backing of the *kashag*, the Tsongdu and the abbots of the three main monasteries. The subsequent Convention of 1904 basically provided that Tibet would acknowledge the provisions of the Anglo-Chinese Treaty of 1890, but without mentioning China. It allowed for

Colonel Younghusband and the Qing Dynasty Amban You Tai of Lhasa
at the races in 1904.

the establishment of a trading post at Gyantse, backed by a small military garrison. The agreement was witnessed only by the *amban* and the Nepalese representative.[15]

By signing such a document without Qing participation, Britain was acknowledging Tibet's treaty-making ability and thus its de facto independence. Specifically, the Convention stipulated that no foreign power, including China or Russia, could occupy or interfere with the government and territory of Tibet without prior consent of the British government. This technically established a type of protectorate, then one of the many flavours of colonialism that typified late British imperial policy. The agreement also allowed for the establishment of trading posts at Gyatse, Gartok (Sgar thog) and Yatung (Gro mo dzong).

Despite the 1904 Convention, the adventures of the Younghusband expedition were not well received back at Whitehall. It seemed to be retrograde to current political thinking. This was made abundantly clear by the army not finding significant Russian influence in Lhasa, a failure of intelligence. The expedition was seen not to have been about security matters after all, and the value of yak tails as trade goods was minimal, to say the least. It made Younghusband and Curzon look as if they were primarily motivated by bravura and revenge. Hundreds of Tibetan lives were lost, and there is clear evidence that some of the gentlemanly British soldiers looted temples along the way, seeding the great public collections that are seen in Britain today.[16]

Back on the road, the sacred procession of the Dalai Lama descended, threading over the northern edge of the plateau, demarcated by the unexplored Qinlian Mountains. In their shadow to the west lay the Taklhamakan and Turfan basins, and the arid Lop Nor Desert. Alpine grasses gave way to sand dunes – snorting Bactrian camels appeared on the horizon. After several weeks out of Lhasa, the Dalai Lama arrived at Kumbum monastery in Amdo, the birthplace of Je Tsongkhapa. Situated at the crossroads of Tibet, Mongol and Manchu settlement, Kumbum was a very important monastery with over 3,000 monks. It was ruled by the Arjia (A kyA hu thog thu) lineage of *tulkus*. Nearby was Koko Nor, Tibet's largest lake, near the border with Mongolia. Here was the miraculous sandalwood tree, with leaves inscribed with Tibetan letters, which, it was said, sprouted from the buried umbilicus of the Gelug founder.

At Kumbum the Dalai Lama was warmly greeted by the abbot and given the finest apartment in the monastery. After a few weeks of auditing the administration of this important Gelug centre, the Dalai Lama and his huge entourage resumed their northeastward progress, crossing a section of the Gobi Desert in the heart of Inner Asia. Holding numerous audiences and teachings en route, the caravan grew in great bounds, fuelled by tribute and gifts given at each stop. Bactrian camels were now being outfitted to carry the great trains of accumulating luggage. By November 1904 the party had swollen to around eight hundred men.

Soon they approached the Great Kural of the Jebtsundampa Hutuktu, the religious hierarch of the Khalkha Mongols. This capital encampment of tribes, affiliated with Genghis Khan's Golden lineage and used since the fall of the Yuan dynasty in China, was known as Urga. A generation later, many of the nomadic tents were replaced by permanent structures and the town renamed Ulaan Baator, 'the Red Hero', by Soviet Communists. With the approach of the Dalai Lama, the Mongol ruler sent a golden palanquin to rendezvous with the advancing caravan. The dusty town reeked of the acrid smoke of fried mutton and juniper incense as the hierarch approached the palace, blessing all with his magic tassel as he sat cross-legged in his chair of state.

This spiritual ruler of Khalkha tribes nervously anticipated the arrival of the spiritual leader of Central Asia. The Eighth Jebtsundampa, later called the Bogn Khan, of the Gelug lineage was perhaps the third highest lama in the system, following the Dalai and Panchen lamas. He was Tibetan by birth and approximately the same age as the Dalai Lama. He was recognized by the Panchen Lama and Twelfth Dalai Lama, and enthroned in the Potala around 1874.[17] The founder of the lineage, the Zanabazar Khan, was a blood descendant of Genghis and considered an incarnation of Taranatha of the Jonang school.[18] The Dalai Lama was met by the Jebtsundampa on a broad field surrounded by mountains. He was led into the encampment of hundreds of white felt yurts while thousands of Mongol Buddhists prostrated themselves before the two hierarchs. Tellingly, the new winter palace of the Jebtsundampa was contained within a multi-temple complex built by the architects of Tsar Nicholas II between 1893 and 1903.

overleaf: Thangka painting depicting the holy sites of Lhasa and its surroundings, late 19th century.

Dizzying rounds of religious teachings, empowerments, celebrations and political discussions followed. Not since Sonam Gyatso had visited the Altan Khan at Hohhot had a Tibetan sovereign visited a Mongol capital. While at Urga, the Dalai Lama met the new Russian minister to China, M. Pokotilov, who brought gifts from the tsar.[19] The Dalai Lama was encouraged by the emperor's telegram:

> A large number of my subjects who profess the Buddhist faith had the happiness of being able to pay homage to their great High Lama during his visit to northern Mongolia, which borders on the Russian Empire. As I rejoice that my subjects have had the opportunity of deriving benefit from your salutary spiritual influence, I beg you to accept the expression of my sincere thanks and my regards.[20]

According to a report from A. D. Khitrovo, the Russian Border Commissioner in Kyakhta Town, the Dalai Lama and the Mongol Hutuktu 'irrevocably decided to secede from China as an independent federal state, carrying out this operation under the patronage and support from Russia, taking care to avoid the bloodshed'.[21] The Dalai Lama insisted that if Russia would not help, he would even ask Britain, his former foe, for assistance. Both the Dalai and Jebtsundampa Lamas feared the Qing was about to declare Mongolia and Tibet provinces of the empire.[22] The Manchu act would presumably show strength to its subjects from a dynasty that was nearly bankrupt.

The British incursion into the heart of Tibet had a sobering effect at court. The emperor sent warlord Zhao Erfeng to subdue and colonize the eastern Tibetan province of Kham. Zhao attacked the monasteries, killing as many monks as possible. New regulations were posted in Kham, including the mandatory adoption of Manchu pigtails and clothing for men and the assumption of Chinese names for all residents.[23]

While at Urga, the Dalai Lama sent Dorjiev off to St Petersburg to seek an audience with Nicholas II to request the emperor's support in entering into priest–patron relationships with both hierarchs. After all, most of the Russian Empire in the east was formerly Mongol territory, and the vast majority of the inhabitants were devout Tibetan Buddhists. And now, substantial portions of the Manchu homeland were also

Russian. Through Prince Esper Ukhtomsky, the Orientalist friend of Nicholas, Dorjiev eventually met the Russian emperor. Both Britain and China were thrown off by hearing of these meetings and the extent of the communications back and forth between St Petersburg and the Dalai Lama. In reality, the tsar, having just gone through a crushing defeat in the Russo-Japanese War and the abortive 1905 Revolution, was in no mood to further Russia's Oriental adventures. He merely gave Dorjiev a typically indecisive answer and sent him on his way. The Russian Empire's days of expansion, begun by the tsar's great-great-grandmother Catherine II, were largely over.

Matters grew tense at Urga. The two great lamas, although outwardly friendly, were polar opposites. Where Thubten Gyatso was an accomplished practitioner of the austere monastic discipline established by Tsongkhapa the Reformer, Ngawang Lobsang Chöje Nyima Tenzin Wangchuk Jebtsun Dampa Lama (Ngag dbang blo bzang chos kyi nyi ma bstan 'dzin dbang phyug rje btsun dam pa bla ma), the Eighth Jebtsundampa, loved drinking wine and smoking, and was actively bisexual.[24] But most sinful of all for a Gelugpa monk, he had a wife, Tsendiin Dondogdulam Khatan (1874–1923), and a son. As we saw from the adventures of the Sixth Dalai Lama, the highest *tulku*s are not necessarily subject to the same sort of karmic logic as a simple Buddhist monk. These apparent aberrations were well tolerated by the Mongol people, as they were by the Tibetans. In fact, the Jebtsundampa's wife was considered his tantric *dakini* consort in *yab yum* union and viewed as an incarnation of White Tara herself. This just added to the confusion, as White Tara is a female aspect of Avalokiteśvara, so grandly incarnated in the male form in Jebtsundampa's current house guest.[25]

Contributing to the uneasiness at the Great Kural, hosting the gods proved to be an expensive affair for the Mongols. Furthermore, the Dalai Lama was the undisputed Head of the Faith, and a celibate, *Vināya*-upholding practitioner of that faith to boot. If the cosmology of the visit was problematic, the day-to-day deference to the superior Dalai Lama grated upon the Jebtsundampa and his court. The Mongol prelate was irritated, among other things, that the Dalai Lama required a higher throne. In this environment, the Dalai Lama would stay a full year. Maintaining a delicately balanced passive aggression, the Jebtsundampa would studiously drink his *kumuss* and smoke his Russian cigarettes in front of the Ocean of the Doctrine. But one day the Mongol monarch snapped – he tore apart the interloper's throne like a pouting eight-year-old whose brother got a slightly bigger slice of pie. The Dalai Lama was also disrespected by the Manchu *ambasa* assigned to Mongolia, which led him to express his displeasure by yelling at them.[26]

In this sad state of affairs, a movement was afoot. One letter arrived from the regent back in Lhasa, who urged the leader to return home, for the British had left. The fallout from the Younghusband debacle included replacing Curzon and modifying the 1904 Convention with the Anglo-Chinese Convention of 1906, to which the Tibetans were not party. It was not so much a reversal of policy as a duplicitous action. Britain simultaneously recognized Tibetan de facto sovereignty and Chinese *de jure* suzerainty in Tibet, a fictitious muddle that would leave scholars trying to tease out the truth ever since.

Frank O'Conner, one of Younghusband's officers, remained at Gyantse as a trade agent. As soon as he was settled in, he travelled over to Shigatse, meeting the Panchen Lama and inviting him to India. The delighted Panchen arrived in Calcutta the next month, visiting the new viceroy Minto and meeting George, Prince of Wales.[27] Britain was still trying to play a friendly Panchen off against an aloof Dalai, a tactic China also utilized.

As the summer rain dripped off the tent poles of the felt yurts of Urga, the Dalai Lama decided it was time to leave the Mongols. It was not very clear where he was headed, but everywhere he progressed he was received as the Head of the Faith, so prestigious was the lineage's legacy. The moveable spiritual feast was also politically convenient. As the Dalai Lama could justify his moves as giving blessings to thousands of Buddhists, he also could assess and manage his empire in the process and, given his personal charisma, attract new followers. The circuit through Inner Asia elicited impatient comments from the Qing government to the foreign legations that they wished he would find a monastery to settle down in. In October 1906 the Dalai Lama was in Ganzhou, a city well known to Marco Polo. By December he had returned to the grand monastery at Kumbum in Amdo and set upon the reform of the administration. He spent nearly a year at the holy place, despite receiving a plea from his government to return to Lhasa.

The Great Game followed the Dalai Lama to the isolated monastery. It was just a matter of time before Thubten Gyatso received a summons from the Guangxu emperor in Beijing to come for an audience. An envoy from Russia next arrived, suggesting he return directly to Lhasa. A message from the British suggested a similar move. But the Dalai Lama did as he saw fit – after all, wasn't he the Imperial Preceptor? Did he not command the reverence of all who came within his presence? Everywhere he went in Inner Asia he was acknowledged as the supreme head of Buddhism. He knew he would have the same effect on the Manchu elite in Beijing, a kindred people. He would continue his extended pilgrimage around the northern Buddhist world, visit the sacred mountain at Wu Tai Shan as did Songtsen Gampo, and accept the gracious invitation from his disciples, the Guangxu emperor and his aunt, the venerable Empress Dowager Cixi. He had heard the rumours of being deposed by the emperor upon his flight to Mongolia: never mind, his position in Inner Asia was not based on any title from China. Not since the Great Fifth had a Dalai Lama visited the court in Beijing. And he was not journeying to the Manchu capital to reclaim anything except his rights as priest to the imperial patron.

While at Kumbum the Dalai Lama learned that Manchu forces were destroying Khampa resistance to the ongoing Chinese annexation. And the Great Game suddenly ended: in August the Dalai Lama sadly learned of the signing of the Anglo-Russian Convention. The Russian Empire, recoiling from its losses in the Far East, was to leave Tibet alone, as was Britain, apart from the special trade and political arrangements forced upon Tibet by its 1904 invasion.[28]

The Qing reverses attitude towards Tibet

As the year 1907 rolled to a frosty conclusion, the Dalai Lama and his party left Amdo for China, arriving at Xi'an, the ancient capital of the Tang. Here he received another request from the Tibetan government to return. He responded by appointing Kalon Paljor Dorje Shatra (Blon chen bshad sgra dpal 'byor rdo rje) as Lonchen, or prime minister. To this the Dalai Lama added the Sholkhang (personal name Dhondup Phuntsog) and the Changkhyim (personal name Ngawang Khyenrab) as triumvirs, with powers over the *kashag*.[29] In January 1908 he sent a friendly letter to Sir John Jordan, British minister to China, indicating that he now wished to have cordial relations with India, blaming the past on obstructionist ministers.[30] His envoys also visited the other Western diplomatic representatives in Beijing. Not surprisingly, the Dalai Lama wished to be received into the imperial capital as a head of state, like the Fifth Dalai Lama. And this insistence was an ultimatum to the Qing, as the priest–patron relationship and the dynasty itself were in their death throes.

But first, to prepare himself spiritually to meet the still dreaded Manchu emperor, the Dalai Lama ascertained that he had to make a pilgrimage to the most holy Buddhist shrine in China, Wu Tai Shan, a site most significant to his predecessor, King Songtsen Gampo. Thubten Gyatso left Xi'an that spring, arriving at the mountain in February 1908.[31] He was accompanied by Qing officials and 3,000 soldiers. The Tibetan leader was welcomed by the local lama, Jasagh, who led him to the palace temple of Pusa Ding on the mountain. The Dalai Lama spent five months on the five holy mountains, consorting with his fellow bodhisattva, Mañjuśrī, the lord of the mountains, god of wisdom and, in his wrathful form, a special protector of Tibet. The emperor himself was, of course, considered a reincarnation of Mañjuśrī – a fortunate wordplay not lost upon the founders of the Manchu dynasty. Amid the rocks and the pines, the Thirteenth Dalai Lama greatly enjoyed his spiritual exercises in this sacred place, among the holiest in Asia. He also took the opportunity in this sacred borderland between Mongolia, Tibet and China to exercise his political clout.

Close to Beijing but out of direct reach, the Dalai Lama used the opportunity to enthrone himself and grant nearly unprecedented audiences to foreign diplomats from the capital. Most important was the first visitor, William Woodville Rockhill, u.s. minister to the Qing Empire. Rockhill left a detailed account of the audience, which was paraphrased in a letter to President Theodore Roosevelt. Rockhill was awed by the meeting. According to Sperling, Rockhill's accounts 'provide us with a portrait of the infectious feelings of esoteric privilege that certainly attended upon his access to the hitherto unapproachable and inaccessible Tibetan "pontiff"'.[32] The Tibetan leader had an audience with the German consul of Tianjin, H. Knipping, who simply froze at being presented to the celestial hierarch. The Dalai Lama met with the puffed-up adventurer-scholar Reginald Johnston, who in a few years would become the erudite tutor of Puyi, the young Xuantung emperor. Johnston, in keeping with the sour attitude of British officialdom after the 1904 Younghusband fiasco, was not impressed with the rather common-looking hierarch. French explorer Henri d'Ollore also had a brief meeting with the Tibetan leader. Carl Gustaf Mannerheim, the Russian diplomat and future president of Finland, had discussions as well. He later met with Japanese intermediaries, who began to coordinate an audience for the Dalai Lama with the Meiji emperor in Tokyo. While the Dalai Lama was holding his international entourage in rapture, local Shangxi officials were grumbling about the crushing burden the august personage and his entourage were causing their treasuries, estimated at $5,000 a day ($123,000 today). Furthermore, it appears that Chinese officials themselves were banned from approaching the lamasery, guarded as it was by Tibetan soldiers.[33]

But the sunsets were coming more quickly now, and the long summer vacation in the grand temples on the cool mountain was ending. The Dalai Lama steeled himself to the demands of the next few weeks. He was to meet the emperor. Not since the first days of the Qing dynasty had a Dalai Lama, the Great Fifth, visited the imperial court. Now near the end of the dynasty, another Dalai Lama would travel to Beijing. It became a great historical event, one which affected the outcome of China's destiny nearly as much as it did Tibet. And His Holiness had an imperial bone to pick with His Majesty: China did not come to the aid of Tibet when it was invaded by the British in 1904. The Manchus had also been late responding to the Gurkha War of 1788–91, and never showed up for the Nepalese invasion of 1855–6. The delicate sense of mutual responsibility inherent in the priest–patron relationship seemed to be unravelling. In Beijing the Dalai Lama would also have the opportunity to meet with foreign representatives, useful as a counterpoint for his dealings with the Chinese government and bolstering, perhaps, the image of Tibet as a free state. To this end Agvan Dorgiev met up with him – the Dalai Lama still hoped the tsar could be influential.

It was September and the leaves of the maples were turning maroon and orange, in concert with the robes of the hundreds of monks and scores of *tulkus* slowly processing with the Great Thirteenth as he descended from the mountains to the lowlands of Shanxi province. The

A train arrives at the final stop (Beijing) on the newly built Beijing–Hankow railway line, *c.* 1905.

hours of tantric meditation on the attributes of Mañjuśrī, the thousands of reading of the *Mañjuśrimulakalpa Sutra*, and the hundreds of thousands of chants of the bodhisattva's mantra 'Om A Ra Pa Ca Na Dhih' had prepared the Ocean of the Doctrine to meet Mañjuśrī's incarnation, the Lord of 10,000 Years. It also fortified him to meet the Guangxu emperor's aunt, prickly Empress Dowager Cixi, de facto ruler of the empire for fifty years. The remarkable events of this meeting, although often understated by historians, were to set the stage for the impasse between Tibet and China for the remainder of the twentieth century and into the twenty-first. Interestingly enough, neither official Qing accounts nor Ganden Phodrang histories emphasize these meetings.

At the railhead at Lingshou on the Beijing–Hankow line the short, swarthy Dalai Lama and his entourage were greeted by a strange sight: a train.[34] An immense, black, frothing locomotive, ten bile-green Pullmans, a penultimate yellow parlour coach from the Qing imperial train and a black security coach were lashed together in a stately line extending down the rails for hundreds of metres. None of the party had seen anything like it – in fact, it had been sent to impress upon the barbarians the superiority of China's technical prowess. His Holiness pushed the gauze curtain of his golden palanquin aside and, dismounting, he walked slowly with his aides the full length of the train, from the last car to the hissing locomotive. A mounted unit of the Blue Bordered Bannermen stood guard along the platform, their perfectly matched black horses snorting clouds of vapour in the chill air.

Anonymous Qing Dynasty Court Painter, *Guangxu Emperor in His Study*, late 19th century.

His hosts had thought of everything. A small throne had been set up in the middle of the car, elevated so the Dalai Lama could see the passing landscape. On a sideboard sat a bowl of ripe persimmons; on another, a bowl of red apples from Chengdu were presented. On the small table in front of his throne perched a jade teacup. The walls, curtains and rugs were festooned in yellow silk; the pillows were covered in a rich brocade. The Manchu official in charge dusted off his sleeves, knelt before the Dalai Lama and excavated a letter from the deep interior of his jacket. He read the short statement, written in the vermilion of the emperor, felicitating the pontiff for an auspicious and happy journey to the capital. The peacock feather at the back of his red tasselled hat bobbed up and down as he carefully pronounced the greeting, causing more than one lama in the entourage to enter a meditative exercise in laughter suppression. The official made a short bow, disappearing with his aides into a car to the front of the train.

The great locomotive and its cars made a short lurch, coughing up a huge cloud of steam and black smoke. It began to sway rhythmically as it gained speed eastward. The unfamiliar metallic sounds of steel wheels, couplers and tie plates joined the incessant shriek of the locomotive whistle up front. The Lord Chamberlain was pale and trembling, yet he pulled himself together enough to pour His Holiness's tea into the tiny jade cup.

The Tibetan ruler took this noisy modern contraption in his stride. As he gazed out the window at the endless terraces of endless fields of millet, his thoughts turned to the ordeal ahead. The Guangxu emperor, just a little older than himself, had been since 1898 the prisoner of his adoptive mother, austere Empress Dowager Cixi, who had ruled China unflinchingly for half a century. Although he was the child of her favourite sister, Cixi had developed a white-hot hatred towards Guangxu after he snubbed the bride she had hand-picked for him. The unfortunate young woman was the poker-faced Xiao Ding Jing, daughter of her younger sister. Cixi wanted to maintain the influence of her own Yehenala clan at court. He despised his chosen wife, a gaunt, prognathic courtesan with little ambition save to please her aunt.

Perhaps because of the structural duplicity of the imperial court, the emperor was called the 'Bag of Lies' back home in Tibet, as the erratic government, twisting and turning at the whim of Cixi, was always seen

Hubert Vos, *Her Imperial Majesty the Empress Dowager of China, Cixi*, 1905–6, oil on canvas.

to misrepresent itself. The Dalai Lama wondered how 'Old Buddha', as Cixi was fond of being addressed by intimates, would react to the head of the Yellow Church: the Gelugpa sect of Tibetan Buddhism. The Manchus had been converted to Tibetan Buddhism, much like the Mongols, long before they added China to their empire. And despite having to propitiate Taoism, practise their own Manchu shamanism, patronize other schools of Māhayāna Buddhism and practise state Confucianism as Sons of Heaven, the Manchu ruling clan were very much Tibetan Buddhist. Whatever political ambitions they had in Tibet would be moderated by their faith in Buddhism and their belief in karmic retribution for unmeritorious acts.

And how would the Dalai Lama, an incarnation of Avalokiteśvara, deal with the Old Buddha, who fancied herself an incarnation of Kuan Yin, also an Avalokiteśvara? As we have seen with the Jebtsundampa's wife and the Dalai Lama, coexisting multiple emanations were certainly possible in the system, but the metaphysical paled at the realization that real work needed to be done by the vigorous young god-king from Tibet and the mother of all dragon ladies. The Qing dynasty had suffered a great decline during the nineteenth century, from the Opium Wars, Taiping Rebellion, Treaty of Chefu and recent Boxer War. They needed to show a tributary who was still the boss in order to demonstrate to the people that they still held the Mandate of Heaven.

The Dalai Lama, on the other hand, was to press the Chinese sovereigns to be granted the right to address the emperor directly in political matters without the *ambasa*, the Manchu high commissioners in Lhasa. This would be equivalent to acting as an equal sovereign, as enacted in the meeting of the Fifth Dalai Lama and the Shinzhi emperor. The proposed arrangement would be perfectly harmonious within Vajrayāna Buddhism; it would not easily be accommodated within the Confucian system, where everything revolves around the emperor. Jade teacup in hand, the Dalai Lama spent the next two days of his journey lost in thought and enjoying the rhythmic swaying of the coaches as they picked through the hill country west of Beijing.

The train skirted around the Great Wall, the barbarian lands left behind. At 3 a.m. on the last leg the train lurched to a stop about 20 kilometres out of Beijing to arrive precisely at the hour court astrologers had deemed auspicious. At 6:30 a.m. on 28 September, the party continued towards the city, speeding through the smoky suburbs, past factories and cabbage fields, as a purple-red sun rose in the east.

The long green, yellow and black train carrying the Buddhist pontiff and his entourage of about two hundred men slowed as it glided through to Pao Ting Fu, the provincial capital. Here a Minister of the Presence greeted the Dalai Lama, accompanied by all the notable dignitaries. The train continued to the southern perimeter of the Tartar City towards Dazhimen Station. At the appointed hour the brakes were applied and the carriages ground to a halt. A row of about twenty officials, including the governor of Beijing and the chairman of the Imperial Household, in fur-lined blue court robes with rank badges, iridescent peacock feathers and sable hats with rank buttons, were stationed directly across from Thubten Gyatso's yellow carriage. The Dalai Lama was surprised to see that during the brief rail journey from Shangxi, official summer dress had already been replaced with winter robes. Standing behind the representatives of the emperor were about fifty others, including aides and members of the diplomatic corps in mourning suits and top hats and lamas from the Yellow Temple in Beijing. On either side of the official delegation stood hundreds of imperial guardsmen, some with swords, some with lances, some with ceremonial bow and arrows – all were on foot.

At the head of the delegation of ministers and princes of the blood were Zaifeng, also known as Prince Chun ii, and his brother Prince Zaitao. They were half-brothers of the Guangxu emperor: Zaifeng was an 'Iron Cap' imperial prince of the first rank;[35] Prince Zaitao, a teenage general. They were sons of Prince Chun i, who had married Cixi's younger sister. As a *heshe qinwang*, Zaifeng was of equal rank to Shunzhi's great-uncle Jirgalang, who escorted the Fifth Dalai Lama into Beijing. Unlike their hapless brother, the two Chun brothers were held in high favour at court. Zaifeng and Zaitao resembled each other like twins. Both had handsome, friendly countenances, and were scholarly and mannerly as befitting their heritage in the Aisin-Gioro clan. Zaifeng, in fact, was one of the few imperial princes who understood Manchu.[36] Clever Cixi had also married off one of her conservative supporters' daughters to Zaifeng, who became the father of her heir, Puyi, a healthy, wilful toddler not yet three. Zaifeng, only nineteen, had been sent to Germany in 1901 to apologize in person before Kaiser Wilhelm ii for the Boxer

Zaifeng, Prince Chun's visit to Saarland, Germany, as Ambassador Extraordinary, September 1901, sent by the emperor to establish, among other diplomatic reasons, economic relations in the coal mining industry.

assassination of the Prussian ambassador. Zaitao was a trusted supporter of the empress dowager and was often sent abroad on ambassadorial missions. Zaitao can be seen in grainy newsreels walking with the kings and emperors of Europe in the funeral procession of King Edward VII in 1910. Sending the impressive young princes rather than elderly bureaucrats and flabby eunuchs showed the vibrancy of the court rather than the decadence and weakness of the Qing that were increasingly evident. The Qing wanted desperately to impress at these meetings.

The Dalai Lama stepped from the railway carriage while incense hung heavily in the air, mixing with steam and smoke from the hissing locomotive. The two princes walked forwards and bowed before the Celestial Presence. Zaifeng first read a message of welcome from Guangxu, followed by a similar greeting from Cixi. They then presented the Dalai Lama with a jade *ju-i* sceptre, wishing him good luck. The head lamas from the two main Tibetan Buddhist temples were brought forth, who presented His Holiness with *khata* (*kha btags*). In turn, the Dalai Lama presented the four with similar silk scarves. Then the ministers of external and internal affairs stepped forward, offering their welcome.[37] The monks from the temple chanted a long-life prayer for the Dalai Lama, followed by short blasts from giant *dung chen* horns and drums.

His Holiness was provided with a covered chair of state, upholstered in yellow, to be carried with his armed escort through the Outer Court of the Forbidden City and several kilometres further to Xi Huang Si, the Western Yellow Temple complex to the north. This monastic cluster, it is recalled, was built for the Fifth Dalai Lama for his visit to the Shunzhi emperor in 1652. It had also been used by the Sixth Panchen Lama in the late eighteenth century on his ill-fated visit to the Qianlong emperor.[38]

At the cry of the captain of the guards, the golden palanquin was picked up by the bearers and began to move eastward. The procession, including the imperial escorts and Tibetan government ministers, passed through the massive Tian An Men (Man., Abkai elhe obure duka, the Gate of Heavenly Peacemaking) into the Imperial City. The procession crossed the great square to the triple Wu Men, the Gate of the Meridian at the entrance to the Forbidden City. They passed through Wu Men on the right, followed the north–south meridian, passed the Hall of Supreme Harmony (the centre of the Earth in Chinese cosmology), and on through the palace ground and out the Gate of Divine Prowess, the Shenwumen. Passing through Jingshan in the Imperial City, the party marched through the Gate of Earthly Peacemaking to the Western Yellow Temple beyond. Clearly, a detour through the Forbidden City, as opposed to a more direct route through the city streets, was designed to impress foreign and tribute-bearing embassies, to which latter category the court was pressing upon the Tibetans. Upon his arrival at the Western Yellow Temple, the Dalai Lama received horses, silks and other precious objects sent from the emperor and empress dowager.

Used to the immense Potala and the sprawling Norbulingka, the Dalai Lama found the Western Yellow Temple to be a rather small affair, one storey with glazed golden tiles and a tidy garden with ornamental pines. However, he wasted no time in setting up his overflowing household in the cosy residence. Many gifts had been provided by the Chinese government: servants, foodstuffs, robes of finest silk brocade. The Tibetan party soon developed a routine at the Huangsu. Officials of both governments met frequently to discuss the matters to be brought up to the throne by the Dalai Lama. Slowly the requests took shape.

A few days after their arrival an official from the Board of Rites appeared at the Yellow Temple to inform the Tibetan leader of the protocol to be used at court. The audience with the Guangxu emperor had been scheduled for 6 October. When the official remarked that, upon presentation of the Dalai Lama to the emperor, the former was instructed to perform kowtow to the latter, His Holiness immediately baulked – when the Great Fifth was met in audience by the Shunzhi emperor in 1653, he was received as an equal sovereign. There was no kowtow then, and there would be none now. It would be *infra dignitatem*: the Dalai Lama was the imperial preceptor, the religious teacher of the Manchu emperor, a mere student. This was a 2,400-year-old rule of Buddhist decorum. Furthermore, the submission of the Dalai Lama to the Son of Heaven would symbolize the submission of Tibet to China, which was of course the primary motivation for calling the Dalai Lama to Beijing; the Dalai Lama was there to demand the opposite. Tibetan and Manchu officials argued heatedly for many unpleasant minutes. The audience had to be postponed. The officials returned to the Huangsu the next day and reached a brilliant compromise. The audiences with the emperor and the empress dowager were rescheduled for two days hence.

Clearly, the Manchu court had read its history of the visit of the Great Fifth Dalai Lama to the court in 1653 and was not about to repeat that reception which had helped cast the Tibetan leader as a co-equal to the throne. Kangxi and Qianlong had realized the naive mistakes of their ancestor Shunzhi. Having been driven into exile by the British invasion in 1904, and in fact deposed, the Dalai Lama was believed to be in a weak position by the court. It would also be timely for the Chinese government to annex Tibet outright, helping to prop up the mandate for the emasculated Manchu throne. The Thirteenth Dalai Lama would not be accorded the high honour of passing over the walls of the Forbidden City as was the Fifth, the thought being at that more ancient time that no mortal should look down upon the sacred head of the Living Buddha. The Dalai Lama would have to enter through the gates, just as any subject would.

The imperial audiences were held at Cixi's reception hall, the Jen Shou Tien in the new Summer Palace. The Tibetan ruler and his ministers arrived from the Huangsu and were escorted to the hall where the illustrious empress dowager held court. The room was small but comfortable. The fabulous old lady was attended in her silken dotage by her niece, the abandoned Empress Xiao Ding Jing (later Empress Dowager Longyu), lady-in-waiting Rongling, the 'Luscious Concubine' of Guangxu, and the portly but thoroughly evil chief eunuch, Li Lianying. Presently, the ageing dowager arose from her glistening red sandalwood throne to meet the Buddhist pontiff at the foot of the dais, the Dalai Lama and his party pertly dipping on one knee. He presented her with a statue of Amitāyus, representing longevity, and a pure white *khata* of the finest quality. They were escorted to a sofa of pink and yellow damask to the right of the throne. For the next half-hour, as tea was served, the two most influential rulers in mainland Asia spoke in near privacy.

Old Buddha, despite her worldly and grasping personality, was superstitious and fearful of the spirits, malevolent and otherwise, which His Holiness was evidently in command of. She treated the Dalai Lama with the greatest deference, as but a humble woman, and presented him and his party with many thoughtful, motherly gifts. The two emanations of the God of Compassion spent that half-hour engaged in conversation relating to the difficulties that the British invasion of Tibet had created for the Dalai Lama's regime. Cixi empathized, but quietly stated that her government had not been able to help at the time – in fact, the imperial court was itself recovering from the massive destruction of the Boxer uprising and invasion by the foreign powers. Speaking through a cloud of incense, she looked forward to a time when the big family of China and Tibet would see closer relations, and the old relationship between Tibet and the Manchus renewed.

After this short conversation, the party left the hall to await the arrival of the emperor. Soon the long procession appeared from the Yulantang, the small Hall of Jade Ripples, his place of house arrest on a peninsula amid the lakes of the Yiheyuan Summer Palace complex.[39] The frail Guangxu emperor arrived in a yellow palanquin carried by two dozen eunuchs, who were also his jailers.

The 37-year-old Lord of 10,000 Years was helped from his chair and slowly walked about sixteen metres towards the Tibetan sovereign and stopped. As upon meeting Cixi, Thubten Gyatso briefly dipped one knee, in the manner members of the foreign diplomatic corps had previously won for use in court. It was a face-saving device by which any foreign sovereign, or their representative, could thereby appropriately greet the emperor without offending the Confucian religious paradigm that places the Huangde at the Centre of Earthly Power. The Treaty of Tientsin of 1858 agreed that foreign representatives were immune from the performance of the kowtow.[40] In the Tibetan context, the Dalai Lama's kneeling could be considered valid in either a foreign or tributary context; faces were saved on both sides.

The Tibetan leader then presented Guangxu with a white *khata*, and the emperor escorted the Dalai Lama to a small sofa on the right side of the throne within the Jen Shou Tien. The two bodhisattvas exchanged pleasantries, the Dalai Lama merely referring to the existence of a written report of matters he wished the Manchu government to consider. The emperor noted that his aunt and his officials would advise him on these matters. Officials of the moment included the traitorous Yuan Shikai, former *amban* of Korea, who ended up betraying not only the emperor and the Qing dynasty, but even the succeeding republic. Princes Zaitao and Zaitung assisted their beloved brother. Clearly, Guangxu was a figurehead, but even the matriarch Cixi needed the emperor to give a *de jure* stamp to all official matters. So cautious, so reluctant, so listless was Guangxu that the round-eyed Dalai Lama felt that he simply could not be the powerful bodhisattva Mañjuśrī, who with his flaming sword could cut the fetters of ignorance.[41]

On 30 October, the 250th anniversary of the Manchu capture of the Mandate of Heaven, the Dalai Lama was feted at an imperial banquet held in his honour. Coming southward from the Huangsu, the Tibetan party arrived at the Ziguang ge, the Hall of Purple Light in Zhingnanhai.[42] This was the august reception chamber used since the middle of the eighteenth century for the visits of foreign diplomats and tributary rulers. The ambiguity of function did not escape the Tibetan hierarch: he could claim that he was received as a foreign head of state; the Chinese could claim that he was received as a subordinate tribute-bearer. At the steps of the two-storey hall, the Dalai Lama dismounted from his golden palanquin, climbed the white marble steps and entered the elaborately decorated wooden building.

The walls of the main chamber at Ziguang ge featured martial portraits of the heroes of the Battle of Qurman of 1759, the campaign that captured Turkestan for the Manchu Empire, becoming the province of Xinjiang with the demise of the Dzungars. Once the area was depopulated, it was resettled by Manchu and Sibe (Xibo) peoples. Genocide like

Yuan Shikai in
European dress,
c. 1900.

that of the Dzungars became a standard operating procedure in the repertoire for future Chinese aggression in Inner Asia. In this boastful audience hall, works made under commission to the Qianlong emperor were displayed, rendered in the unique Euro-Chinese style by Jesuit priests Jean Denis Attiret and Giuseppe Castiglione and local artists, showing the Qing capture of Formosa, the campaign against Burma and the seizure of Annam. The bold symbolism of Manchu martial valour and conquest was unmistakable to the Tibetan party and especially to Thubten Gyatso.

The Dalai Lama was hosted by the Guanglusi, a department of the Board of Rites, in the adjacent dining hall.[43] Although a lavish under-taking, with a great quantity of game such as wild boar, pheasant and partridge from Manchuria, complemented with fresh seafood sped in from the coast such as abalone, prawns and shark fins, it was only a grade-five banquet. The finest spreads were intended for ancestral sacrifice; even the great holidays such as New Year, winter solstice and imperial weddings only mustered a grade-four.[44] No doubt the Dalai Lama was presented with foodstuffs that he had scarcely imagined existed, but much was clearly Manchu and quite familiar to many East Asians, like pickled vegetables with red pepper. Like Tibetans and Mongols, the Manchus ate a variety of dairy products. But the feeling of cultural sympathy and respect between the old nomadic horsemen of Inner Asia – the Manchus, Mongols and Tibetans – that had been so strongly expressed in the courts of the seventeenth and eighteenth centuries had largely evaporated. The Manchurian dream that had produced the Great Qing was unravelling before the eyes of the Thirteenth Dalai Lama and all his ministers. What of the core of the relationship between the Buddhist Manchu bannermen and the head of Buddhism?, thought the Dalai Lama as he watched the poor drugged emperor being fed millet porridge by his attendants.

Although the niceties of florid court courtesies were ladled on heavily by the Chinese administration, and the Dalai Lama was a perfect guest, everyone in the Manchu government, the foreign diplomatic corps and Thubten Gyatso himself were acutely aware that the Manchu dynasty was nearing its end. It was an open secret that the emperor was in fact a prisoner in his own palace, put there by his paranoid and uncompromising aunt Cixi. That he was always ill led many to believe that he was slowly being poisoned, which in fact he was. Historians are divided as to who actually gave the order to assassinate the emperor – Cixi, Yuan Shikai and the chief eunuch Li all had compelling reasons to remove Guangxu permanently.

Horrendous events began to happen quickly. On 1 November the Old Buddha threw an uncontrollable, red-faced tantrum that panicked the imperial court.[45] It was clear to those at the Forbidden City that the irascible empress dowager was living out her final days. Her last nights were troubled with dreams of ghosts beckoning her to her mausoleum in the Eastern Tombs. In a panic, she summoned loyal Prince Qing to visit the tomb to propitiate the spirits. The Guangxu emperor had been waiting too, with orders to execute his jailers upon Cixi's death. With vultures pacing about her bedside, the empress dowager had the Dalai Lama perform a long-life ceremony in her presence on what would be her last birthday, 3 November.[46]

Following this, the mortally ill emperor and empress dowager presented the Dalai Lama with a title clearly subordinate to the one the Great Fifth had been honoured with by the Shunzhi emperor. Whereas in 1653 the Dalai Lama was awarded the golden tablet inscribed in Manchu, Chinese and Tibetan, 'Most Excellent, Self-existing Buddha of the West, Universal Ruler of the Buddhist faith, Holder of the Thunderbolt, Oceanic Lama', this had lapsed when he was deposed in 1904. The rulers wished to show their magnanimity with a restoration. Now he was proclaimed the 'Sincerely Obedient, Reincarnation-helping, Most Excellent, Self-existing Buddha of the West'.[47] The ancient reference to the *chakravartin* was dropped, as it clearly implied sovereignty. Although it was a calculated snub, it did not affect Thubten Gyatso's sense of pride.[48] He was, in fact, a self-existent *tulku*, the Presence – as in the seventeenth century, he needed no such title from the emperor to make it so. In the realm of Buddhist theology, should the emperor be an emanation of Mañjuśrī, he was an equal; there was no alternative paradigm for Tibetan spiritual sensibilities. Furthermore, a condescending imperial edict was published:

> When His Holiness has returned to Tibet, he must be careful to obey the laws of the Sovereign State of China, and he must promulgate to all the goodwill of the Court of China. He must exhort the Tibetans to be obedient and to follow the path of rectitude. He must follow the established custom of memorializing Us, through the Imperial Amban, and respectfully await Our Will.[49]

The Dalai Lama continued to press the basic points of his written memorial to the throne: requesting the right to petition the throne directly without having to go through the Manchu *amban* in Lhasa. It was continually denied. He also pressed to have Chinese troops removed from Kham. It fell upon deaf ears. China had been torn apart by internal and external aggression for decades: the Taiping Revolt, the Opium Wars, the Boxer Rebellion, the loss of territories and interference by Japan, Britain and Russia. The dynasty, as all dynasties of China including the present People's Republic, had to demonstrate that it still held the Mandate of Heaven. It did this by territorial expansion.[50] It trumpeted its mandate through places such as the Hall of Purple Light. Having been routed in the east, the imperial government turned to reining in the territories in the west. Tibet, and its former tributaries of Bhutan, Ladakh, Sikkim and Nepal, were low-hanging fruit for the desperate Manchu regime trying to demonstrate that it still had divine favour. The humiliation of the defeat by Japan and the European powers, which set about carving up China, would not ease even until the twenty-first century. The breathless dragon had to seize the pearl, but it would not be until the autumn of 1950 that China finally won.

In the Forbidden City, extraordinary events fell upon one another. Having experienced the first glimmers of her own finite mortality with a fit of apoplexy on 1 November, the empress dowager suffered a major paralytic stroke on 12 November that disfigured her face and slurred her speech. The frantic court realized that Cixi might well predecease Guangxu, a catastrophe. All those who had participated in the 1898 *coup d'état* now were in mortal peril of the emperor's revenge. Guangxu wrote in his diary that day that it looked as if he would survive Cixi. In this case, he would give the order to behead both Yuan Shikai and chief eunuch Li Lianying.[51] Intrigue and rumour being the very definition of the 'Great Within', the imperial court immediately got word of the emperor's intentions. Sometime between the first and the twelfth the order was given to finish off the twelfth Qing monarch instead. His doctors were dismissed, and his ministering was put into the hands of Li Lianying.[52]

On 13 November, the screaming toddler Puyi was brought before Cixi and the dying emperor, who had now slipped into a coma. The emperor retained consciousness long enough to remark that Puyi was too young to take over the reins of the empire, then fell back into blackness. The Guangxu emperor died on 14 November in the presence of the ailing dowager, the Empress Xiao Ding Jing, the Lustrous Concubine, the imperial princes and Li Lianying. He died in great agony, having been apparently poisoned with massive doses of arsenic.[53]

Very soon afterwards Cixi held a Grand Council, where she presented the new emperor, Puyi, the eldest son of her nephew Zaifeng, Prince Chun II. Clearly, he had been her choice for some time now, as she had had the child brought to her previously.[54] The Manchu court had a tradition of deathbed heir appointments, clearly to help prevent long-simmering rivalries within the Aisin-Gioro clan.[55] Cixi also appointed Zaifeng as regent. The widowed Empress Xiao Ding Jing became the co-regent as Empress Dowager Longyu, with Cixi becoming the grand empress dowager for the remaining hours of her life.

Prince Zaifeng immediately contacted the Dalai Lama residing at the Western Yellow Temple to inform him of the apocalyptic tragedies unfolding at the palace.[56] The regent wanted to have Yuan Shikai executed instantly, but vacillated; with the mediating advice of Empress Dowager Longyu the corrupt official was merely sent to his estates to nurse a concocted illness in January. Yuan would use the stay to plot his final treachery against his masters.

As he prepared to return to the Great Within, the Dalai Lama could scarcely believe that Guangxu, a young man nearly his own age, could pass into the Great Beyond so quickly. While he immediately suspected an assassination, he kept his thoughts to himself. Instead, he quickly began preparations for the myriad of Buddhist prayers to help the dead find a good reincarnation. Monks began to chant the Pure Land sutras of Amitābha, which were used to help the deceased to find re-birth in the Sukhavati, the western paradise, of which the Dalai Lama, as Avalokiteśvara, was of course the chief active bodhisattva. He also prepared Long Life prayers for Empress Dowager Cixi, now barely clinging to life. One can empathize with the general predicament of the Great Thirteenth during these venomous intrigues. The Japanese monk Ekai Kawaguchi, visiting the Lhasa court a bit earlier, remarked, '[The Dalai Lama] is so dangerously situated . . . he is obliged to pay the greatest attention to what is offered him to eat, lest some poison should have been put in.'[57]

At midnight little Puyi, still shaken by his meetings with Cixi and Guangzu in their death throes, was taken to the Hall of Supreme Harmony in the heart of the Forbidden City. With his father Zaifeng by his side and the Dalai Lama in attendance,[58] the frightened child was placed on the Dragon Throne, rising a full 2 metres (6 ft) above the floor, now having become the Centre of the World. The theatre of the imperial tableau was designed to strike awe in the most worldly of outsiders. Every surface was layered in deep symbolic meaning. The carved caption above the throne cautioned all in archaic Chinese that 'the Emperor has established this highest throne upon his empire' – all belongs to the Great Centre. Special bricks burnished to a dark golden colour covered the floor. The dais was encircled by six huge gold-lacquered pillars of exceedingly rare *nanmu* wood painted with dragons. The great chair of red sandalwood was encrusted with golden, writhing dragons. Around the throne stood two cloisonné bronze cranes, an elephant-shaped incense burner snorting out redolent clouds of sandalwood incense, and spindly tripods in the shape of mythical beasts. The scroll to the left read: 'The Celestial Emperor descends his will to exhort all subjects and peasants to practise proper conduct confronting the countenance of His Majesty.' The banner to the right of the throne read: 'The exegetics of the Ancestors' words inspire later generations to faithfully serve one's country to repay His Majesty for his kindness.'[59] Directly above the throne was an elaborate caisson, adorned with radiant mirrors and two imperial dragons chasing flaming pearls. The tennis-ball-sized glass balls were coated with mercury. The central Huang Di pearl was said to be able to detect any usurper of the imperial power. If anyone who was not the descendant of the Yellow Emperor seized the throne, it would drop down and crush him.

It was all the stuff of nightmares for a tired three-year-old. The toddler, crying through most of the noisy, terrifying ceremony, surrounded by all-too-realistic dragons on all sides of the throne, was invested with a heavy, ill-fitting gold and pearl crown. Prince Zaifeng did his best to pacify his son as the ancient jade seal was applied to the document announcing to heaven the accession of the twelfth emperor of the Qing. 'Don't worry, it will be over soon,' Zaifeng said prophetically to the boy. The giant pearl did not fall on the child, but Puyi would be the last of the celestial rulers. The wide-eyed Thirteenth Dalai Lama took it all in, having seen, through his various emanations, the beginning and the end of the ambitious Manchu Empire.

The new emperor issued his first edict through his father, announcing his succession to the foreign legations and to the world. Zaifeng was careful to note praise for his late, ill-treated brother:

I have the honour to inform Your Excellency that on the 21st day of the 10th moon [14 November 1908] at the yu-ke [5–7 p.m.] hour, the late Emperor ascended on the dragon to be a guest on high. We have received the command of Tze-hsi, etc., the Great Empress Dowager to enter on the succession as Emperor. We lamented to Earth and Heaven. We stretched out our hands, wailing our insufficiency. Prostrate we reflect on how the late Emperor occupied the Imperial Throne for thirty-four years, reverently following the customs of his ancestors, receiving the gracious instruction of the Empress Dowager, exerting himself to the utmost, not failing one day to revere Heaven and observe the laws of his ancestors, devoting himself with diligence to the affairs of government and loving the people, appointing the virtuous to office, changing the laws of the land to make the country powerful, considering new methods of government which arouse the admiration of both Chinese and foreigners. All who have blood and breath cannot but mourn and be moved to the extreme point. We weep tears of blood and beat upon our heart. How can we bear to express our feelings!

But we think upon our heavy responsibility and our weakness, and we must depend upon the great and small civil and military officials of Peking and the provinces to show public spirit and patriotism, and aid in the government. The viceroys and governors should harmonize the people and arrange carefully methods of government to comfort the spirit of the late Emperor in heaven. This is our earnest expectation.
(Seal of the Xuantong Emperor)[60]

Regardless of her true actions at the death of the Guangxu emperor, Cixi showed deep devastation at his demise, which no doubt underscored her own mortality and revealed her precarious karmic footing in the cosmos. Whispers and rumours attended every moment of her being, from the time she assumed the regency in 1861 over her son, the Tonzhi emperor, to her last breath.

Her fragility and desolation apparently did not curb her essential grasping nature to the vast Chinese populace: at lunch, it was said, the Grand Empress Dowager could not resist a large helping of crab apples and clotted cream, whereby a resultant severe attack of dysentery brought her near imminent death. In fact, Cixi had had a massive stroke, having suffered a minor one three days before. The chief eunuch had told her that the foreign legations suspected foul play in the death of Guangxu, and that they wished to enquire as to the cause of the late emperor's death. Upon hearing this news, the empress dowager collapsed.[61] She was taken to her deathbed where she was dressed in the Robes of Longevity in the Hall of the Graceful Bird in the Zhongnanhai. In her valedictory statement sent to the foreign ministers, she stated that she took to her deathbed from her grief over the demise of the Guangxu emperor, and she gave her stamp to the next reign:

> The Prince Regent and all the officials of Peking and the provinces should exert themselves to strengthen the foundations of our empire. Let the Emperor now succeeding to the throne make his country's affairs of first importance and moderate his sorrow, diligently attending to his studies so that he may in future illustrate the instruction which he has received. This is my devout hope.
> (Seal of the Grand Empress Dowager)[62]

She was content, at least, that she had installed yet another boy emperor of her choice, that she was able to assassinate Guangxu before he could take his revenge and discredit her for all eternity. Comforted with the demon-vanquishing presence of the Dalai Lama, she nevertheless remained a conflicted soul to the very end, telling her heirs never again to let a woman rule the empire. At the Hour of the Goat (1–3 p.m.), she turned her face southward and died on 15 November.[63] The ruler of 400 million people for nearly half a century was no more. With his patroness dead, the chief eunuch Li Lianying skedaddled out of the Forbidden City, never returning. The Dalai Lama was informed of the cataclysmic death, and prayers were subsequently started for a fine rebirth of Cixi.

A second edict was issued by Puyi to the legations, which was penned to reflect filial piety:

> We received in our early childhood the love and care of Tze-hsi, etc., the Great Empress Dowager. Our gratitude is boundless. We have received the command to succeed to the throne and we fully expected that the gentle Empress Dowager would be vigorous and reach a hundred years so that we might be cherished and made glad and reverently receive her instructions so that our government might be established and the state made firm.

But her toil by day and night gradually weakened her. Medicine was constantly administered in the hope that she might recover. Contrary to our hopes, on the 21st day of the moon at the wei-k'o [1–3 p.m.] she took the fairy ride and ascended to the far country. We cried out and mourned how frantically! We learn from her testamentary statement that the period of full mourning is to be limited to twenty-seven days. We certainly cannot be satisfied with this. Full mourning must be worn for one hundred days and half mourning for twenty-seven months, by which our grief may be partly expressed. The order to restrain grief so that the affairs of the empire may be of first importance we dare not disregard, as it is her parting command. We will strive to be temperate so as to comfort the spirit of the late Empress in Heaven.
(Seal of the Huantong Emperor)[64]

In preparation for her eventual funeral, the empress dowager's garments had been embroidered with the characters of 'long life', 'good fortune' and the eight auspicious symbols of Buddhism. The body was wrapped in five layers of silk coverlets into which were woven secret *dharani* incantations in five shades of gold. Eight extra layers of silk covered with dragons were laid over the coverlets.[65] The same was arranged for the Guangxu emperor. The bodies were placed in coffins of *nanmu* wood, to receive 49 coats of lacquer, followed by a final coat of gold lacquer.

Both coffins were removed from their respective palaces for storage at the Guandedian, the Temple of Visiting Virtue located northeast of the Forbidden City, at Jingshan, until all arrangements could be made for burial at the Eastern Qing Tombs. The Dalai Lama and 108 Tibetan monks initiated the Buddhist funeral rites at the Yong he (Dga' ldan byin chags gling) temple monastery.[66] For the emperor, 108 Tibetan Buddhist and 108 Chan Buddhist monks continued a recitation of the sutras in segments for 21 days at the Guandedian. Tantric rituals propitiating the hungry *preta* were also held, and monks circumambulated the coffins chanting mantras. This continued as the coffins were sealed with their fifty layers of lacquer.[67] Because of the winter cold the layers of lacquer had to wait until warm spells, dragging on into the summer of 1909, long after the Dalai Lama and his party had returned to Tibet. Later that year the empress dowager was finally buried at her glorious mausoleum

Mausoleum of Empress Dowager Cixi in Eastern Qing tombs complex,
Zunhua, Hebei province.

in the Eastern Tombs. Her coffin had been filled with pearls. The Guangxu emperor's interment was delayed even longer, in fact into the Republic (1912).⁶⁸

At appropriate moments in the great drama, the Dalai Lama held talks with Prince Regent Zaifeng, asking to have direct representation with the emperor upon return to Lhasa. He also asked that the Chinese troops meddling in Kham be removed. But officialdom still insisted that the Dalai Lama communicate to the emperor through the *ambasa* stationed in Lhasa. Quite often during these audiences Zaifeng sat on the Dragon Throne with Puyi in his lap. Both parties could only agree that China and Tibet would work more closely together in the future. When the rounds of prayers for the guidance of the rebirth of the Guangxu emperor and Cixi were concluded in mid-December, Thubten Gyatso prepared to return to Tibet.

During this interlude the Great Thirteenth was also able to meet with foreign delegations, although Chinese officials attempted to control access to him at the Huangsu. Sir John Jordan and the entire staff of the British Mission to Beijing were received in audience. Jordan never wanted the Dalai Lama to come to Beijing, as it would point out Tibetan weakness after the 1904 British invasion, incite Chinese aggression towards the region, and potentially embarrass Great Britain.[69] The Dalai Lama, sitting on a yellow throne in the reception hall, received the *khatas* of Jordan and his staff. Having been humiliated by the ministers of the Manchu emperor, in apparent disrespect of the priest–patron covenant, and having failed to interest the Russian tsar into supporting Tibet, the Dalai Lama was reaching out to yet another emperor. In referring to the British invasion in 1904, an event for which the Dalai Lama was still in exile, now in Beijing, he gave a message of conciliation to the British minister to be conveyed to King-Emperor Edward VII in London: 'Some time ago events occurred which were not of my creating; they belong to the past, and it is my sincere desire that peace and friendship should exist between the two neighbouring countries [Tibet and India].'[70]

Sir John was dismissed from the Oceanic Presence and sent the message to London. It was an olive branch, and clearly a solicitation for a new patron, as the Dalai Lama had told the Jebtsundampa in Urga. The Dalai Lama also met with the Japanese ambassador, Gonsuke Hayashe, and again with the American minister, W. W. Rockhill, who brought greetings from President Theodore Roosevelt.[71] The Dalai Lama granted visits from the Russian minister, and the India Office's Colonel Frank O'Connor, political agent for Sikkim, who brought about a reunion with the young crown prince of Sikkim, Sidkeong Tulku Namgyal, now on a world tour. They had been friends since they were children and the royal Namgyal family was in Lhasa.

His work done in Beijing, the Dalai Lama and his entourage left the Western Yellow Temple on 21 December 1908. It had been a most remarkable autumn, but the heady and time-consuming events in Beijing had made a subsequent state trip to Japan impossible. The Dalai Lama had deeply admired the progressive modernization of Japan by the Meiji emperor, which he saw as another great Buddhist empire.[72] He was aware of the reform movement by the progressive King Chulalongkorn in Thailand and encouraged the modern ideas of Sidkeong of Sikkim. He had been aware of Guangxu's Hundred Days' Reforms that attempted to bring a Meiji-like modernization to China and saw more clearly than almost everyone how reactionary Cixi had destroyed the emperor and his reforms.

Departing Beijing, Thubten Gyatso blessed the little emperor and was escorted by Prince Regent Zaifeng, Prince Zaitao and other Manchu and Mongolian noblemen, who marched on foot to the station while His Holiness rode in his golden palanquin. At the platform, the Dalai Lama bid farewell to the regent with the suggestion that he leave some Tibetan language teachers behind in Beijing to instruct the Chinese, and to send some students from Lhasa to Beijing to learn the Chinese language. This was taken very favourably by Prince Zaifeng.[73]

Several cars of the imperial train had again been made available for the Dalai Lama and his entourage. With a blast, the locomotive slowly chuffed out of a capital full of mourning, confusion and great anxiety. In a few hours, the Dalai Lama could see the mountain ranges of the west appearing, and soon after his train roared through Henan province. He would travel via Luoyang, Xi'an, Lanzhou and Xining. After five years of exile, he was returning home to govern in a manner that had not been seen in Tibet for hundreds of years. His royal processions through Mongolia, Amdo and China had given him confidence in his ability as a secular and spiritual ruler of Inner Asia. In every monastery and village he sped through, thousands of people threw themselves in the dust as he passed. And he did this without pike or sword, but by the Law of the Dharma alone.

The Dalai Lama had been an intimate, nearly unique historical witness to the treachery, greed and corruption of the Manchu court, which was the ancient signal that the end of the dynasty was at hand. In fact, there was probably no other person, outside or inside the Forbidden City, who had such clear knowledge of the death of Guangxu and Cixi. He also saw the limits to the help he could expect to receive from the new regent Zaifeng and the boy emperor. He was witness to the greatness of Chinese arts and culture, the refinement of manners still practised at court, and the pride of martial valour and Buddhist ideals that were at the heart of the old alliance between Mongol, Manchu and Tibetan aristocrats. The last was the very essence of the priest–patron relationship to which the Dalai Lama had appealed. Even autocratic but superstitious old Cixi dared not anger the Dalai Lama as head of the faith. Thubten

Gyatso learned how advanced the outside world was relative to Tibet, with its telephones and telegraphs, railways, steamships, motorcars, photography and weaponry. The Dalai Lama was determined to modernize his country where he could.

The West was aware of the strategy of China to lasso Tibet closer into the empire, especially after the British invasion in 1904 and the subsequent Anglo-Chinese Agreement of 1906. The Beijing correspondent for the London *Times* wrote prematurely, '[The Dalai Lama's] visit has coincided with the end of his temporal power, but he has been treated with the dignity befitting his spiritual office.'[74] The reconquest of Tibet would symbolically prove that the Manchus were still legitimate to the Chinese masses that had started grumbling for a republic. It had seemed to them that Britain had nearly conquered Tibet for itself, having already turned Sikkim and Bhutan into colonies. The Dalai Lama had other ideas.

The official biography of the Thirteenth Dalai Lama reported the Mongolian and Chinese encounter in a careful, taciturn manner:

> I was given wonderful receptions in both these countries [Mongolia and China], and in Peking the Emperor and Empress received me graciously and showed me great honor. I informed them of our situation, and they showed deep sympathy.
>
> But while I was there they both passed away and the new Emperor, Shon-ton [Huantong, that is, Puyi], was installed. I held some talks with him, and then left to return to Tibet.
>
> Yet even as I traveled, the Chinese amban sent false reports to the Emperor and as a result a Chinese army under Lui Chan began to invade from the east.[75]

The Tibetan party reached the railhead in Inner Mongolia in a few days and exchanged the cosseted yellow parlour cars for gilded sedan chair and sturdy ponies. The Dalai Lama brushed the chair aside, preferring to ride like any khan would, on a swift steppes pony. Winding through mountain ranges and vast steppes, past salt lakes, the Tibetans returned to Kumbum monastery in Amdo. The Dalai Lama found monastic discipline to have lapsed since he was there the previous year. He punished the abbot and set up direct administration of this important Gelugpa centre. It appeared to be a calculated preview of the degree of personal control the Thirteenth Dalai Lama would exercise from here on.

The Dalai Lama stayed at Kumbum nearly a year, and while there learned that Manchu troops were already moving into Kham with the aim of political annexation. Zhao Erfeng, the last appointed imperial *amban* in Tibet, was chewing through Kham, destroying monasteries and building roads to tie the eastern region closer to China. Zhao also convinced the Qing government that troops were needed in Tibet proper to prevent another invasion by the British. The Manchu government agreed and sent an army of 2,000 men to Lhasa. Zhao, on the other hand, continued his butchery in Kham. By August 1910, he had taken Dzayul and was trying to extend his administration to the Powo country to the east.[76]

Upon hearing these actions, the Dalai Lama reflected on the duplicity of the imperial government. Surely the emperor, a four-year-old boy, and the regent, his kindly father, were ill-advised. Surely the treachery at the court rested with the ministers, some of whom might not be working in the best interests of the Qing, namely the 'retired' Yuan Shikai. The Dalai Lama resumed his frustrated efforts of eliciting foreign support. He cabled Beijing with a strongly worded cease and desist request, but to no effect. Another telegram was sent, addressed to Great Britain and 'all of Europe'. The Ganden Phodrang government in Lhasa tried to contact the emperor through the *amban*, but the latter refused to cooperate, prompting them to send an envoy to Calcutta to cable Beijing directly. Still there was no response.[77] Rather than flee the invasion, this time the Dalai Lama decided to return to Lhasa to better assess the situation.

Having been absent for five years, the Tibetan leader returned to his capital on 25 December 1910. He was presented with a new seal prepared by the people of Tibet itself, referring to him holding the full Buddhist doctrine on earth by the prophecy of the Buddha. It was a demonstration of self-determination by the Tibetan people. During this brief time in Lhasa, the Dalai Lama established a foreign ministry and began to issue silver coins that for the first time bore the name Ganden Phodrang. Nevertheless, the city was rife with rumours; a sense of apocalyptic doom hung heavily over the Barkhor. The Dalai Lama remained sequestered in the hulking Potala. He listened to the confabulations of Amban Zhao, which were made evident in February when 2,000 Chinese

View of the Potala Palace from the west gate into Lhasa, 1903–4, photograph by
John C. White.

marched into the city, firing on both the Norbulingka and Potala. Their
leader bore a letter which promised that the Dalai Lama could retain his
spiritual title but indicated nothing of his political one. Realizing that he
soon could become prisoner in his own palace, having seen for himself
how even the imperial Aisin-Gioro family was not beyond imprisoning
and killing their own leader, he decided to flee again. At midnight his
staff packed; by first light the Tibetan sovereign left with his ministers
and his seals, this time heading south to the British Empire in India.
The day after the *amban* realized that the Dalai Lama and his ministers
had fled, Zhao sent an army of about two hundred men in hot pursuit.

The Dalai Lama had sunk to profound depths of anxiety and
desperation, having made the decision to cross the high Himalayan
passes in the dead of winter. He would appeal directly to an enemy, the
thoroughly foreign British viceroy in Calcutta. The Dalai Lama further
hoped to be able to sail from India to China, where he would return to
Beijing to appeal his case directly to the Huantong emperor and his
father, the regent. To the Dalai Lama now, as in the times of the Great

overleaf: Dzuluk in East Sikkim, through which the Dalai Lama would have had to
pass on his way to India, in order to cross the Jelep La mountain pass.

Fifth, Phagpa and Altan Khan, the relationship between Tibet and its protectors was not a matter of abstract codes and strictures, but rather of personal ties of friendship and loyalty. Although the Manchu throne knew well the utility of all its empire's religious institutions as potential tools of statecraft, the Aisin-Gioro and most of the other banner clans were personal practitioners of Vajrayāna Buddhism as well as Inner Asian shamanism. The Dalai Lama felt he had established a friendship with Prince Regent Zaifeng, and within that spirit he would air his grievances. Zaifeng had become somewhat of a reformer, initiating many of the reforms that his brother Guangxu was blocked from accomplishing. This included work towards a constitution.

Fearing the appearance of Chinese troops at every turn in the road, the Tibetan party galloped southward, crossing the Tsangpo River at Chaksam Ferry. Here he left behind a faithful attendant, Jensey ('favourite') Namgang, and his party, who managed to delay the pursuing Chinese force. The Dalai Lama slipped past the sacred lake of Yamdruk to the monastery of Samding with its female *tulku*, the Dorje Phagmo. Here he sent a message to the British agent at Gyantse, Basil Gould, indicating that they might seek sanctuary in India. Jensey and his men, riding fast ponies, kept up a rear guard with the party as they climbed steadily over Gamta La. At times the Chinese were only 16 km (10 mi.) away. They bypassed Gyantse, Tibet's third largest town, which was being occupied by a Chinese garrison.[78] Here, the Dalai Lama glanced over at the *dzong* above the settlement and reflected that five years before it had been a major battleground between Tibetan and British forces under Colonel Younghusband. Now the tables were turned: he was headed straight into the mouth of the lion to seek support. The Dalai Lama could not have failed to see the karmic ramifications of this transformation.

To avoid tipping off any Chinese troops that may have been lurking about town, the Tibetan party galloped around Gyantse, not resting until reaching a small farm several kilometres distant, where the startled peasants tried their best to accommodate the nervous royal personage and his ministers.

The divine caravan swiftly headed up the northern escarpment of the lofty mountain Chomolhari in a raging blizzard. Encountering the curious stares of wild yaks, the fleeing Chogyal bolted up the steep trail to Sikkim, dodging drifts and icy patches. Locals, upon realization of the approach of the Holy Presence, threw themselves on to the snow as the sturdy Central Asian ponies and their riders clambered past.

Thubten Gyatso was appreciative that he was still relatively young and fit to suffer the hardships of the winter passage. He pondered how long the sickly Guangxu emperor would have fared. He remembered how Cixi, Guangxu and his wife Xiao Ding Jing had to disguise themselves as peasants riding trundle carts to Xi'an when they left for temporary exile during the Boxer Uprising. The Dalai Lama, being of farming stock, never felt awkward among common people. Despite icy rocks, piercing winds, hunger and thirst, it was far preferable to be at flight than a gilded prisoner in the gloomy Potala.

The Tibetan leader finally entered the border town of Phari, one of the highest permanent habitations in the world. Here the few Chinese were held back by the local villagers as the Dalai Lama stayed with the telegrapher, a Mr Rosemeyer of the government of India.[79] At this point the party could head 64 km (40 mi.) southwest into Sikkim or turn east for 3 km (2 mi.) to Bhutan. Both countries were now protectorates of the British Raj; both countries were once dependencies of Tibet. Here the Tibetan leader performed a *mo* divination to decide whether to cross into Sikkim or enter Bhutan.[80]

Sikkim was chosen, and the party headed down the Chumbi Valley and up to Yatung. The Dalai Lama sought shelter at the small British cantonment headed by administrator David Macdonald. They learned that the Chinese forces had arrived at Phari. The British soldiers stationed there made sure no Chinese soldiers entered. Thubten Gyatso rested for a day, then resumed the flight on the steep trail to Dzelep La, where they finally crossed the border into the British Empire. The Dalai Lama's luck had held, and he was free to continue his pursuit of the British viceroy and to visit the emperor in Beijing. If he was free, his people were free. Fifty years later, the fourteenth emanation would adopt a similar strategy but would choose a route to the east to confound Chinese pursuers.

At midnight the Tibetan party arrived at Gnatong in Sikkim, where they met the two British agents in charge. Although Macdonald had telegraphed the day before, it still struck the agents as incredulous. Shorn of his royal vestments and golden palanquins, a parched, hungry and

Nicholas Roerich, *Jelep La, Tibetan Frontier*, 1936, oil on canvas.

thoroughly dishevelled Dalai Lama sipped a cup of tea before collapsing on the telegrapher's bed.

Regaining their strength, the party soon moved down the trail in the safety of the highlands of Sikkim. The Dalai Lama stayed a few days at Kalimpong as the guest of Raja Kazi Ugyen of Bhutan,[81] blessing the hundreds of villagers. Meanwhile, the rear guard, under the command of Jensey Namgang, had arrived safely at Phari. There he was given assistance by the local *dzong pon* (*rdzong dpon*) and made the next leg safely to Yatung. At this village Namgang disguised himself as a mail carrier and rode with two others over the pass and into Sikkim, weighted down with mail sacks destined for India.[82]

Sikkim was much lower and warmer than the high plains of southern Tibet, and the party quickly reached Darjeeling, arriving on 21 February. He had successfully fled over the Himalaya, one step ahead of a pursuing Chinese army, in the dead of winter. He was soon united with Jensey Namgang, the hero of the hour, who was heaped with rewards by a grateful Dalai Lama, including ennoblement, promotion as general of the Tibetan Army, and marriage into a noble family with the name Tsarong.

Darjeeling, being a summer capital of British India, was fully fortified with garrisons, weapons, ammunitions, supplies, transportation and communications. The Dalai Lama was first put up in a centrally located hotel. He was made welcome by the British and the ruling family of Sikkim, his friend Crown Prince Sidkeong Tulku Namgyal, with whom he had last met in Beijing in 1908.[83]

Here the Dalai Lama learned of a Qing edict posted on the streets of Lhasa and throughout diplomatic outposts. The rudeness of the wording would seem to lend credibility that it was not the work of Prince Regent Zaifeng. Perhaps the imperial court was unaware of its unnecessary severity – in fact, it bears the unmistakably duplicitous stamp of Yuan Shikai, who had been pulling strings behind the court to position himself as ruler. On 25 February 1910, the Chinese government, in the name of the Xuantong emperor, had the Dalai Lama deposed again, this time even stripping his status as a *tulku*:

> The Dalai Lama of Tibet has received abundant favours from the hands of Our Imperial predecessors. He should have devoutly cultivated the precepts of religion in accordance with established precedent in order to propagate the doctrines of the Yellow Church.
>
> But, ever since he assumed control of the administration, he has shown himself [to be] extravagant, lewd, slothful, vicious and perverse without parallel, violent and disobedient to the Imperial Commands, and oppressive towards the Tibetans.
>
> In July, 1904, he fled during the troubles and was denounced by the Imperial Amban to Us as lacking in reliability. A Decree was then issued depriving him temporarily of his Titles. He proceeded to Urga, whence he returned again to Sining. We, mindful of his distant flight, and hoping that he would repent and reform his evil ways, ordered the local officials to pay him due attention. The year before last he came to Peking, was received in Audience, granted new Titles, and presented with gifts.
>
> On his way back to Tibet he loitered and caused trouble; yet every indulgence was shown to him in order to manifest Our compassion. In Our generosity we forgave the past. Szechuan troops have now been sent into Tibet for the special purpose of

preserving order and protecting the Trade Marts. There was no reason for the Tibetans to be suspicious of their intentions. Now the Dalai Lama spread rumours, became rebellious, defamed the Amban, refused supplies, and would not listen to reason.

When the Amban telegraphed that the Dalai Lama had fled during the night of February 12 on the arrival of Szechuan troops, We commanded that steps be taken to bring him back. At present, however, his whereabouts are unknown. He has been guilty of treachery and has placed himself beyond the pale of Our Imperial favour. He is not fit to be a Reincarnation of Buddha. Let him, therefore, be deprived of his titles and his position as Dalai Lama as punishment. Henceforth, no matter where he may go, no matter where he may reside, whether in Tibet or elsewhere, let him be treated as an ordinary individual. Let the Imperial Amban at once cause a search to be made for male children bearing miraculous signs and let him inscribe their names on tablets and place them in the Golden Urn, so that one may be drawn

The Thirteenth Dalai Lama and Sir Charles Bell, with an attendant standing between them, *c.* 1907.

out as the true Reincarnation of previous Dalai Lamas. Let the matter be reported to Us, so that Our Imperial favour may be bestowed upon the selected child, who will thus continue the propagation of the doctrine and the glorification of the Church.

We reward Virtue that Vice may suffer. You, lamas and laymen of Tibet, are Our children. Let all obey the laws and preserve the Peace. Let none disregard Our desire to support the Yellow Church and maintain the tranquility of Our frontier territories.

(Seal of the Xuantong Emperor)[84]

The Dalai Lama learnt of being treated as an insolent teenager by a four-year-old boy as he met the British agent assigned to Sikkim and Bhutan, Charles Bell. The Dalai Lama decided then to invoke the 1904 Lhasa Convention to be able to appeal directly to the British, and to henceforth ignore China. The Chinese then attempted to place Tibet in the hands of the Panchen Lama, which was refused by Tashilhumpo. Through Bell, who would become his close friend, the ruler of Tibet was to plead his case to the British king-emperor. Bell, as well as Prince Sidkeong, spoke fluent Lhasa dialect Tibetan, which made direct communication between the principals possible.

An invitation was received by the Dalai Lama from Viceroy Minto to visit Calcutta. Bell, the Dalai Lama, Prince Sidkeong Namgyal, his younger half-brother Tashi and the Tibetan leader's ministers boarded the winding narrow-gauge train to the plains. Railways were no longer a novelty for him, but the Dalai Lama nevertheless enjoyed the swaying journey to the capital of the Indian Raj. The party stayed in Hastings House, the official guest house of the viceroy; Bell was bivouacked in the annex. The presence of the great holy man from Tibet was quite a spectacle in Calcutta, and he was given many sightseeing tours of the capital, as the Panchen had been previously entertained.

In Calcutta the Dalai Lama presented to Lord Minto the case of Chinese duplicity and reminded him of Tibet's rights under the 1904 Anglo-Chinese Agreement to deal directly with the British. The government of China could not be trusted, explained the Dalai Lama, because it had ignored the assurances given to him by the late empress dowager and Guangxu.

Although the Tibetan leader was treated with profound respect, the official policy of Britain towards Tibet now tilted from duplicity to one of neutrality. Britain had really sacrificed Tibet to keep Nepal, Bhutan, Sikkim and Ladakh within its sphere of interest, especially since Russia no longer seemed interested in territorial expansion. The British Empire itself was also entering a period of consolidation rather than aggrandizement. The Dalai Lama, however, cautioned the viceroy that once China felt secure in Tibet, they would march southward and claim these border states, too. He feared that the invasion of South Asia would be analogous to the Muslim invasions of India centuries before, when most of the great monastic centres of Buddhism, such as Nalanda, were destroyed. The Dalai Lama's insight proved correct, for China did lodge its claim for the former dependencies of Tibet as its own tribute-bearing realms. Except for changes in administration in China and India, Britain's decision to abandon Tibet to China in exchange for the southern border states remains the core of international policy towards Tibet to this day.

It was superstitious Empress Dowager Cixi herself who guaranteed that the Dalai Lama's rule in Tibet would be respected, accounting no doubt for much of his frustration. The truth was that by now the Manchu government was losing control over the empire. Whatever sentiment the Dragon Throne had for the Dalai Lama, Prince Regent Zaifeng could hardly enforce the promises of his dead aunt with massive Han nationalism and anti-Manchu hatred being unleashed throughout the land.

Unable to control the unofficial power sources around the throne, Prince Regent Zaifeng had to recall the hated Yuan Shikai from exile. But the self-serving and probable regicide Yuan resumed his course of betrayal to the dynasty, embracing many of the ideals that were broadcast by the republican leader Sun Yat-sen. The most significant one was the replacement of the Manchu alliance in Inner Asia, the core of its 'foreignness', with a multi-ethnic, nationalist China ruled by the Han majority. The component members of the Qing Empire would become simply minorities in a Chinese nation state. Clearly, this was not to the benefit of the Tibetan, Mongol and Manchu leadership that had been the privileged elite of the empire.

The Manchu government realized that it had seriously underestimated Tibet. The Tibetan people themselves ignored the two imperial deposition orders, further establishing the sovereignty of the country. In a frustrated reversal, the Qing government instructed Amban Lien Yu in Lhasa to dispatch an envoy to the Dalai Lama at Darjeeling to offer to restore his titles. He sent his private secretary, Lo Qingqi.[85] Instead of meeting the official, the Dalai Lama issued the following letter:

> 13 day, 9th month, Iron-dog year (September 1910)
> I received through you an urgent message from Peking political and military departments asking me to return to Lhasa . . . The Manchu Emperors have always shown great care for the welfare of the successive Dalai Lamas, and the Dalai Lamas have reciprocated these feelings of friendship. We have always had each other's best interests at heart . . . In the Wood-dragon year [1904], when the British expedition arrived in Tibet, I did not consider taking any assistance except from Peking. When at Peking, I met the Emperor and his aunt, and they showed me great sympathy. The Emperor committed himself to taking care of the welfare of Tibet. On the strength of the Emperor's word, I returned to Tibet, only to find that on our eastern borders, large bodies of Chinese troops had massed and many of our subjects had been killed. Monasteries were destroyed and the people's rights suppressed. I am sure that you are fully aware of this . . . At Kalimpong, I came to know that the Manchu Emperor had already issued orders that I had been deposed from office. This was published in the Indian newspapers, and even in Lhasa, posters were put up announcing that I was now an ordinary person and that a new Dalai Lama would soon be chosen. Since the Emperor had done everything on the recommendation of the Manchu Amban in Lhasa, without considering the independence of Tibet and the religious relationship between our two countries, I feel there is no further use in my negotiating directly with China. I have lost confidence in China and in finding any solution in consultation with the Chinese.
>
> I have contacted the British because the 1904 Convention permits us to deal directly with them. The Chinese are responsible for this action of mine . . . You are fully aware of this inexcusable illegal action taken by your troops; yet you inform

me and my ministers that the situation in Tibet is peaceful and that the status quo is being maintained. I know that this has been said to persuade me to return and also I know that it is false.

Because of the above, it is not possible for China and Tibet to have the same relationship as before. In order for us to negotiate, a third party is necessary; therefore we should both request the British government to act as an intermediary. Our future policy will be based on the outcome of discussions between ourselves, the Chinese and the British. Are you able to agree to the participation of the British in these discussions? [If not] I am handing you a letter containing the above facts, written in both the Manchu and Tibetan languages, which I would like you to forward to the Emperor.

(Seal of the Dalai Lama)[86]

By refusing the imperial largesse, the Dalai Lama broke with the centuries-old personal relationship between Buddhist hierarch and emperor. His action established a new strategy of using non-Chinese powers to help broker the relationship between China and Tibet. This policy is still used by the Tibetan government-in-exile.

The Panchen Lama was invited by the Chinese to take up residence in Lhasa, albeit with the design to eventually offer him the administration of Tibet. The local populace, however, sternly resisted such an attempt, and threw rocks and mud on the procession of the arriving Panchen and the *amban*. Amban Lien Yu dispatched Lo Qingqi in February 1910 to eastern Tibet to continue to suppress the Khampas in Powo. His 1,000-strong army was soon reinforced with Zhao Erfeng's troops from Dzayul. The Chinese troops were unable to sustain their early successes against the Pome tribesmen, who had launched a guerilla war against them. By late 1911, they were recalled to Lhasa, tired, defeated and ready to turn on their leaders.

Having spent close to two years in India, the Dalai Lama was confident that his messages to Britain were now completely clear. He had abandoned his original plan to sail to China to plead his case to the emperor, for the emperor no longer seemed to be in charge. The Dalai Lama now manoeuvred for Tibet to be considered a protectorate of India, like Sikkim and Bhutan, and he did not back down until he received a polite but clear rejection of British interference by the government of the new King George V. Although by 1911 the apparent Russian threat to the stability of the region had faded, Britain was still hesitant to fully colonize Tibet. Maintaining the fiction of Chinese suzerainty was far cheaper than sending garrisons and supplies over the Himalayan passes to maintain a legal protectorate. The border between empires would be drawn at Sikkim, Bhutan and Ladakh, not at Tibet.

The Dalai Lama learned much Western statecraft during his stay with the British. His friendship with Bell facilitated a deep understanding between the West and Tibet that had eluded Western explorers of the region for centuries. Who once was Tibet's aggressive bogeyman became a respected, if somewhat reluctant, patron in the eyes of the Tibetan people. Friendly Westerners, if not their official representatives, would become the new patrons of the Tibetan people.

The Dalai Lama spent much of his time visiting the holy places in India and Nepal, accumulating merit for himself and his subjects. Eventually, though, it became clear to him that his work was finished in the south. After nearly seven years in exile, it was time to go home. He had ten thousand ideas how to build his state. First and foremost, Tibet needed an army. This would be a challenge: being the worldly throne of Buddhism, Tibet had no wish to maintain a strong army that could karmically befoul its purity, but it was clear no one else would defend the realm. It had been the role of the emperor in Beijing to protect the religious state, which in turn contributed significantly to maintaining the legitimacy of the imperial dynasty, especially among the Mongol and other northern tribes. This no longer worked; the Dalai Lama saw first-hand how the emperor and regent had no power to maintain the old military and religious alliance. There were forces at hand that were demanding a new Chinese construct, one that clearly was not to Tibet's advantage. With all the resources he had available, the Dalai Lama was determined to make a clean break.

He did not have to wait long: on 10 October the Wuchang Uprising marked the beginning of the Xinhai Revolution in China. Town by town, province by province went over to the new republican army and Qing forces were slaughtered. The empire fell apart. On 1 December 1911, the Khalkha Mongols declared their independence from the Manchu Empire under a monarchy with the Eighth Jebtsundamba Khutuktu becoming emperor, or Bogd Khan, on the 29th. In a desperate attempt to maintain control, the powerful but traitorous Yuan Shikai was declared prime minister, and Prince Regent Zaifeng was forced to retire. But rather than support the Qing, Yuan proceeded to negotiate a deal with the republican leader, Sun Yat-sen. Yuan would arrange for the abdication of the Xuantong emperor in exchange for becoming the president of the new Republic of China. On 12 February 1912 two thousand years of imperial rule was wiped away, as the agonized new Regent Empress Dowager Longyu agreed to the abdication of her six-year-old nephew.[87]

The news hit the Dalai Lama like a thunderclap. Indeed, this seemed karmic retribution for years of imperial abuse of Tibet. Chinese forces, many disgruntled by their defeat in Powo, mutinied in Lhasa; returning to Sichuan, Amban Zhao was tortured and beheaded by his own troops. The Dalai Lama now gave an order to fight and expel all the Chinese. He also instructed two officials in Lhasa to establish a war department, and at once despatched the hero of Chaksam Ferry, Tsarong, to Lhasa to stir up Tibetans to take military advantage of the divided Chinese.[88] Clearly, this was a change in karmic strategy for the Tibetan state.

The Dalai Lama was excited about the dramatic turn of affairs and clearly his leadership was needed back home. The long exile may not have resulted in establishing new priest–patron relationships with the great powers in the traditional manner, but it did establish the public

Chinese forces leaving Gyantse on deportation to India, 1912. Tibetan women threw dust after them and clapped their hands, a mode of expelling devils.

Zhao Erfeng, Amban
of Tibet, *c.* 1910.

face of a real Tibet in the world, something which had not been done
before. It was a strategy that the Fourteenth Dalai Lama would adopt
as well.

Returning to Kalimpong, the Dalai Lama continued to receive
hundreds of devout Buddhists. The development of Sikkim as a protectorate of Britain seemed to have some appeal to the Dalai Lama as a
model for the future, and Bell, succeeding John Claude White in 1908
as political agent for Sikkim, was earnest in his convictions. White had
taken a personal interest in the education of Crown Prince Sidkeong
Tulku and had sent him to Oxford University to finish his education.
Then he was given a grand tour in 1908 to meet the monarchs of Asia,
seeing both his old friend the Dalai Lama and the Manchu emperor in
Beijing. Sidkeong, a worldly polyglot, was well groomed by the British
to become an ideal native ruler within the Raj system. Like Bell, he
remained in attendance of the Dalai Lama for much of his stay in

Kalimpong. Intelligent, knowledgeable, warm and compassionate, the slight young crown prince was progressive and exceptionally charming.

Ex ore leonis

In the wee hours of a humid June night in 1912, sturdy Tibetan ponies were drawn up to the residence of His Holiness provided by Raja Kazi Ugyen and loaded down with the tonnes of baggage accumulated by the Ganden Phodrang during its two-year exile in India. Before he left, the Dalai Lama ennobled Raja Kazi with the hereditary title of *rimshi* for his hospitality.[89] Here at Kalimpong, the Golden Chair of State was made ready.

At Gnatong the Dalai Lama's friends – Bell, King Thutob (Don grub) and Crown Prince Sidkeong Tulku, soon to be king himself – saw the holy man off. The haul up the Jelap La pass to Chumbi Valley in Tibet was an easy one compared with the outbound journey. The party proceeded through Yatong, where they stayed with the administrator David Macdonald for several days,[90] meeting up with the Dalai Lama's old

teacher and emissary Agvan Dorjiev. Upbraided, Macdonald had the audacity to ask the Dalai Lama to dismiss Dorjiev. Surprising the British, Thubten Gyatso complied: Dorjiev was left packing for Mongolia, but not before he had been given another secret mission by the Dalai Lama. The Tibetan ruler proceeded to Gyantse and across the Tsangpo where Jensey Namgang had so successfully held back the advancing Chinese army. The Dalai Lama and his ministers continued on to the sacred scorpion-shaped lake of Yamdrok and the 'Diamond Sow's' famous monastery of Samding (Bsam Iding), built out on a peninsula.

Some Chinese troops still had not been flushed out of Lhasa, about 108 km (70 mi.) to the northeast, so the Dalai Lama waited at Samding. Here the government availed itself on the hospitality of the abbess Dorje Phagmo for nearly two months. Dorje Phagmo, of the Bodongpa school, was the holiest woman in Vajrayāna Buddhism. A *tulku* of fifteenth-century mystic Chokyi Dronma, she was considered the rein-carnation of the Diamond Sow Vajravārahī, consort of the tantric deity Heruka.[91] With the Jebtsundamba Khutuktu of Mongolia, the Dorje Phagmo is considered the third highest incarnation in Tibetan Buddhism,

Samding monastery, 2013.

The Eleventh Dorje Phagmo at Samding monastery, November 1920.

following the Panchen and Dalai Lamas. Samding, the Temple of Soaring Meditation, hosted nuns as well as monks on the shores of the mirror-lake of Yamdrok. Here, His Holiness was given the abbess's accommodation upstairs while she moved to more humble quarters on the ground floor.

It took almost a year to remove all the Chinese from Tibet. The Kashag and Drepung monastery supported the continued presence of the Chinese, as did the Panchen Lama, who had even moved into the Norbulingka. The fighting was much like a civil war. The Chinese were eventually defeated, and the members of the *kashag* who sided with the Chinese were executed.

From Ü-tsang, Chinese prisoners were given safe passage back to China through Sikkim. While at Samding, the Dalai Lama received a message from the remaining *amban*, Lien Yu, requesting his representative at Lhasa to witness his surrender. It was time for the Dalai Lama to re-enter the capital.

Sir Charles Bell summed up the perspectives and issues rather well, and it has stood the test of time:

> To cut short these episodes that favour one side or the other, it seems that since 1720 China had more power in Tibet than the Dalai Lama and other Tibetans admit, but a great deal less than

she herself claims. The Tibetan claim is nearer to the truth. But China can make its case known to the world; Tibet cannot do so. And the world judges accordingly, after hearing the evidence on one side only.[92]

It was now Great Britain, rather than the Dalai Lama, who would keep Tibet sealed. For years it was not even possible for Bell to visit Lhasa, despite the Dalai Lama's repeated invitations.

The final break

In January 1913 the Thirteenth Dalai Lama processed triumphantly into the Tibetan capital, a sea of yellow banners and black horses. After seven years without his presence, the city dwellers were happy beyond measure. On 11 January 1913 Dorjiev's secret mission came to fruition. Mongolia and Tibet signed a treaty that recognized each other's independence. The treaty itself assumed a somewhat mythical standing in international law until 2007, when the government of Mongolia made the document available for scholarly study.[93] The British were uneasy about the agreement, which could possibly allow Russian Mongols to enter a war against China. Political agent Bell and others passively entered into a campaign of disinformation that would question Dorjiev's authority to sign the treaty, and indeed its very existence. The existence of a valid treaty of recognition between two subjects of international law would upset Whitehall's fabrication of convenience that China was a suzerain power over the two countries. Misinforming the world about the existence of the agreement was also in the interest of China's confabulation of sovereignty over Tibet. The treaty was subsequently conveniently ignored for nearly a century.

The minister plenipotentiary for the Dalai Lama, Agvan Dorjiev, had concluded the accord with the newly independent Mongolian state at Urga. Its preamble sums up the events of the previous two years:

Our two States, Mongolia and Tibet, having come out from under the supremacy/domination of the Manchu Empire/Qing State and separated from China, have each formed their independent States . . .

Agvan Dorjiev, *c.* 1913.

Article 1. The Monarch of the State of Tibet, Dalai Lama, approves and recognizes the formation of an independent State of Mongolia, and the proclamation of Jebtsundamba Lama, leader of the Yellow religion, as Monarch of the State on the ninth day of the eleventh month of the year of the pig.

Article 2. The Monarch of the State of Mongolia, Jebtsundamba Lama, approves and recognizes the formation of an independent State established by Tibetans, and proclamation of the Dalai Lama as Monarch of the State.[94]

These declarations were entirely lawful, according to consensus in international law. In fact, in 2010 the International Court of Justice ruled in the case of Kosovo that unilateral independence declarations, indeed even secession attempts, are not illegal.[95] The mutual recognition of the two Gelug hierarchs clearly marked a path of no-return for the Buddhist states of Mongolia and Tibet.

The Dalai Lama soon followed with a clearly written edict to the Tibetan people. On 13 February 1913, nearly exactly a year after the

Xuantong emperor was forced to abdicate, the Dalai Lama issued the following proclamation to his people. It is recognized as the Tibetan declaration of independence:

> I, the Dalai Lama, most omniscient possessor of the Buddhist faith, whose title was conferred by the Lord Buddha's command[96] from the glorious land of India, speaks to you as follows:
>
> I am speaking to all classes of Tibetan people. Lord Buddha, from the glorious country of India, prophesied that the reincarnations of Avalokiteśvara, through successive rulers from the early religious kings to the present day, would look after the welfare of Tibet.
>
> During the time of Genghis Khan and Altan Khan of the Mongols, the Ming dynasty of the Chinese, and the Ch'ing dynasty of the Manchus, Tibet and China co-operated on the basis of benefactor and priest relationship. A few years ago, the Chinese authorities in Szechuan and Yunnan endeavored to colonize our territory. They brought large numbers of troops into central Tibet on the pretext of policing the trade marts. I, therefore, left Lhasa with my ministers for the Indo-Tibetan border, hoping to clarify to the Manchu Emperor by wire that the existing relationship between Tibet and China had been that of patron and priest and had not been based on the subordination of one to the other. There was no other choice for me but to cross the border, because Chinese troops were following with the intention of taking me alive or dead.
>
> On my arrival in India, I dispatched several telegrams to the Emperor; but his reply to my demands was delayed by corrupt officials in Peking. Meanwhile, the Manchu Empire collapsed. The Tibetans were encouraged to expel the Chinese from central Tibet. I, too, returned safely to my rightful and sacred country, and I am now in the course of driving out the remnants of Chinese troops from Do Kham in eastern Tibet. Now, the Chinese intention of colonizing Tibet under the patron–priest relationship has faded like a rainbow in the sky . . .
>
> Your duties to the government and to the people will have been achieved when you have executed all that I have said here.

This letter must be posted and proclaimed in every district of Tibet, and a copy kept in the records of the offices in every district.

> From the Potala Palace
> (Seal of the Dalai Lama)[97]

China has ever since maintained that both these declarations were penned by the British and Russians and are in violation of China's concept of territorial integrity.[98] In the Tibetan declaration, the entire history of Tibet is encapsulated as a prophecy of Lord Buddha and, most notably, states that the successive incarnations of Avalokiteśvara are the lineage authorized to rule Tibet. The document is consistent with centuries of Tibetan assessments on the nature of its state.

Never does the Dalai Lama denounce the Manchu ruling family (Guangxu, Cixi, Xuantong and Zaifeng) for abrogating the spirit of the priest–patron relationship; he always blames corrupt officials. In the opening years of the twentieth century three strong personalities would meet, interact and in the process determine the course of Tibet, Mongolia and the Manchu Empire. The Thirteenth Dalai Lama, the Eighth Jebtsundampa of Mongolia and Prince Zaifeng of Qing dynasty China, all young men thrown into the cauldron of imperial gamesmanship, would survive the encounter. Their intercourse underscores the personal nature of the priest–patron relationship over the institutional and demonstrates the fragility of the lofty idealism that was once the core of the Manchu Empire. To have denounced the emperor himself would call into question the infallibility of a religious system that, as Buddha prophesied, created the line of *chogyal* to rule Tibet. The Dalai Lama's authority springs from this, not from any secular ruler or martial conquest.

The concept of a Han-dominated 'Greater China' as successor to the Manchu Empire was a philosophical concept created by Sun Yat-sen. The republican revolution was a nationalist one: to overthrow a foreign dynasty and replace it with a secular, representative government of the Han majority. Not content to let the outlier territories fall away and to merely create a strong China proper, however, Sun and his successors claimed the entire empire. The 'five races' were now to be 'one family'. This was a Qing innovation at the height of its power, however. But under Sun Yat-sen's philosophy, it relegated the Mongols, Manchus,

Uighurs and Tibetans into minorities in a Han-dominated nation state.

The Dalai Lama moved quickly to consolidate his newly independent country. Leaders of the government and army during the successful uprising that dispelled the Chinese were rewarded with titles. The young commander of his forces, Tsarong, was given the title *dzasa*.

Yuan Shikai, who wrote of a greater republican China idea in the abdication edict of the Xuantong emperor, sent two friendly letters to the Dalai Lama restoring his titles, which had been stripped from him upon the Tibetan leader's exile to India. The Dalai Lama communicated back that he needed no such titles, as he intended to exercise secular and religious authority himself. In fact, he had written the tsar with the request to recognize Tibet's independence under the Dalai Lama's authority, and to possibly provide protection from Chinese intervention. Nicholas II, occupied elsewhere, was not interested.[99]

Hedging his bets, the Dalai Lama also exchanged gifts and letters directly with King George V, through the official Lungshar, who was entrusted to chaperone four boys sent to Rugby School for a Western education.[100] Similarly, Chogyal Thutob of Sikkim, who had become friends with King George when he first visited India, arranged with Claude White to send Crown Prince Sidkeong to Oxford to be educated. King George returned a message to the Dalai Lama, indicating that Britain would soon meet with representatives of his government, Tibet, and China to try to resolve issues. This tripartite conference, which met at the summer capital of the British Raj, would be known as the Simla Convention. Mahārāja Sidkeong would also attend, partly as an interpreter, partly for the British to show off their new, Oxford-educated Chogyal.

Britain was intent on creating the fiction that Tibet was vaguely submissive to a Chinese suzerainty. China was satisfied with nothing less than making Tibet a province of China. And Tibet thought itself now independent. Under international law, which was then and is now a work in progress, Tibet satisfied the requirements of statehood: it had a government, it had a stable population, and it possessed territory. Furthermore, after 1912, it had not even a vestige of Chinese control. The Simla conference would be perhaps too little too late to satisfy anyone. But for the first time, the three parties did sit down and talk with each other.

Simla Convention, October 1913. Rear, middle, left: Archibald Rose and to the right Charles Bell. Front, left to right: Wangchuk Tsering, Chinese delegates B. D. Bruce, Ifan Chen, Sir Henry McMahon, Tibetan delegates Lonchen Shatra, Trimon and Tenpa Dhargay (known as the Dronyer Chenmo).

The minister with plenipotentiary powers for the Ganden Phodrang was the Lonchen Shatra, among the highest-ranking Tibetan aristocrats. The position of Tibet as an independent state reached its apogee in the position statement presented at Simla. It had not stated this in such language before, nor was it ever as adamant about the future of the state:

> Firstly, the relationship between the Manchu Emperor and the Protector, Dalai Lama the fifth, became like that of the disciple towards the teacher. The sole aim of the then Government of China being to earn merit for this and for the next life, they helped and honoured the successive Dalai Lamas and treated the monks of all the monasteries with respect . . .
>
> Tibet and China have never been under each other and will never associate with each other in the future. It is decided that Tibet is an independent State and that the precious Protector, the Dalai Lama, is the Ruler of Tibet, in all temporal as well as in spiritual affairs. Tibet repudiates the Anglo-Chinese Convention concluded at Peking on 27 April 1906 . . . as she did not send a representative for this Convention nor did she affix

her seal on it. It is therefore decided it is not binding on the three Governments.[101]

The Chinese, in their commencement statement, were polar opposites:

> In 1206 Tibet was again subdued by Genghis Khan, who incorporated it into his wide-spread Empire. Tibet remained in this relation to China during the time of the Ming Dynasty...
>
> As regards the recent relations between China and Tibet which have resulted in such a misunderstanding as now exists between the two peoples, it is not China that can be blamed, but it is entirely due to the conduct of His Holiness the Dalai Lama himself...
>
> It is hereby agreed by the undersigned that Tibet forms an integral part of the territory of the Republic of China, that no attempts shall be made by Tibet or Great Britain to interrupt the continuity of this territorial integrity, and that China's rights of every description which have existed in consequence of this territorial integrity shall be respected by Tibet and recognized by Great Britain.[102]

This assumes that the title to Tibetan sovereignty passed to China during the Yuan dynasty; Tibetan history contends that China was then a mere province of the Mongol Empire and could not have claimed another associate state of the larger empire, and no such relationship was made during the Ming dynasty. Remarkably, through the era of British decolonization, Chinese warlordism, Second World War occupation and the Communist Revolution, this has basically remained the Chinese claim to Tibet. At Simla, China conjured up boundaries between the two regions far to the west of the Tibetan line: in fact, only 160 km (100 mi.) east of Lhasa.

Britain's interests were served by creating an impotent buffer state aligned with China, which would not be allowed to intrigue with other powers, mainly Russia. Its model for Chinese suzerainty seems to be the then evolving dominion concept which was applied to Canada, Australia and other self-governing realms within the British Empire. Here, the shared monarch retains in personal union the crowns of those gradually independent dominions. Was Britain aware of the personal aspect of the priest–patron relationship between China and Tibet?[103] The term suzerainty also referred to the supposed tributary relationship between the Chinese Empire and peripheral monarchies such as Burma, Korea and Annam. The term is also burdened with somewhat inappropriate connotations derived from European feudalism. But the most logical explanation of the British intent was to have China recognize Tibet as a protectorate in the same manner as it had created and patronized subordinate monarchies in the Indian Raj. Sikkim was a good example.

The parties finally agreed to split Tibet into an outer and inner region. The solution was to follow the precedent that was used in Mongolia during much of the Qing, and in Manchuria after the 1858 Treaty of Aigun with Russia. Mongolia was partitioned into an Inner Mongolia, which was ruled directly by the central government, and an Outer Mongolia that was self-governing. This Outer Tibet would be run along the lines of the old empire: China would be responsible for Tibet's foreign policy, but would refrain from local administration, including the selection of the ruling *tulku*. Inner Tibet would be ruled directly from China.

After spirited haggling, the borders between the three states were determined. The boundary between eastern India and Tibet is now known as the McMahon Line after the British plenipotentiary. The former Tibetan territories of Tawang and Monyul, which extend to northern Burma, would hence be given to India. It is disputed now, as ultimately the Chinese delegate, Ifan Chen, was not permitted by his superiors to sign for the Republic. China, interpreting the convention itself as proof of continued British intrigue, insisted on nothing less that turning Tibet into a province. Britain and Tibet, however, signed the document in 1914 and, until the invasion of Tibet in 1950, based their foreign policies towards each other upon these articles of the Simla Convention. Despite being a tripartite conference, it resulted in a bilateral agreement between the world's then superpower and Tibet, and further contributed to an international understanding that Tibet had treaty-making powers, a demonstration of statehood.

Given the fact that the Chinese government did not sign the agreement, Sir Henry McMahon and the Lonchen Shatra signed the document with a clause that stated, 'The powers granted to China under the Convention shall not be recognized by Great Britain and Tibet until and unless the Government of China ratifies the Convention.'[104] Since China did not accept the agreement, China cannot subsequently claim legal suzerainty over Tibet, nor is the McMahon Line binding. The terms of the original, non-ratified agreement between Britain, China and Tibet, however, are much like the current request of the Fourteenth Dalai Lama for 'genuine autonomy' and internal self-rule for Tibet.

Soon after the Simla Convention, the Dalai Lama lost his reform-minded ally and cohort in Sikkim. Chogyal Sidkeong Tulku died under mysterious circumstances at his palace in Gangtok.[105]

War on the eastern frontier

Despite the ambiguity of the Simla Convention, the reality of the state of Tibet was no pipe dream. The Tibetan army had pushed Chinese forces completely out of Ü-tsang, proving that they could defend themselves. It was soon time to secure the eastern borders from further incursion by Chinese republican forces. The Ganden Phodrang, at the outset of the First World War, offered to send troops to India to help support the British war effort as an ally. The Dalai Lama, upon reviewing Chinese, Mongol, Japanese, Russian and British military drills, chose to emulate the British system. Subsequently, regiments were trained according to British methods. Some officers were sent to India for training in artillery and machine-gun operations.[106] No longer could the Tibetan state rely upon a proxy militia.

What drove the Chinese to the conference table at Simla was the increasing massing of Tibetan troops in Kham. The Dalai Lama was determined, with his new army, to wrest that traditional province back from China, which it had carved up under Qianlong almost two centuries before and had more recently been decimated by Zhao Erfeng. In 1917 the Dalai Lama sent a full *kalon*, Lama Jamba Tendar and six generals (*mda' dpon*) to Kham with instructions to drive out the Chinese. The fighting was fierce, and three of the generals, Phulungwa, Jingpa and Tailing, died in battle. After many months of fighting, the Chinese capital of Kham (or Sikang) was captured. Following the strategy of the expulsion of Chinese troops from Lhasa after the Chinese Revolution of 1912, prisoners were deported from Tibet through India. Left at the border, they had to find their own way home. This had the effect of preserving life while defusing any sort of instant recovery of capitulated Chinese troops. The commander of the Chinese troops, humiliated by defeat, was pensioned off and allowed to settle at Dowa *dzong* in southern Tibet.[107] Chamdo became the headquarters of Jamba Tendar as governor-general of Kham. The Tibetan forces recaptured Markham, Draya, Sangyen, Gojo and Derge, and occupied parts of Yunnan.

Suing for peace, the Chinese asked the British to arrange a truce. Eric Teichman, British consular agent for northwest China, was sent to negotiate. A new border was drawn up in 1918 that followed the course of the Upper Yangtse. Tibet regained significant territory by the ceasefire, but by the agreement Tibet lost its ancient claim to Lithang, Batang, Dhartsedo and Nyarong.

Warlord Zhang Xun had briefly restored the Xuantong emperor to the throne in July 1917. As the empires of Germany and Austria-Hungary fell in the autumn of 1918, the Chinese and Tibetans ceased hostilities. The increasing power of Tibet under the rule of the Thirteenth Dalai Lama was thus largely ignored by the Western powers in the process of concluding their Great War. The Sino-Tibetan war of 1917–18 was won decisively by Tibet, thus demonstrating an ability to defend itself.

Free of Chinese intervention, the Dalai Lama continued to bring out the trappings of an independent nation. Thubten Gyatso issued Tibet's first postage stamps and paper currency, both printed from carved wood blocks, in addition to the newly valued gold and silver coins bearing the name of Ganden Phodrang. And the Dalai Lama continued to build the army under Tsarong Dzasa. The Tibetan army at the time was only about 3,000 men – he moved quickly to train an additional 1,000. Having been impressed with the sharp drill of British soldiers in India, and most conscious that the British Empire was the sole great power of the world, the Dalai Lama sought to develop his army along British lines. British advisors were brought in; recruits were given khaki jodhpurs, pith helmets, riding crops and British arms. Officers learned to drink sweet tea. The national anthem for Tibet was adopted to be played to the tune of 'God Save the King' by a newly formulated Tibetan marching band. Telegraph and wireless radio broadcasting were further developed. A Western-style school was opened in Lhasa, with a curriculum that included a worldwide perspective. The Dalai Lama sent Chamba Tendar Shape to Kham as governor-general with orders to raise a local militia. A frontier between China and Tibet was established on the divide between the Salween and Mekong rivers.

A return to xenophobia

The Dalai Lama's modernization and centralization policies did not go over well with many of the monastic institutions. Drepung, Sera, Tashilhumpo and Ganden, with their thousands of Gelug monks, were quite used to running their great estates autonomously. The same could be said for the Nyingma, Sakya, Kagyu and Bonpa monasteries throughout the entire Tibetan Buddhist cultural region. And the kingdoms of western Tibet and Kham often acted independently of Lhasa. Xenophobia had served the theocratic government well; the Manchu Empire, like the previous Mongol protectorate, was a convenient way of protecting Tibet's integrity without the expense of keeping a standing army or incurring the karmic consequences of killing. The *raison d'état* for Tibet, after all, was to serve as light in an unenlightened world, a holy place where the full doctrine was being preserved and transmitted for the benefit of all. It is at the heart of the idea of the Tibetan state.

Unfortunately, it was also clear to the Dalai Lama that this philosophical view of Tibet was anachronistic and impractical in the modern world. The best way now to preserve the religion, maintain border security, and allow for the propagation of the doctrine was to secure Tibet as a nation state, educate the people, and continue to build bridges with the great powers: these were the basic ideas of the Thirteenth Dalai Lama.

Having seen first-hand how lax even the great Gelug monastery of Kumbum had been and having shaken his golden *dorje* at the Mongol Jebtsundampa for his scandalous behaviour, the Dalai Lama was keen on tightening the noose around the local Lhasa monasteries. Some of the 'seven seals' had even opposed his defenestration of the Chinese authorities upon his return from India. Ganden and Drepung were seen as pro-Chinese; Sera, on the other hand, had fought for the restoration of the Ganden Phodrang.

The monastic culture was still wary of the Dalai Lama's British advisors, such as Sir Charles Bell. For many monks, at least the Chinese were Buddhist. Many resented the power of Tsarong Dzasa, who was looked upon as an interloper by some aristocratic families. The greatest factor in monastic resistance, however, was the military build-up. Having a standing Tibetan army was not an ideal in the dovish minds of many of the great abbots, even though they had expelled the Chinese. The flash point came as the Dalai Lama decided to tax the wealthy monasteries, as the Ganden Phodrang was nearly bankrupt from the recent wars with the British and the Chinese. The monasteries, not used to being tapped by a central government, were generally horrified at the thought of having to pay taxes to the Ganden Phodrang. Sera stood strongly behind the Dalai Lama, but Drepung and Ganden were incensed. In 1921 the Dalai Lama acted by arresting three of the more irascible Drepung abbots and giving them a good thrashing. Like angry red ants, the monks of Drepung stormed out of their monasteries and headed directly for the Norbulinka. Skilled perhaps better in passive aggression rather than martial valour, the monks resorted to pulling up flowers, urinating and defecating in the gardens.[108] Next day the Dalai Lama sent his crack new army to lay siege to Drepung. Ganden fell in with the government. Drepung capitulated. The Dalai Lama then paraded his new army through downtown Lhasa and quietly replaced the Drepung abbots with his own appointments.

The government of Tsang under the Panchen Lama proved to be a far more difficult challenge to the Dalai Lama than his local Gelug monks. China and Britain had played a divide-and-rule game with the Panchen and Dalai Lamas nearly since the beginning of the Gelug institution, taking advantage of the ancient rupture between Tsang and Ü. Despite their great authority, the Dalai Lamas could hardly dismiss the Panchens, and vice versa, for they were bound by the sacred strictures of teacher and student, which alternated over the generations of successive *tulku*s. Their recent history was not promising: while the Dalai Lama fled the Younghusband invasion and was trying to establish foreign relations with Mongolia and Russia and improve communications with the Qing, the Panchen Lama was being feted by Viceroy Minto and the Prince of Wales in Calcutta. There was testosterone-fuelled barracks talk during the Curzon–Younghusband episode that Tsang be made a separate state by Britain under the friendly Panchen. The Panchen even tried to send his own representative to the Simla talks, but was rebuffed by the Ganden Phodrang. The Dalai Lama first insisted that Tsang pay one-quarter of the total costs of expelling the Chinese and the wars with

Britain. In 1917 Thubten Gyatso demanded taxes from certain Tsang estates in Gyatse, despite ancient agreements contrary to this practice. In 1923 he increased this to include all of Tsang.[109] Tashilhumpo pleaded with Lhasa, saying that they did not have the funds to satisfy the tax obligations. The Panchen responded with a threat:

> His Serenity the Tashi Lama states that he is unable to meet the demands made upon him and proposed to submit a representation to His Holiness the Dalai Lama on the subject. If his request is granted, things will then of course be all right; but if not, His Serenity wished to know whether the Government of India will mediate between himself and His Holiness the Dalai Lama as he states that his only hope is the assistance of the Government of India.[110]

Despite the Panchen's protests, the Dalai Lama pressed his demands. For Lungshar and the Dalai Lama, it was not just a matter of filling the national treasury, but to assert Ganden Phodrang's authority over Tsang and much of western Tibet. This was a deep structural fissure in Tibet, going back to the break-up of the Yarlung dynasty with the assassination of Lang Darma in the ninth century. It would persist to the present day with two Panchens: a Dalai Lama-recognized one (Dge 'dun chos kyi nyi ma) and a Chinese one (Rgyal mtshan nor bu) determined by the Chinese Golden Urn lottery. In December 1923 the Sixth Panchen caved in and jumped into the waiting arms of the Chinese, fleeing Shigatse and going into exile in Mongolia and Kham. The Dalai Lama responded by publicly denouncing the Panchen, calling him a 'moth attracted to a flame' and not suitable to be an incarnation of Amitābha.[111] Furthermore, he sent Lungshar in hot pursuit, and appointed an administrator over Tashilhumpo. He did not catch the Panchen Lama, who ended up at Lanzhou in former Kham territory.

Of the four boys who were educated in England, Rigzin Dorje Ringang was assigned the task of introducing electric lighting in Lhasa and at the Norbulingka. Wandu Norbu Kyibuk was assigned to improve the telegraphic network begun by the British. Chaperone Lungshar himself became finance secretary and civilian leader of the military department.[112] He also helped to establish the English school for

Tibetan boys in Gyantse. The school only lasted three years, however, due to pressure from the monastic community who felt an English education would be detrimental to the boys' development of Buddhist values.

The Chinese government repeatedly tried to re-establish communications with Tibet. In 1927 a letter from General Chiang Kai-shek was sent to the Dalai Lama through an abbot returning from Beijing.[113] It was an offer to fully support the Dalai Lama's office, provided Tibet agreed to become a province of China. It was, of course, rebuffed by the Dalai Lama. Similarly, Buriat Mongols arrived from Soviet-controlled Mongolia, oddly seeking to interest the Dalai Lama in their Communist form of government. Having seen how the Soviets had destroyed the monasteries of Mongolia and Russia, he sent the Buriats packing.

During the early 1920s, the ruling clique of Tibet consisted of Tsarong, Tsepon Lungshar and Kuchar Kunphela, all in support of the Thirteenth Dalai Lama. The three were bold, innovative and somewhat unorthodox, which aroused great jealousy throughout the old, landed aristocracy and the higher ranks of the lamas, including many Gelug abbots. It would just be a matter of time before these reactionary forces would bring them down.

The first to go would be Tsarong, the military genius who literally saved the Dalai Lama and the Ganden Phodrang upon his second exile to India. While the Thirteenth Dalai Lama, through his travels, had become more worldly and politically adroit in dealing with foreigners, he also had difficulty in controlling his new, British-equipped army. The essence of the internal problem stemmed from the army's resentment of the new police force, which appeared to be better paid and had sharper uniforms. Rumour and innuendo passed back and forth until some police officers were punished by Commander-in-Chief Tsarong. This action, which involved the death of one of the officers, may have been beyond Tsarong's authority. Many at the top believed that this arrogance was part of a military plot to overthrow the Dalai Lama's secular powers. Realizing that something had to be done, the Tibetan ruler demoted Tsarong and other officers. The Dalai Lama's favourite thus began a slow deflation of his brilliant military career. Thubten Gyatso felt it was better to reduce the power of the army than risk a coup. Tsarong was appointed head of the mint and printing office.

The new favourite was Thubden Kumbela, a young monk from a humble background who became totally dedicated to the Dalai Lama. In addition to providing the constant attendance to his master that Tsarong once did, Kumbela developed a special military regiment consisting of the sons of nobility named the Drong Drak Magar and housed in Drapchi (Grwa bzhi) base in Lhasa.[114] The noble youths Dapon Yuthok ('turquoise roof') Tashi Dondup, and Prince Jigme Taring Namgyal ('Jigs med sum rtsen dbang po rnam rgyal), nephew of Sidkeong, were trained in Gyantse in recruitment and machine guns, respectively, and were assigned to the Drapchi regiment.[115] The Drong Drak Magar was to become a source of power for Kumbela, who was now the second most powerful man in Tibet. He fed his soldiers well on dried yak and made sure the likes of Yuthok and Jigme Taring had the sharpest uniforms from Calcutta. But it was not popular for aristocratic sons to be conscripted into the military. As K. K. Dhondup has written, 'Kunphela had succeeded in building . . . an extremely vulnerable conclave of young soldiers ready to desert their post and return home at the slightest excuse and provocation.'[116] The unhappy regiment fuelled resentment towards the Dalai Lama's favourite, one which crafty Lungshar would use to full advantage.

The peace in Kham was shattered in 1930. When a dispute between two monasteries broke out just east of the border with China along the Yangtse, local Sichuan warlord Liu Wenhui decided to take advantage of the uncertainty by attacking Dargyag monastery. This pulled the Tibetan troops out of Derge, and they began to march in the old quest of capturing the traditional border town of Tachienlu (modern Kangding). The Kuomingtang was powerless to interfere with Liu, who was virtually an independent ruler of Sichuan. The Nationalists did manage to obtain a ceasefire for a brief period, just enough, however, for Liu to regain his strength and attack again. The Tibetans retreated to the Yangtse line and made a truce with China, not informing the Ganden Phodrang. They were subsequently demoted by the Dalai Lama.[117]

Meanwhile, another warlord, Ma Bufang, who controlled Qinghai (Amdo) province, began a similar attack on a monastery which engaged local Tibetan troops. A battle ensued at Dan Chokorgon that defeated the Tibetans, who retreated to Chamdo, Riwoche and Tengchen. Shiqu, Dengke and other counties were retaken and dispossessed from the

Tibetans. Nanking arranged for ceasefires, and hostilities ended in 1933 for both Liu and Ma.

Death of the Thirteenth Dalai Lama

The strong, determined, battle-worn Thirteenth Dalai Lama carefully maintained his authority over it all. For the first time in centuries, Tibet was now as centralized as it had ever been, even though it had lost the southern kingdoms to the British and half of Amdo and parts of Kham to the Chinese. Nevertheless, for a whole decade, there was peace in Kham and the borders held.

In fact, the Thirteenth was much more of a *chogyal* of Tibet than even the Great Fifth, as the position of king then had not been incorporated into the position of Dalai Lama. The patron khan, Altan, was given that title, and later the Qing emperors claimed the khanship of Inner Asia. Thubten Gyatso's greatest challenge was to erase much of the fiction in London and the West that Tibet was somehow suzerain to China, and the Nationalist fiction that his country was an integral part of the Republic of China since the Yuan dynasty. By making personal contact with Mongolia, Russia, Great Britain, Japan and the United States, meeting dharma-seekers such as Alexandra David-Neel, and living outside of his country for long periods of time, the Dalai Lama was establishing a precedent for his successor, Tenzin Gyatso, in his position as a world moral leader. His actions constructed the prototype by which the authority of the Dalai Lama continues to exist regardless of territorial rule and without Chinese support or authority. This is the paradigm that continues to animate the Ganden Phodrang in exile.

The Dalai Lama closely watched the destruction of the great Russian Empire at the hands of the Bolsheviks, the assassination of Nicholas II, the mystical 'White Khan' of the Western Buddhists, and the destruction of the Buddhist monastery in St Petersburg established by his friend and teacher, Dorjiev. He saw the erosion of power of the Jebtsundampa Hutuktu Bogn Khan in Urga, the takeover of that country by atheist Soviets (1921), and the destruction of its monasteries. He had strong premonitions that the same could happen to Tibet.

The Thirteenth Dalai Lama, having a sharp, clairvoyant vision of the looming catastrophe that would soon befall his country, decided to die early to ensure that his incarnation was mature when the holocaust struck, according to many Tibetans' thinking. In fact, the Nechung Oracle administered deathbed medicine to the Dalai Lama, which, rather than restoring him, apparently hastened his demise. Before Thubten Gyatso died on 17 December 1933, he cautioned in a valedictory message:

> It may happen that here in the centre of Tibet the Religion and the secular administration may be attacked both from the outside and from the inside. Unless we can guard our own country, it will now happen that the Dalai and Panchen Lamas, the Father and the Son, the Holders of the Faith, the glorious Rebirths, will be broken down and left without a name. As regards the monasteries and the monks and nuns, their lands and other properties will be destroyed. The administrative customs of the Three Religious Kings [Songtsen Gampo, Song Detsen and Ralpachen] will be weakened. The officers of State, ecclesiastical and secular, will find their lands seized and their other property confiscated, and they themselves made to serve their enemies, or wander about the country as beggars do. All beings will be sunk in great hardship and in overpowering fear; the days and the nights will drag on slowly in suffering.[118]

Indeed, with the demise of the Thirteenth Dalai Lama the state governed by the Ganden Phodrang once again entered a viperous period of regency from which it would not recover, at least within the sovereign nation state of Tibet. By the time the Fourteenth Dalai Lama took the full reins of the government, it was too late.

The Tibetan government sent notices of the passing of the Dalai Lama to Great Britain and China. While King George v expressed his nation's sorrow and respect, Chiang Kai-shek used the opportunity to attempt to restore Chinese influence in the country, on the pretext of sending a condolence mission to Lhasa. Presently China had little to show for its republican revolution: Outer Mongolia, Tibet and Manchukuo[119] were independent, and much of the rest of the border areas were in chaos. Reunifying China was a major goal. The Tibet government was deeply divided whether they should invite the condolence party or not, and the line was among those who favoured continued independence and those that saw rapprochement with China as the more practical route. In the end, the Kuomingtang condolence mission was invited.

General Huang Mu-sung left Nanking with orders to reel Tibet back into the nation. Huang arrived with a party of about eighty and spent the first weeks visiting holy temples and presenting gifts. The Tibetan *kashag*, when the appropriate time came, responded by demanding that the territories China occupied in Kham and Amdo be returned. It also called for a restoration of the priest–patron relationship and complete internal autonomy. However, the Tsongdu rejected joining China.[120] The government told Huang that Tibet was independent. In the end, a wireless operator was the only Chinese person allowed to remain. He was touted as a resident representative back in Nanking, thus saving face. For the Tibetan government, it seemed as if they relished the best of both worlds: to be independent yet also be the recipient of the largesse of China. This indecision would continue to grow with the demise of the Great Thirteenth and the ensuing regency that greatly reduced the effectiveness of the new Tibetan state.

SIX

A Bright and Sparkling Lama

The failure of the Tibetan state in the mid-twentieth century is exceptionally well documented through the works of Melvyn Goldstein, Tsering Shakya and others.[1] In summary, however, it seems that the Tibetan ideology of the state had difficulty matching the realpolitik of ethnic ethnogenesis at the end of several imperial experiments, such as the Qing, Russian and British empires. Tibet as a theocracy was reluctant to build an effective standing army that could be called upon to wage war and thus sully the state's role as an abode of the pure Bodhidharma. The Marxist definition of the state as an entity that holds a monopoly of lethal power found ethical difficulty in a post-priest–patron Tibet. And for much of the early twentieth century, Tibet was governed by a *tulku* regent in a manner perhaps more befitting a monastic estate than a new nation immersed in an increasingly post-colonial international milieu.

Tibet's last hope

About 100 km (60 mi.) north of Lhasa is a monastery, battered, destroyed and rebuilt several times. This weary institution continued to exist simply because the historical memory that helps to fabricate the Tibetan state is long indeed. The monastery, called Reting (Rwa sdgreng), is not just a thousand years old; its existence memorializes the very foundation of the second introduction of Buddhism to Tibet, the creation of the distinctive religio-secular government, and the establishment of the monastic school which was crucial in the development of the Gelug government of Tibet. Reting monastery's incarnate lama, the Reting Rinpoche, had a short tradition of becoming the regent of Tibet during the interregna of two Dalai Lamas, the Eleventh and Fourteenth.

Reting monastery, 2008.

The Fifth Reting became the root guru of the child, for he was the one who found the Fourteenth Dalai Lama through his own spiritual acuity and physical action.

The milieu of Reting Rinpoche is remembered as a world of transparent glazes of the palette of Kanwal Krishna, of red brocade, and a happy world of social rounds with jolly resident British agents and German explorers of the 1930s. It was also the time of growing, fatal sectarianism, of selfishness, ignorance and blunders that would eventually lead to the end of the hard-fought independence of the Tibetan state.

The problem of interregna in Tibet was largely created by the break in absolute authority that the death of a totalizing figure such as the Dalai Lama necessitated. Unlike in hereditary monarchies, where the succeeding sovereign is usually immediately present, even as a minor, a Tibetan regency required waiting for the ruler to reincarnate, grow old enough to be communicative, and then for the religious establishment to infallibly discover the new *tulku* from the universe of all male toddlers. At that point the new sovereign was still highly restricted from exercising any authority as he was being socialized into the religio-secular government, receiving countless empowerments from his preceptors in strict, unquestioning student–teacher relationships. Effective leadership after the passing of a Dalai Lama could take an entire generation to be realized. The lack of an authority on a par with the Dalai Lama exacerbated sectarian differences during times of regency; it was in almost all cases a time of uncertainty, turmoil and abuse of power. The second Reting regency would, in fact, plunge Tibet into civil war just as the country faced the unprecedented fury of the People's Liberation Army of China's new Communist leadership. Throughout the nineteenth century, only the Eleventh Dalai Lama reached maturity, and he died soon after, unable to consolidate his power.

At the passing of the Thirteenth Dalai Lama in 1933, the Fifth Reting *tulku*, Thubten Jamphel Yeshe Gyaltsen, was a petite young man, sparkling and charismatic. As a child, Thubten had showed signs of his divine nature:

> One day his mother asked him to watch a pot of *thukpa* soup on the fire so that it would not boil over as she had to leave the kitchen. When the fire was getting high and the soup threatened to boil over, the child tied the snout of the stone pot together with his mother's shoe laces. Later he announced well in advance the arrival of the search party who were coming to look for him. He started making preparations for their arrival, driving wooden

The British mission entertain the Cabinet under an awning at the Dekyi Lingka in September 1936. Young high-ranking Tibetan girls, often referred to as 'Chang girls' by Mission members, serve the guests.

phurbas (ritual daggers) into a stone face for many horses and mules to be tethered to.²

According to Bell, the Thirteenth Dalai Lama had had a very clear idea who should become the Fifth Reting Rinpoche, telling his ministers in 1915:

About the incarnation of him, you had better search in a country situated in the southern direction from Reting monastery, and

Reting Rinpoche (seated), regent of Tibet, *c.* 1936. Standing next to him was a member of the Ldab ldob, a group who acted as both bodyguards and monastic police.

in the exact southern direction from the Lhasa Temple, a prosperous country which has been blessed by many scholars and sages. There are three forests and a green meadow surrounded by a river which flows slowly. In the vicinity you may ask for a boy who was born in the year of the Water Mouse (1912) to a father born in Hare year, and the boy may be a very wonderful one. If you examine carefully according to this instruction, you will find the real lama, and he will do much beneficial work for Buddhism and for the people.[3]

The Thirteenth Dalai Lama showed Reting favour by gifting him his divination dice and texts,[4] which indicated to some that he should be the regent of Tibet, the one who would be primarily responsible for finding the next incarnation of the Dalai lineage.

Although the Panchen Lama is traditionally assigned to the vital task of finding the new Dalai Lama, the long falling out with the Thirteenth Dalai Lama left the Panchen in permanent exile in China (and dying in 1937). No lay official was considered spiritually realized enough to perform this most delicate vocation – it fell to the highest *tulkus* of the land. In the absence of the Panchen, the job of regent devolved to the Reting, Ganden and other previously serving lineages, especially of the highest, Gyetru (rgyal sprul) Hutuktu rank. Due to practical geographic matters, it fell to young Reting, the Ganden Triba (throne-holder) Minyang Ami Yeshe Wangden, the ex-throne holder Chama Chosrak, and a popular Gelug lama, Phurbucho Rinpoche.[5] The authorities were unable to decide, so left it to the supernatural: they held a drawing of lots. Reting's name was selected. On 23 February 1934 24-year-old Thubten Jamphel became the regent of Tibet.[6] With this frail young man, its destiny was decided.

The importance of the Reting lineage to the Ganden Phodrang is related to the reinstatement of Buddhism in Tibet at the turn of the second millennium. The Reting line can be traced directly to this event and the appearance of the great Indian teacher Atiśa. From the second introduction of Buddhism, Tibet would never again let the secular aristocracy dominate the government of the state.

Young and naive but highly intelligent, curious and fun loving, the Reting Rinpoche soon caught on to the ins and outs of ruling Tibet.

However, the crafty *tulku* began to insist that all officials submit to his dictates unquestioningly, or suffer dismissal and forfeiture of their estates.

The regent's primary responsibilities were to see to the completion of the golden stupa in the Potala to house the mummified body of the Thirteenth Dalai Lama, and to lead the search for his reincarnation. Other than that, much of Reting's work could easily be delegated. Not used to following advice, the regent began to consolidate his powers. Especially vulnerable were reformers in the government, such as Lungshar, who had sent the four boys to England to be educated and helped to establish an English school in Gyantse in 1923. In 1934 Lungshar attempted to reform the Kashag, making it more responsible to the representative National Assembly, the Tsongdu, under the 'Union for Happiness' Party. Many in the deeply conservative religious establishment were highly offended by any thoughts of change. After all, the Gelug worldview supported the notion that the Dalai Lama and his religio-secular government were uniquely the holders of the complete Buddhist teachings in an unbroken heritage leading back to Gautama Siddhartha himself. There could be very little deviation in the overall structure of those lineages. Some saw Lungshar's attempted reforms as the Bolshevik conspiracy prophesied in the Thirteenth Dalai Lama's valedictory address. Reting sat passively at the side while Lungshar was dismissed from his government position and blinded for his efforts, dying shortly after release from prison. It was a clear message to the aristocracy that modernization of Tibet was in direct conflict with the maintenance of orthodoxy. It is widely felt that this lack of ability to meet ever-more rapid worldwide political change is the primary reason for the downfall of the Tibetan state in the mid-twentieth century.[7]

The regent's first major responsibility was accomplished with much success. A new chapel was built in the Red Palace of the Potala for the construction of the stupa. As the long process of mummification was completed, the huge reliquary, one of the largest jewel-encrusted gold artefacts ever built, was finished, the Dalai Lama's body entombed, and the whole consecrated by Reting. Studded with diamonds, carved jade objects, turquoise nuggets, and massive chunks of red coral and gem agate, the 14-metre-high tomb was covered in over 750 kg of solid gold plates.[8] It was dubbed Gelek Dod jo, 'Glorious like a Wish-fulfilling Cow'.[9]

The Potala palace from the east, February 1937, photograph by Frederick Spencer Chapman showing the round-walled watchtower, Taktshang Gormo. Nomad pilgrims can be seen in the foreground walking away from Lhasa.

The second task confronting Reting was much more difficult, and tapped into the full, convoluted worldview of Tibetan metempsychosis. The new incarnation of the Dalai Lama had to be found, brought to Lhasa and installed as ruler of the state. Upon the success, or failure, of the project rested no less than the continued independence of Tibet. The failure to recognize and install a Dalai Lama would have given the Chinese Republic currency in their hubristic claims to facilitate and authorize the appointment of the Tibetan hierarch, a perquisite that the secular government claimed it inherited from the Manchu emperors.

Reting chose to visit the oracular lake of the Protector goddess Palden Lhamo, leaving for Lake Lhamo Latso in Chokhor gyal southeast of Lhasa in 1935. Here at 5,230 m (17,000 ft) he performed an intensive *sadhana* with his party for several days. The high-elevation glacial lake is turquoise in colour, with a wind-rippled surface. The magical pond had been sought out by Tibetan regents and other high lamas from the very founding of the Dalai Lama lineage. Reting was accompanied by Trimon Shape, chief minister of the Kashag. At the conclusion of his *sadhana*, the regent rode down from his camp on a yak, accompanied by only a few attendants. Here he saw in the lake three groups of *dbu can* letters, 'a', 'ka', and 'ma'. He envisioned a three-storeyed monastery, with a turquoise first floor and a golden roof. From the east side of the monastery he saw a thin path leading to a small house with a similar turquoise roof. No one else in the party had visions, and the regent kept the revelation secret for over a year. Reting returned to Lhasa via Rame, his hometown.

In the summer of 1936, Reting convened the National Assembly and revealed to them the contents of his visions at Lhamo Latso. 'A' stood for Amdo, the easternmost province of Tibet, now under control of the Chinese. Other omens suggested a similar direction. During its embalming, the Thirteenth Dalai Lama's corpse twice turned its head to the east. In the throne hall of the Potala, an unusual star-shaped fungus mysteriously appeared on an east-facing pillar.[10] The state oracles were noted to have thrown their scarves to the east.

The assembly authorized three search teams to head for the eastern provinces. Each consisted of an incarnate lama and all had instructions to investigate the various omens that the regent had discerned. The Amdo group, headed by the seventeenth abbot of Sera Je, Tsenzhab Kyutsang Jampa Monlam, met with the still-exiled Panchen Lama, who advised them to visit the renowned Kumbum monastery, where the Thirteenth Dalai Lama spent so much time. He also provided three names of promising boys. Arriving at Kumbum in the spring of 1937, lay official Kheme Sonam Wangdu remarked that the main building of the monastery resembled the one in Reting's dream. The boy from nearby Taktse was visited. Kyutsang Rinpoche disguised himself as a servant. Immediately the boy identified him as 'Sera Lama', and wanted his rosary, which had belonged to the Thirteenth Dalai Lama. The party returned to Kumbum and telegraphed their request to further test the Taktse boy. The request was granted, and the party returned to the village by a lower road, which brought them to a scene that resembled Reting's vision of the house with a blue roof. The parents of the boy knew what the party was up to, as an older son had already been recognized as a *tulku*.[11] The boy was then shown pairs of rosaries, walking sticks and *damaru* drums; one of each pair had belonged to the Thirteenth Dalai Lama. The boy unerringly picked out the correct articles.

The party was convinced that they had found the true incarnation. But the cohort had to keep their conclusion secret, as the local Muslim warlord, Ma Bufang, might use the opportunity to hold the boy for ransom or 'invade' Tibet by sending an armed escort to Lhasa. The party simply told Ma that the Taktse boy was a candidate with the others. Eventually Ma saw through the ruse and demanded about £8,000 sterling. Then Kumbum monastery wanted to detain the boy to give blessings before the party returned to Lhasa. Ma finally allowed the child to leave, provided another £15,000 were obtained. Kumbum also demanded religious texts and relics from the Thirteenth Dalai Lama. By now the Kuomingtang government had become involved, ostensibly to push the fiction that they were responsible for the final selection. Finally, the search party arranged for a group of Muslim traders to pay off Ma, escort the 'candidate' to Lhasa, and be repaid in rupees by the Tibetan government upon their arrival. The party left Amdo in July 1939. To forestall any idea that the Chinese authorized the appointment of the Taktse boy, or any other candidate, the Tibetan government declared the child to be the Fourteenth Dalai Lama on 23 August 1939 while the party was still en route.[12] Trying to save face, the Chinese government, after receiving an invitation to the enthronement set for 22 February 1940, and having extracted permission from Reting to 'examine' the Taktse boy on 1 February 1940, announced to the world they had 'approved' the selection of the new Dalai Lama.[13]

By late September the new sovereign's entourage had reached the border at Nagchuka. Ganden Phodrang officials met the four-year-old boy at nearby Gashi Nakha, where the Kalon Bonsho offered a *khata* and the *mendel tensum mandala* recognizing him as the Fourteenth Dalai Lama.[14]

As the team approached the Tibetan capital, Reting Rinpoche rode out from his monastery to greet the new *tulku* that he and his government had successfully discovered. As was customary, the huge cavalcade stopped at Rekya and at Dogu Thang, on the plains just outside Lhasa.[15] A huge encampment, looking every bit as much as the Grand Kural of Urga or the hunting parties of the Manchu emperors, was established so the rest of the government and the abbots of the great monasteries could do reverence to their returning leader.

On 8 October 1939 the new Dalai Lama arrived in Lhasa, led by the Reting Rinpoche and his entourage. The Dalai Lama first visited the Jokhang and then moved on to the summer palace of Norbulingka. A few weeks later Reting took the Dalai Lama again to the Jokhang, and performed the tonsure and naming ceremony, adding his own name to 'the Lord, Ocean of Wisdom': Lhamo Dhondup became Jetsun Jamphel Ngawang Lobsang Yeshe Tenzin Gyatso. It was the high point of Regent Reting's career.

Reting was very interested in the renowned Nyingma teachings of Khenpo Ngagi Wangpo, who was then the abbot of Kathok monastery. The old abbot recommended a hermit named Chatrul to give the teachings.[16] Chatrul Rinpoche stayed with Reting Rinpoche for two years, giving him many transmissions and instructions, including the ear-whispered and profound Dzogpa Chenpo teachings. Reting Rinpoche would not let him leave. But Chatrul Rinpoche foresaw that trouble would come to Reting Rinpoche.

In early 1940 the Tibetan government invited the governments of India and China and the kings of Nepal, Bhutan and Sikkim to attend the installation of the new Dalai Lama in Lhasa, to be held on 22 February. Sir Basil Gould, political officer of Sikkim, represented Britain; Wu Chung-hsin represented Nanking. Tibetan and foreign officials, as well as historians, have squabbled to the present day over who among the guests were given precedence. It was an occasion, however, which the fading British Raj wished to record in great detail. Kodachrome movies were taken of the great event, and Indian artist Kanwal Krishna was commissioned to paint portraits of many of the dignitaries.[17] The ceremony itself involved a splendid procession from the Norbulingka to the Potala, where the little boy was placed on the golden Snow Lion throne in the main audience chamber. Then, the officials, in precedence according to their rank, filed past presenting their *khatags* and gifts. The ceremony took several days. Among other objects, Gould presented the Dalai Lama with a Meccano Erector set.[18]

Reting's downfall

Following the dismissal of Trimon, the success of the construction of the Thirteenth Dalai Lama's stupa and, above all, the discovery of the Fourteenth Dalai Lama, Reting's power had vastly multiplied. Feeling unfettered, he brashly removed the highly accomplished Yuthok as commander of the bodyguard; he dismissed his official co-ruler, Langdun, shortly after this, learning that he had kept information about the Taktse candidate away from the regent, supporting his own candidate, a boy who eventually became the Ditru Rinpoche. Reting had threatened to resign himself, prompting the abbots of the three great monasteries to appeal to the National Assembly and the Kashag to remove Langdun.

Jealousies at court also multiplied. The business manager of the Reting office complained that the regent spent too much money flying kites. This office, in fact, was one of the largest trading companies in Tibet, and Reting was becoming vastly wealthy. Reting simply replaced his whistleblowing manager and continued flying kites. Reting seemed to be developing a reputation of using his high position for personal gain. By 1938, Phünkang Jetrungla, the *tse drung* (monk official) son of Yabshi Phunkang Tashi Dorje Kung, had reputedly become Reting's lover. It is claimed that the young man's aristocratic father was made a *shape* in 1939 as a result, passing over others to whom he had promised the position. Continuing his wilfulness, Reting dismissed the head of the treasury for not arranging a private loan and did so at a Lhamo at the Reting *labrang* in front of hundreds of people. In his place he appointed Cogtray, whose wife Namgyal Tsedron was reputedly in a sexual relationship with Reting.

The headstrong regent had built a small mansion, the Shide Drokhang, in Lhasa with a beautiful garden in which to entertain parties of friends and members of the British mission. Reting loved animals, including the dogs brought by the British officers as gifts. Many birdcages filled the gardens. Reting also shared a passion for horses with the new Dalai Lama's father. Singing, picnics and games were as common at Shide Drokhang as chanting of the sutras. Cinema and recorded music were provided by the British agents.

In early 1939, while awaiting the arrival of the new Dalai Lama from Amdo, Reting was visited by a German expedition consisting of ornithologist Ernst Schäfer, racial anthropologist Bruno Beger, and other scientists and photographers. They were in part supported by the Nazi ss leader Heinrich Himmler. The expedition was constituted as a holistic study of the people, botany, zoology and geography of Tibet. It also was charged with working on the racial theory that pure Aryans had once settled Tibet, and that they seemed to be represented in the Tibetan nobility. The British agents were incensed by the sudden appearance of Nazis and did everything they could to disrupt the Germans.

Meeting in the Potala, the entire German party was enthralled with the regent. Schäfer referred to the Reting's prominent ears as his 'mystical antennae'. Reting and his court were similarly intrigued with the Germans, especially the Nazi government's use of the traditional Buddhist swastika symbol. At the audience, Reting was guarded, as usual, by two enormous Ldab ldob.[19] Clad in rough red homespun, they stood in menacing contrast to tiny Reting in his exquisite brocades. The dramatic tableau was typical of the regent's signature presentations. When handsome, young Phünkang Jetrungla appeared, it prompted eagle-eyed Beger to recognize the more intimate nature of his relationship with the regent.[20] Reting took the party to see the auspicious fungus in the throne room that pointed to the direction the new Dalai Lama had been found.

Photograph from the Tibetan expedition led by Ernst Schäfer showing members of the team sit down around a table with locals, in a room adorned by a swastika and the ss logo.

Reting Rinpoche and Bruno Beger, 1939, photograph by Ernst Schäfer.

Reting politely listened to the party's babble about the achievements of the Germans and their search for origins of the 'Master Race', but became increasingly smitten by the tall, athletic, blond, 26-year-old Beger. The mischievous regent asked the German to stay behind as a bodyguard – Berger demurred but Reting persisted. The regent was also fascinated with Schäfer's beard, stroking it repeatedly, much to the surprise of all.[21]

Working for the Ahnenerbe, the Nazi cryptohistorical think-tank, Beger's main task on the expedition was to make anthropometric measurements of Tibetans' bodies, collecting data that might indicate Aryan origins. He also made meticulous notes of the sexual habits of his various hosts. Beger is quiet on his methods of how he obtained such intimate information, but his male and female admirers, it is noted, were captivated by his 'golden hair and turquoise eyes'.[22] Beger made the acquaintance of Tsarong, Jigme Taring and the 'Rugby boys' who had been educated in England. One, Mondro, developed quite an obsession with the Germans, Beger in particular, plying him with liquor then attempting

Bruno Beger conducting anthropometric studies in Sikkim, photograph by Ernst Krause.

to sleep with him.[23] Beger also attended to the medical needs of Tibetans, making him that much more popular.[24]

Sex and the single monk

As Reting became more autocratic, critics took aim at him through his weakest characteristic, his active sexuality. For all its fun-loving, high-living atmosphere in the Lhasa of the Jazz Age, the dour Gelug hierarchy, with its adherence to strict Vinaya principles, added a puritanical streak to Tibetan mores. In addition to trolling the halls of the monasteries, working his way through the handsomest monks, lusty Reting apparently had relationships with several women. Besides Namgyal Tsedron, he reputedly had a polyandrous arrangement with Tseyang, his half-brother's wife, and a son was born of the union.[25] All of this, which was pretty much an open secret in Lhasa, came to light precisely when Reting's star had reached its zenith and begun to set.

Tantra, of course, seems all about sex. But it is also about breaking the normative rules and, rather than negating polluting aspects of the world, embracing them as tools for understanding the divine essence in oneself. This behaviour goes beyond the elaborate and self-negating Vinaya rules that regulate monastic life. Very high Gelug lamas, such as Reting, the Jebtsundampa and the Sixth Dalai Lama, although technically celibate monks, were popularly believed to have reached such an advanced state of practice, having purified their karmic burden through countless lifetimes, that they no longer suffered its effects. This may have been particularly true for the Reting *tulku*, being the incarnation of Dromtön, the main disciple of Atiśa who reconciled tantric practice within monasticism. Much of the violent sexual imagery of the Heruka, Hevajra and Candamahārosana tantra evolved over time in Tibet to be considered symbolic rather than literal; the underlying base of the system suggests no difference between external and internal reality. 'Breaking the rules', as well practised by the ancient Nyingma *nagpo* before Atiśa, forced the monastic practitioner to consider the transformative nature of the tantra's 'skilful means' in which to acquire wisdom and achieve enlightenment. The Dalai Lama himself has elaborated:

> In Tibetan Buddhism, especially if you look at the iconography of the deities with their consorts, you can see a lot of very explicit sexual symbolism which often gives the wrong impression. Actually, in this case the sexual organ is utilized, but the energy movement which is taking place is, in the end, fully controlled. The energy should never be let out. This energy must be controlled and eventually returned to other parts of the body. What is required for a Tantric practitioner is to develop the capacity to utilize one's faculties of bliss and the blissful experiences which are specifically generated due to the flow of regenerative fluids within one's own energy channels. It is crucial to have the ability to protect oneself from the fault of emission. It is not just a purely ordinary sexual act.[26]

Whether or not Reting actually practised with a *yab-yum* partner was irrelevant, as far as the non-dual philosophy of the tantric system espoused. He was simply above all this in the minds of most Tibetans.

For monastic dalliance, homosexuality has much less stigma than heterosexuality among celibate monasteries. However, like the concept of tantra, it is largely understood within the monastic tradition and not outside of it. Like most traditional cultures with a strong patriarchal orientation and strong division of gender role expectations, Tibetan society largely swept the topic of same-sex affection under the carpet and far away from outsiders' eyes. Indeed, until recent times, there was no proper word for it. Being all-male communities, the larger monasteries, especially the celibate Gelugpa, developed a type of institutionalized homosexuality to help control the lustier of the monks and to maintain discipline.[27] These were, of course, the Ldab ldob, the hypermasculine cadre that policed the monasteries and performed much of the manual labour. They often wore their hair in long locks, carried gigantic keys as weapons, painted their faces in fearsome lampblack, and were distinguished by their formidable size, physique and violent temper. Aggressive, sauntering about with macho gaits, they loved sports and athletic competitions. Ldab ldob had a reputation for being pederasts; schoolboys would often band together to defend themselves from being accosted or kidnapped. These were the same bodyguards Reting chose to display to his foreign and domestic visitors, forming a striking contrast with the ethereal regent.

It was gossip regarding his heterosexual alliances that proved much more difficult for Reting. Although such arrangements were entirely permissible in the older schools of Tibetan Buddhism and certainly among *nagpa* practitioners, the imposition of strict Vinaya rules by reformers such as Tsongkhapa proscribed relations between women and virtuous monks. This is not because the sexuality was necessarily bad, but, like in European monasticism and priestly celibacy, women's ability to have children can potentially turn the monk away from dedication to his studies, his meditations and his loyalty to his brethren in consideration of his family. The Sarma movement in Tibet was a once-and-for-all break in the power of biological heredity to determine leadership of the state. Religious institutions, which developed into a self-reproducing system of reincarnation, were destined to remain at the pinnacle of power in Tibet.

One of the monk
policemen (Ldab
ldob), bearing
his heavy staff,
photograph by
Heinrich Harrer.

The system also introduced several structural weaknesses which
continue to plague the government of Tibet. In addition to the long interregna that occur with the death of a Dalai Lama and other high ecclesiastic
personages, the inter-lineage milieu is subject to wide sectarianism,
competition and dissention, the antithesis of the processes that nurture
state formation. Within the lineages themselves, individual *tulku* could
be subjected to external criticism that, through perceived transgressions
of the Vinaya, they were no longer 'pure vessels' for the continued residence of the unbroken Dharma teachings, the source of all authority. All
three of these systemic weaknesses were to affect the rule of Regent
Reting.

The Fourteenth Dalai Lama seated on the throne during his official enthronement ceremony in Lhasa, 22 February 1940.

One precipitating crisis that Reting and all the abbots and monk-officials were acutely aware of was the upcoming taking of novice vows by the young Dalai Lama. He was to receive his vows as a *getsul* with 36 precepts and begin his formal religious education. Among these was the usual Gelug vow of celibacy. The preceptor for initiating one into these vows had to be a practitioner of the virtue himself in order to maintain an unbroken lineage. Since Reting was the Dalai Lama's senior tutor and root guru, this presented a problem. Reting could not delegate such an important duty. Nor could he openly admit that he was a sexually active being, even though it could be accepted tacitly by the people since he was a high *tulku*. Resignation as regent was the only recourse.

Reting's advisors came up with an ingenious plan of action. Reting would resign with the understanding that he would return in a few years, after the Dalai Lama had been initiated. He would go off into retreat to avert an assumed danger to his life. The government would appoint an old, minor lama who would be more than happy to be relieved of his duties after a few years. Taktra, Reting's root lama, was just the man to do this, the advisors felt.

Unfortunately, during this time Reting continued an unpopular course of dismissing high officials. Although many of the abbots of the great monasteries supported giving Reting many governmental estates for his services in finding the Fourteenth Dalai Lama, other officials felt it was robbing the Dalai Lama of his inheritance. Khyungram, a senior lay official, was one who was most adamant about not giving Reting too much. Reting took deep offence at making such discussions public and found cause to dismiss him. Reting found documents that seemed critical of his administration, resulting in the confiscation of Khyungram's estates and the social demotion of his family. Khyungram himself was exiled to western Tibet.[28] Rather than enhancing his power base, the dismissal of the official seemed vindictive and further eroded Reting's popularity. The regent then blundered into goading the Sera Mey abbot to resign, ostensibly to replace him with a favourite. The monks of the college rose up in defiance, however, and refused to accept Reting's appointment. Critical posters and street songs started appearing around Lhasa that alluded to Reting's greed. A popular Tibetan idiom was heard, 'After eating the mountain, hunger is not satiated. After drinking the oceans, thirst is not quenched.'[29] Support for Reting was rapidly disappearing. However, his resignation allowed the dissatisfaction with Reting to surface, and the new regent was not going to be a patsy.

In early 1941 the young regent abdicated and returned to Reting monastery confident that he would be reinstated after a few years. Taktra quietly assumed full control. The ascetic old lama immediately began to take a high moral stance and 'instil decency' in the highest levels of government. The law and order regent denounced the practice by which his office could profit from trade, thus indirectly insulting Reting. He curbed the excessive demands of Yabshi Taktse Kung, the Dalai Lama's father. With various adroit appointments, a Taktra party was slowly being built. But in retreat, Reting made sure he was not ignored.

In 1943 Reting received the party of Ilya Tolstoy and Brooke Dolan sent from the United States on behalf of President Franklin Roosevelt. The u.s. Office of Strategic Services (precursor of the CIA) wished to send a survey team to Tibet to design a road from India to supply its ally China during the Second World War. China, of course, gave its permission and Tibet refused, no doubt to show it was independent and neutral in the war. The southern Burma Road had been cut off when the Japanese took Burma in 1942. It was only under the guise of bringing respects from President Roosevelt that the Tolstoy party succeeded. The road was to extend from the Indian railhead at Digboi in the Indian Northeast Frontier Agency to Dzayul in Tibet, across the north side of the Hkakabo Razi range (headwaters of the Irrawaddy), to Yunnan in China. It was never built, the Allies having taken northern Burma in 1945 and established the Ledo Road through Myitkyina. Between 1942 and 1945, Allies had to fly supplies to China 'over the hump'.

Chatrul Rinpoche, upon leaving Reting, was still convinced that Reting was in serious danger. According to one of his students:

Chatrul Rinpoche went into solitary retreat to hold a special meditation puja in order to save Reting Rinpoche's life. After 18 days, when his Tsampa was finished, he wanted at least to make some hot water to sustain him. But just as he was about to build a fire, an eagle came and dropped food for him. Days later, Rinpoche again built a fire to make some hot water. Some villagers saw the smoke and came to find out who was there. Rinpoche's practice, which required strict solitude, was thus interrupted. At that moment, he knew that the life of the Reting Rinpoche could not be saved and that he would be assassinated.

He also knew, according to Guru Rinpoche's prophecy, that this would mean the end of Tibet's independence. For in his prophecy, the Great Lotus-Born [Padmasambhava] had stated that the Reting Rinpoche had a special and close connection to him, that he was a direct counterforce to Mao and Tibet's last hope.[30]

It is uncertain whether Reting had a written agreement with Taktra for the latter to relinquish the regency after a few years. Melvyn Goldstein suggests that if there were any written documents to this effect, they may be in the closed archives in Lhasa.[31] Regardless, Reting and his party were shocked when Taktra betrayed Reting in 1944 when he tried to resume the regency. In December of that year, Reting entered Lhasa in a magnificent procession crafted from all the accumulated wealth of the Reting *labrang* to shock and awe the government and populace. Reting proceeded to lobby other lamas for their support, then confronted his old teacher in Lhasa at Photrang Sarpa. Using the accustomed polite language, Reting emphasized that the heavy responsibilities of being regent must be weighing upon his older teacher, implying that he might benefit from being relieved of this responsibility.[32] Taktra refused to become engaged in any sort of conversation, completely deflating a still hopeful Reting. After Tibetan New Year, a chastened Reting returned home, not to appear again until he was arrested for treason by the government.

In no small measure, the monks at Sera Je, Reting's college, were incensed at the treatment of their former regent and beloved classmate. A growing dispute over taxes and revenues was exacerbated by Taktra's insensitive dismissal of Reting. An altercation occurred between a district commissioner and the local Sera Je monks. When the commissioner refused to collect loans due from estate peasants to Sera Je, tempers flared and the monks beat him to death. The government arrested the monks and some of their relatives. The impasse reached a critical point during the Monlam prayer festival in Lhasa after New Year 1945, when all the monastic community traditionally assumed control of the capital for the duration. The Sera Je lamas decided to boycott the event unless the monks and relatives involved in the beating were released. Fearing a confrontation with Ganden Phodrang, they began to arm themselves. When the government dismissed the abbot of Sera Je and started beating its monks, Reting was determined to lead Sera in all-out war against Taktra.

Taktra clearly was aware of the threat. He dismissed the monk official Phünkang Jetrungla, Reting's lover.[33] Then he intimidated Cogtray, whose wife was assumed to be Reting's mistress. As a result, Cogtray resigned from government service. Another Reting supporter, Phünkang Shape, was dismissed for trivial reasons and was replaced by Reting's bitterest enemy, Lhalu, son of Lungshar, who had been blinded by the government under Reting. And then the Lord Chamberlain, Ngawang Tenzin, was removed.[34]

Reting realized that he had to forcibly overthrow Taktra, so Reting and his supporters decided to assassinate him. A bomb parcel was sent to the regent, allegedly from Dzasa Yuthok, governor of Kham. The delivery was delayed, and as a result of a curious boy opening the box, it exploded with no harm to Taktra.

From attempted murder, Reting and his advisors then moved to treason: they contacted the Kuomingtang for their assistance. An agreement was made with Chiang Kai-shek (Jiang Zhongzhen) that if the cabal would recognize China's coveted rights in Tibet, China would support returning Reting to the regency.[35] Furthermore, Reting would cede the occupied territory in Kham to China. He requested troops, equipment and airplanes to stage the coup.[36]

Reting's message was intercepted and brought to the attention of the Tibetan government. These were far more damning accusations than the ex-regent's kite flying and chasing blond Germans. A tearful Taktra agreed that Reting had to be arrested and brought to Lhasa. He sent Surkhang and Lhalu, with an army of two hundred men, to Reting monastery. Reting was informed before the army arrived, but declined to go into exile to China, noting that the northern route across the Changtang would be too cold for his son Panam by Tseyang, his half-brother's polyandrous wife.

Reting was arrested at his monastery and was thoroughly searched – the powerful *Nam chug phurpa* (a meteoric *vajra*) was found on him and removed.[37] He was relegated to ride a mule back to Lhasa. At the same time, Sera Je again rose in revolt against the government. The new abbot, Tendar, was appointed by Taktra after the first revolt. Tendar appeared not overly concerned about the closing of the Reting *labrang*. This hostility to Reting infuriated the monks. That evening, Ldab ldob monks burst into the private apartments of the abbot, chasing him across rooftops. Tendar was hacked to death. The rebellious monks then moved on to Lhasa, burning officials' houses and storming the Reting *labrang* to get the arms stored there. The government officials moved over to the Potala and the gates were closed after them. The next day the abbots of the three great monasteries, who were attending a meeting of the Tsongdu, were detained in Lhasa. It was feared that if they returned to their monasteries, they could well join the Sera Je war against the government. Back at Reting, the monks mounted an offensive against the troops that had been left there.

The arresting party, with Reting in their possession, passed directly in front of Sera Je monastery, where they were attacked by its monks. This was the biggest battle of the rebellion, and although considerable fire was exchanged, the troops and their prisoner got through. Reting was thrown into dark Sharcenchog prison in the Potala, under orders to be killed if supporters appeared to free him. From living high above the city amid the Potala's golden roofs and sunshine, the ex-regent was led to a cell in the palace's deepest recesses, surrounded by 4-metre (13 ft) thick walls. The Reting *labrang* was sealed on 15 April 1947. As he was being led away to appear before the regent and sent to prison,[38] the Reting Dzasa sarcastically remarked, 'Today we are going to get our reward for the discovery and enthronement of the true Dalai Lama.'[39]

Reting stewed for several days before being hauled before the Tsongdu. An eyewitness recalled the event and the impact upon the young Dalai Lama:

A few days after his imprisonment, Reting Rinpochey [*sic*] was interrogated by the members of the assembly. He had to walk from his prison to the assembly room for these sessions and passed below the room where Gyalwa Rinpochey [Dalai Lama] was studying his lessons, on the ninth floor of his palace. I was in a corner of the room, sewing. Suddenly someone came in and I heard them talking in low voices. Gyalwa Rinpochey was looking out of the window and I heard him say, 'Genla [teacher] is coming.' Then he quickly went up the stairs. I realized that they were bringing in Reting Rinpochey. I swiftly ran down to an intersection in the stairs and hid behind a pillar. Reting Rinpochey appeared, escorted by armed soldiers and monks and lay officials. He wore his Regent's robes and his yellow rainbow boots, but his hair looked overgrown and in disarray. I couldn't help thinking, 'He was the most powerful man in Tibet and now he has been reduced to this.' I was almost sure that

Gyalwa Rinpochey had run upstairs to get a better look at his former teacher and hoped that he wouldn't ask for too many explanations or that he be brought before him.[40]

Initially denying everything, when Reting was presented with damning letters he had written to various officials, he attempted to plea bargain his fate. Reting tried to deliver letters to the Trijang Rinpoche, the junior tutor of the Dalai Lama, the Lord Chamberlain, and to Kapshöba Shape, the latter having a veiled threat. Then Reting's two closest associates, Reting Dzasa and Khardo Rinpoche, confessed. On 27 April 1947 the Tsongdu sent a letter to H. E. Richardson of the British mission, explaining their actions. It was also the day when the governmental forces crushed the final resistance at Sera Je, arresting the main leaders of the revolt.

With the incriminating letters written in the hand of the ex-regent the case against Reting was unequivocal, but the assembly could not decide on a punishment. Attempted murder of the ruler and the treason of selling Tibet to China were among the most serious crimes ever encountered in Tibet. The crimes were compromised by the fact that Reting was among the highest incarnate lamas, and responsible for discovering and enthroning their current Dalai Lama. It seemed to be a hopeless dilemma.

Reting was having difficulty adjusting to his cramped confinement. Complaining of headaches, he asked to be transferred to larger quarters. This was refused, but a Tibetan doctor was sent. He diagnosed a nervous condition that the ex-regent had been suffering from for a number of years, and recommend a medicine called *A kar so lang*. The Tsongdu agreed to dispense the pills. On 7 May Reting took two of the pills, even though they looked a bit suspicious. The lama's health worsened that evening, but despite this he was administered a third pill. Retching and screaming in pain, Reting requested a Western doctor. This was refused. Reting's breathing became rapid as he thrashed about in pain. Reting Rinpoche's agony reverberated throughout the dank halls of the Potala until shortly after midnight. He died at 1:00 a.m.[41]

The Tsongdu called for an investigating committee from the government, the monasteries and Reting *labrang* to examine the corpse. They found no overt signs of abuse, except for a small bruise on Reting's backside. The former regent lay in state at Shide monastery, and thousands came to pay last respects to the well-loved, special lama. His body was cremated, destroying any evidence of the suspected poisoning.

To date no one has confessed to an assassination; the apparent poisoning is structurally very similar to the demise of the Guangxu emperor 39 years before, which occurred practically behind the back of the Thirteenth Dalai Lama. Research indicates that at that time, no one, collectively or individually, felt they had the authority to authorize an execution except Regent Taktra or his *dzasa* acting in his name. Indeed, Taktra's aide Kesang Ngawang was the one who had brought Reting's pills.

While the two regents fought to the death, the one in whose name government decisions were made was playing with his Erector set, studying and watching the goings-on with his telescope from atop the Potala. When the thirteen-year-old Dalai Lama found out about the death of Reting, however, he was extremely upset. His father, the Yabshe Kung, had also died recently. Many felt that he, a good friend of Reting, was also poisoned. In any case, the events severely strained the relationship between the Taktra government and the family of the Dalai Lama.[42] The Fourteenth Dalai Lama recalled:

> Reting . . . made a request that he be allowed to see me. Unfortunately, this was refused on my behalf, and he died in prison not long afterwards. Naturally, as a minor, I had very little opportunity to become involved in judicial matters, but looking back, I sometimes wonder whether in this case I might not have been able to do something. Had I intervened in some way, it is possible that the destruction of Reting monastery, one of the oldest and most beautiful in Tibet, might have been prevented. All in all the whole affair was very silly. Yet, despite his mistakes, I still retain a deep personal respect for Reting Rinpoche as my first tutor and guru. After his death, his names were dropped from mine – until I restored them many years later on the instructions of the oracle.[43]

The current Dalai Lama has never refuted the religious teachings of Reting, but qualifies some of his other actions:

However, if you become aware of mistakes your lama has made or he has done things you do not approve of, that does not mean that you should lose faith. For example, I myself have received considerable teachings from Reting Dorjechang, and many teachings from Taktra Rinpoche too. Both of them are my lamas. But [my faith does not extend to] all their deeds. I am referring to what actually happened. In a letter written in his own hand Reting Rinpoche approved a plot to take the life of Kyabje Taktra Rinpoche. I have seen it myself. This is how it happened. A number of documents were seized and among them were found letters Reting Rinpoche had written personally to people like Nyungne Lama in Lhasa. My late abbot himself showed them to me. It was apparent from these letters that when Nyungne Lama, Kharto Rinpoche and others had first sought Reting's approval of their plans, he had repeatedly counseled and advised them to exercise restraint. But the letters seem to indicate that, by and by, as if to the perception of ordinary sentient beings dependent arising had gone wrong, Reting Rinpoche himself developed a desire to get rid of Taktra Rinpoche. This was clear from the documents and there is no problem in saying so.

For us Buddhists there is no contradiction here. I don't feel at all uncomfortable about saying this. Reting Rinpoche's hand written letter says, 'Take care that the old monk (referring to Taktra Rinpoche) does not escape.' This is completely wrong. I don't even try to imagine that this was correct. Even so, I don't view these actions as a cause for my losing faith in him. I have unwavering faith in Reting Rinpoche. However, mistaken actions such as these I recognize as mistakes. I don't think of these as the Lama's so called 'inestimable deeds'.[44]

Shortly after Reting's death, the army retook Reting monastery. Troops desecrated and looted the compound, and the *tulku*'s beautiful residence was levelled, ending the Sera Je War. For some, it was nothing less than the destruction of the Kadampa itself. Such was the nature of a Ganden Phodrang that would in a few short years face the immeasurable might of the People's Liberation Army.

Reting Rinpoche is to some a cultural hero, like the libertine Sixth Dalai Lama, a mischievous, brilliant being who always had Tibet's (and his own) best interests at heart. Recently, a simulated date game website has appeared, 'Reting Rinpoche's Dating Sim',[45] wherein the young regent has to fight his way through the distractions of the religious hierarchy and perfect himself through debate, obtaining wisdom and courage, to gain social currency and meet up with a beautiful foreign girl.

SEVEN

Conquest

It should be clear that the immediate and outstanding cause of 'the demise of the Lamaist State' was the violent military invasion of Tibet by Communist China's overwhelmingly superior military force, and not the moral or political failings of the Tibetan ruling class or society.

JAMYANG NORBU[1]

A dead former regent, an old and unpopular successor – this was the state of affairs in 1947 in Tibet, which was facing the greatest challenge to its existence in history. In 1950 it would be invaded and annexed by a refulgent People's Republic of China. For some, Tibet seemed a failed state, a nation hobbled by the impracticality of its own idealism; for others, Tibet had been a backstop of empire, conveniently discarded when no longer needed.

Many external perspectives towards the eradication of Tibet seem Orientalistic: the ancient land and its political system a classic example of the mystic, occulted East. For generations, Western and Chinese historians have introduced their work on Tibet through contrasting statements. The romance of a forbidden, isolated kingdom is presented within the paradigm of Shangri-La mysticism, then counterbalanced with descriptions of Tibet's sudden cultural destruction/liberation in the wake of the occupation of the country by the People's Liberation Army. It is as if Tibet and its culture were as delicate and ephemeral as a hothouse Tibetan blue poppy, which fades and wilts at first exposure to the outside world. It should be of no great surprise that both Chinese and Western positivist attitudes towards the failure of the Tibetan state are similar: they have a common root in the Enlightenment and Marxism.

Exile followed by inevitable assimilation makes for colourful copy in the Western popular press, yet it hardly captures the reality of Tibetan nationalism, for the business of any nationalism is to show the outside world that a certain people still exist. Therefore, the idea of the 'demise' of the Tibetan state in the 1950–59 period is itself problematic, as the Ganden Phodrang has continued to exist, in exile, for over sixty years.

During the mid-twentieth century, while the rest of the world was shedding its colonies, China was in the process of trying to annex theirs. Britain, which had granted India independence in August 1947, was thoroughly dedicated to retrenchment. It had been financially exhausted in the Second World War, and it was too costly now to maintain an over-extended world empire. Its policy towards Tibet had become even more duplicitous than ever; its political agents in Tibet became increasingly frustrated by Britain's inability to recognize the de facto independence of the country and the moral and treaty obligations supporting the administration of the Dalai Lama. Nevertheless, Britain assured Tibet that relations would continue as before following Indian independence and the Tibetans had a right to appeal to the high commissioner resident in New Delhi.

In 1947 the Tibetan government sent a trade mission to India, China, the United States and Great Britain. Finance minister Tsepon W. D. Shakabpa headed the group. Its focus was to secure trade arrangements, primarily with India, receive payment in hard currency instead of rupees, and to purchase gold bullion to shore up the Tibetan srang. In addition, it was an opportunity to demonstrate to the world the independence of Tibet and to seek appropriate recognition.[2] The Ganden Phodrang issued Shakabpa and his party with Tibetan passports.[3] Tibet's trade produce then consisted primarily of wool, yak tails and musk. Since the Indian rupee was no longer considered a free currency, the Tibetan government felt it needed hard currency backed in gold.

The trade mission had enormous implications for the Ganden Phodrang. While Shakabpa reported the successes of the trip in a matter-of-fact manner,[4] with the Tibetans being accepted everywhere in due course as representatives of a sovereign state, the situation seems to have been much more complex. Intricate negotiations ensued, causing confusion due to the duplicitous manner in which the various foreign governments dealt with the Tibetans trying to act on the international stage. First, the Tibetan government had not then recognized the government of India as the successor to the British Raj. This caused great difficulty, but eventually they met with former Viceroy Mountbatten, Mohandas Gandhi and Prime Minister Nehru, who helped to clarify new India's position. While in India the Tibetan diplomats tried to attain the necessary visas for the United Kingdom and United States; Goldstein provides evidence of how confused both states' policies were towards Tibet.[5] In general, those diplomats who knew something about Tibet were generally inclined towards granting visas; those who did not were noncommittal or worse. They were advised by both the UK and USA embassies to obtain their visas in China. In China they met newly re-elected President Chiang Kai-shek and discussed the tea trade. They were advised not to travel any further, nor to continue to use Tibetan passports. These 'suggestions' were ignored, the mission even declining a $50,000 bribe to use Chinese passports.[6] The next step was to travel to the United States, which presented another double bind, according to Goldstein: 'The U.S. Embassy [in Nanjing] would not issue visas until the Tibetans had obtained exit visas from China. However, the Chinese would not issue these on the Tibetan passports and the Tibetans did not want to travel to the United States on Chinese passports.'[7] The delegation broke the impasse by leaving China through British-governed Hong Kong on Chinese exit visas stamped on Chinese passports they had secured at Calcutta. In Hong Kong they discarded them, and obtained visas for both the UK and USA on their Tibetan passports.

The trade party continued on to the United States through Hawaii and San Francisco, meeting Secretary of State George Marshall in Washington. The Chinese diplomatic corps was in an uproar. The Chinese embassy was upset that they were refused permission to accompany the Tibetan delegation on their calls in Washington. The United States, as had Britain in the past, was treating Tibet as an independent state for some things and as an integral part of China for others. The United States was grateful for the assistance that Tibet had lent for downed fliers supplying troops in China during the Second World War, and were not about to insult them; however, the Kuomingtang had been a strong ally during the war and there was no desire to offend China. A hoped-for meeting with President Truman had to be scrapped, because a compromise could not be reached between the Chinese, Tibetan and American officials. Shakabpa and his party were able to meet Marshall, however, on an unofficial basis.

The trade mission overstayed its visa to the UK with all the diplomatic wrangling that had occurred since leaving Hong Kong. When they applied in New York, the British Consulate General would not reissue a visa on their Tibetan passports, citing a 'technical error' in the original issuance by their ambassador in Hong Kong. The Tibetans subsequently cancelled their sailing to England in protest. On appeal to the British ambassador to Washington, the Foreign Office simply authorized amending the date of the original visa, thus avoiding having to issue new visas. Shakabpa then asked for audiences with the king and queen to present gifts from the Dalai Lama. While the British finally agreed to meet them as an official trade delegation, it was the Lord Chamberlain who provided an audience instead of King George VI, who was ill.[8] Shakabpa suspected, wrongly, that this was Foreign Office subterfuge. The trade mission also met with the prime minister, as 'distinguished visitors' rather than political officials. This byzantine, official/unofficial manner of dealing with Tibetan dignitaries respectfully, without unduly upsetting the Chinese, would become a standard pattern of hosting the exiled Fourteenth Dalai Lama on his peripatetic foreign travels, especially after his 1989 Nobel Peace Prize award in recognition of his universal appeal as a world moral leader.

The eleventh hour

By the end of the Second Sino-Japanese War (Second World War), the Communist Party under Mao Zedong had assumed an edge over the Kuomingtang that was led by Chiang Kai-shek. Mao had previously set up a state, the Soviet Chinese Republic, from 1931 to 1937 with the backing of the Soviet Union. The Soviet Union, which had taken over the rest of Manchuria from Puyi's Manchukuo at the end of the war, handed the territory over to Mao, giving him a great strategic advantage. Chiang was supported by Khampa regiments, among others, but since the war was not able to continue receiving support from the Allies for the protracted civil war. This was largely due to strong evidence of corruption and morale issues among the Kuomingtang. From his northern stronghold, Mao's army moved southward, crossing the Yangtse in April 1949. On 23 April they seized Nanjing, the Kuomingtang capital. Chiang's forces retreated to Chengdu, then retreated to Taiwan in December. At that time Taiwan was still technically an occupied territory of Japan. Tibetans began buying rupees in expectation of the worst. Not wishing to have to accept the credentials of Communists, in July 1949 the Kashag expelled the temporary Chinese mission that had arrived as a condolence party for the Thirteenth Dalai Lama. They were given an escort to the Indian border.

Groups of Tibetan government officials were cobbled together to try to secure foreign assistance for travelling to United States, United Kingdom, India and Nepal, with an additional embassy for China. The British mission was to include a request for sponsorship into the United Nations.[9] As a gesture of friendship, the Tibetan government allowed passage of the missionary Morse family from Dzayul in Kham to Burma.[10] The United States, fearing an immediate Communist invasion of Tibet, did not offer any sort of support. This was echoed by Great Britain, who, throwing salt in the wound, reminded the Ganden Phodrang that any petition for UN membership would most likely be vetoed by China, a member of the Security Council. India also felt that the Communist takeover of Tibet was inevitable, and any resistance by India would prove futile.

On 1 October 1949 Mao proclaimed the People's Republic of China in Beijing. Chiang declared that his exiled government, and its two million mainland refugees, constituted the official Republic of China from Taiwan. The Communist People's Liberation Army had steadily grown throughout the war, and was approximately four million in 1949. It seemed strategically valuable to take advantage of the army's size and recent successes to fulfil the old Nationalist dream of annexing Tibet. In fact, it had begun broadcasting intentions of 'liberating' Tibet from 'imperialistic' forces as early as September 1949. Clearly, this came as a great shock to the Ganden Phodrang, who responded by sending radio messages indicating that as there were no longer any British or other foreign agencies in Tibet, there was no need to liberate them.

Through Indian independence, Britain could conveniently dump the issue on the new government of India, headed by the Congress Party's Jawaharlal Nehru. Having seen China as a sister victim of Western imperialism, and the Congress Party itself a moderate socialist political organization, Nehru wished to forge closer ties with the new China. 'Hindi–Chini bhai bhai' (Hindu–Chinese brotherhood) became the slogan of India's attempted seduction. But Nehru had not shirked when it came to his own country's national aspirations a generation before:

> We believe that it is the inalienable right of the Indian people, as of any other people, to have freedom and to enjoy the fruits of their toil and have the necessities of life, so that they may have full opportunities of growth. We believe also that if any government deprives a people of these rights and oppresses them the people have a further right to alter it or abolish it.[11]

Tibet's foreign diplomatic efforts fell upon deaf ears. In Delhi, the Chinese ambassador informed the Tibetan representative that Tibet had to become a part of China. The message was duly forwarded to the Kashag. 'No' was the response.[12]

Mao's strategy was to eliminate warlords throughout the western regions, people like Liu and Ma who had maintained virtually independent states in Sichuan and Qinghai, parts of old Kham and Amdo respectively. His strategy throughout China was to utilize the apparent disaffection of tenant farmers with their landlords to provide popular support for his revolution. He did not vary this strategy in the invasion of Tibet but decided to proceed slowly with social change. He felt that the simple farmer and nomad would eventually turn on their aristocratic and monastic overlords should they be given the opportunity. In January 1950 Mao had a meeting with Joseph Stalin in which the former stated his wish to occupy Tibet. Stalin assured the Chinese leader of continued Soviet support. Mao also wanted Mongolia back, but that was not acceptable to the Soviet leader.

In 1950 Ngapo Ngawang Jigme was appointed the new governor-general of Kham by the Ganden Phodrang. Realizing that there were only 3,500 elderly soldiers in the Tibetan army in Kham, Ngapo gave a realistic assessment that the Chinese army was much too powerful to oppose. The Reting and Taktra regencies had not done much to secure a powerful army: in fact, quite the opposite. Constant fears of having a too powerful army had plagued Lhasa since the early career of Tsarong Dzasa. Ngapo entered his tenure as governor with aims to negotiate with rather than intimidate the new Communist state to the east. Still, he had his orders to defend Tibet. To help improve communications, the

Englishman Robert Ford was hired by the government to operate the telegraph system out of Chamdo. This is the primary reason Lhasa had heard about the Communist 'liberation' plans. Ford had spent much of 1948 establishing Tibet's first broadcasting station, Radio Lhasa. This was followed by other broadcasting stations at Chamdo and Nagchuka along Tibet's northern border with China.

In the autumn of 1950, Shakabpa and Thubten Gyalpo were appointed by the Ganden Phodrang to negotiate with China on the status of Tibet. They were to reiterate that Tibet was an independent state, bound to China in the past by the priest–patron relationship. The party arrived in India to arrange for visas to China. Prime Minister Nehru seemed perturbed by the presence of the Tibetan diplomats. On 8 September, Shakabpa met with Nehru and expressed his desire for India to mediate between China and Tibet. Shakabpa then insisted on using the language of independence, Nehru with continuing suzerainty to China. Pressed, Nehru fumed and said:

China never accepted the Simla Convention. The Chinese believe that Tibet is a part of China. Tibet thinks that because China didn't accept Simla, it is independent, but at that time Tibet did not make any clear decisions. That was a mistake. And later when you had the time and the opportunity to do something you did nothing and this was a mistake.[13]

The Ganden Phodrang did develop further international ties during the 1920s and '30s but lacked many political resources during the weak regency period. Nehru certainly had a point, especially the failure of Tibet to develop diplomatically with the new state of India.

Later, a cooler Nehru arranged for a meeting of the Tibetans with the incoming ambassador from China to India, Yuan Chungsien. The Tibetan party began talks with Yuan on 16 September. Very little was accomplished. Yuan presented the Tibetan party with an ultimatum: 1) accept that Tibet is part of China; 2) turn over the Tibetan army to China; 3) all political and trade matters with foreign countries must be handled by China.[14] Shakabpa cabled China's demands to his government in Lhasa. The Ganden Phodrang told Shakabpa not to accept Yuan's ultimatum, and to stall for the time being.

On 5 October 1950, while Tibetan officials waited to deliver a response to Yuan in New Delhi, the People's Liberation Army crossed the border at the Yangtse River and through four points of entry began the invasion of Tibet. There were considerable delays in getting the word back to Lhasa: first, the transmitter was at Chamdo and not on the border. Second, the Kashag was apparently having its annual picnic and could not be bothered. Ngopo was livid: 'Shit on their picnic!' was his aide-de-camp's transmission to his counterpart in Lhasa.[15] Much valuable time was lost, and by the time it acted it could only instruct the Kham governor to flee. Chamdo fell; the local Khampas, many of whom were fighting on the Chinese side, began looting. Ford, initially left behind, was arrested for being an 'imperialist' and spent the next five years in prison. The Ganden Phodrang finally began acting, protesting the action to the government of India and then to the United Nations.

Ngapo returned to Chamdo and personally surrendered on 19 October. The Chinese continued pushing west, meeting no resistance. All of Kham was 'peacefully liberated'. The Dalai Lama's brother, Takster Rinpoche, fled

The People's Liberation Army troops marching towards the Tibet border, 1950.

the Chinese-dominated Kumbum monastery in Amdo and arrived in Lhasa. Reporting to his brother, he continued to India and soon was in New York, where he could represent his country to the United States. Ngapo would be educated about Communism from the Khampa Puntsong Wangyal (Phun tshog dbang rgyal) and generally treated well.

The cascading news coming from the east prompted the Ganden Phodrang to invite the Nechung and Gadong oracles to advise the government on the correct course of action. After some confusing interpretations, both oracles agreed that the Dalai Lama should assume full powers.[16] Taktra had to resign. On 17 November 1950 a sixteen-year-old boy, with the weight of an entire country on his shoulders, had to face Mao Zedong. He would rule a free Tibet for only six months.

No one in Lhasa really knew what a Communist China meant. The Thirteenth Dalai Lama knew well the threat from the Soviet actions in Mongolia, but he had been gone for seventeen years. For many, the Chinese demands on Tibet were no more than what they had been during the times of Kublai and Phagpa, Shunzhi and Thubten Gyatso – the head of Tibet would become the imperial preceptor as before in exchange for material sponsorship of the religio-political establishment. For many in Lhasa, the secularism of the Kuomingtang had not been the issue; the Nationalists' corruption and weakness that caused warlords to arise and terrorize much of Kham and Amdo had been the problem, and the Communists seemed to be morally competent, at least. To some, it did not matter so much that Tibet was considered a part of China as long as the monasteries continued to provide spiritual benefit to sentient beings. For many, that was the *raison d'être* for Tibet in the first place. Few realized that the particular type of secular nationalism under Mao would soon show a violently atheist, anti-traditional fury that would destroy most of the cultural traditions and centuries-old institutions in Tibet, as well as in China proper. No one knew that the failure of radical social reorganization such as the Great Leap Forward would kill tens of millions in widespread famine throughout the People's Republic. Mao's strategy in Tibet was to try to split the religious establishment from the political segment, and he did this by promising support for the monastic community. The new Panchen Lama, 'discovered' entirely by the Chinese, was the poster child for this effort. Geda Trulku of Kanze was another lama who supported the Chinese occupation. He was murdered in Chamdo, believed by some to be the work of the Tibetan administration.[17] Reting was also believed to have been pro-Chinese.

The Ganden Phodrang decided to appeal directly to the United Nations, and sent Shakabpa to Kalimpong to best utilize the telegraph there. The first message to the United Nations Secretariat was thought to be from a non-government agency rather than a diplomatic one, so it was not given appropriate attention. Once Shakabpa's position was acknowledged, none of the big powers wished to irritate China by sponsoring a Tibetan complaint. It was little El Salvador that eventually sponsored a proposal to hear the protest of Tibet.

The El Salvador initiative ignited a flurry of diplomatic exchanges that underscored the generations of misinformation that had been accumulating about this Tibet which had suddenly been thrust upon the world's attention. The El Salvador draft condemned China's unprovoked act. It provided for a committee to advise the General Assembly at the request of the government of Tibet. Great Britain, the United States and India were forced to review their understandings and provide leadership in the crisis. First, the British Foreign Office examined whether Tibet was eligible to apply for an appeal under Article 35 (2), which required the party to be a state, and not necessarily a member. In a letter from the Foreign Office to the high commissioner in India, the British cited the Simla Convention, with the interpretation that

> If, therefore, China repudiated the Convention in its entirely, as her present actions clearly show she has done [that is, the invasion], she has no right whatever over Tibet, not even to a nominal suzerainty. Since 1913 Tibet has not only enjoyed full control over her internal affairs but also has maintained direct relations with other states. She must therefore be regarded as a state to which Article 35 (2) of the Charter applies.
>
> Our recognition of Chinese suzerainty over Tibet after 1914 was conditional on the recognition by China of Tibetan autonomy.[18]

The British delegation to the UN, however, immediately reversed this position, suggesting that they 'argue to the general effect that the legal situation is *extremely obscure* and that in any case Tibet cannot be considered as a fully independent country [emphasis added]'.[19]

The Indian government, realizing that all eyes were on it, mildly condemned the invasion, saying, rather remarkably, that the invasion was not in the interest of peace. China reacted sharply, stating that the Tibet problem was entirely a domestic issue, a formula for shrugging off human rights violations that is used to the present day. In any case, India decided not to support Tibet's appeal at the United Nations.

A precipitating incident for placing Tibet on the back burner of world politics was the invasion of South Korea by the Soviet- and Chinese-backed Communist government of North Korea, which had begun in July 1950. However, it was just that incident that helped the United States to reconsider its policy towards Tibet. The United States had been a strong ally of the Republic of China headed by the now-defeated Kuomingtang. The peaceful pontificate of the Dalai Lama, being annexed without provocation by the new Communist People's Republic of China, could become a useful symbol in the rhetoric of the Cold War.

On 7 January 1951 the Dalai Lama's court had moved to the town of Yatung, to be close to the border with Sikkim should the need to flee into exile arise. Initially, the Dalai Lama was opposed to agreeing that Tibet was part of China. It is what the oracles had cautioned. It was decided that Ngapo would go to Beijing to negotiate with authorities the meaning of 'liberation'. Ngapo left in April. He opened with a statement on the traditional independence of Tibet, clarifying the priest–patron relationship. He was bluntly told by Communist Party officials that the status of Tibet was not being negotiated: Tibet had always been a part of China, end of story. Under threat of further army movement into Tibet, Ngapo was told to accept the facts of history and cooperate with the new Communist regime.

The United States wished to support Tibet, but was aware that the new government of India would be problematic should direct military aid be offered. Logistically it would have been impossible for the u.s. to supply troops or military supplies to Tibet without Indian cooperation. The United States government therefore took a rather non-committal attitude in their dealings with Tibetan officials in order not to raise expectations. The United States, however, contacted the British government for their assessment of the feasibility of the Western powers supporting Tibet against Communist aggression. Communist control of Lhasa might continue through to Nepal, Bhutan and India.[20] Early 'Domino Theory' thinking, characteristic of later Cold War strategy (such as that expressed by Eisenhower in 1954), was already being formed.[21] The United States concluded that covertly supporting guerrilla activity in Tibet might be the best strategy, given that Britain was backing away entirely from previous responsibilities, the logistical problem and India being unwilling to side with the West.

At the United Nations, Britain was to follow India's lead in shelving the proposal by El Salvador to bring the Tibet invasion to the floor of the General Assembly. The Indian argument was that Tibet was already engaged in peaceful negotiations with China, and that any punitive condemnation of China might jeopardize those talks, and even seem to support China's claim that 'imperialist forces' were interfering in the affair.

Ngapo had kept the official seal of a Kashag minister with him, but in secret. The Chinese simply made their own seals for Ngapo to use. Another issue was the acceptance of Chokyi Gyaltsen as the Tenth Panchen Lama. China had promoted this pro-Chinese young man. The Ganden Phodrang refused to recognize him until the traditional religious tests were done, which Ngapo understood well. Finally, however, the Dalai Lama relented, threw a divination by lottery, and the results concurred with Chinese wishes.

With no way out, Ngapo signed away his country's independence in Beijing on 23 May 1951. The Seventeen Point Agreement basically stated that Tibet was part of China, and that the government of the Ganden Phodrang would continue to operate in an autonomous manner. Radio Beijing broadcast that Tibet had agreed to be liberated. The Ganden Phodrang first learned that their independence had vanished through this announcement. The pro-annexation and pro-independence factions in the government belaboured whether or not to ratify the agreement in exile at Yatung.

While in his liminal world at Yatung, the Dalai Lama received an interesting letter. Unsigned and on Indian paper, the letter claimed to be from the American ambassador to India. It was indeed from Loy Henderson, who had acted upon the advice of Heinrich Harrer. The Austrian had just arrived in India from his seven years in Tibet as a war

Ngapo Ngawang
Jigme signing the
Seventeen Point
Agreement in
Beijing without
the Dalai Lama's
authority, 23 May
1951.

refugee. Harrer was, of course, good friends with young Tenzin Gyatso. The letter was written so as not to be traceable should it fall into Chinese hands. It suggested that the Dalai Lama seek asylum in Ceylon, or possibly the United States itself, and to send his treasury there as well. The initiative had the backing of the u.s. State Department. Secretary of State Dean Acheson, after the issuance of the Seventeen Point Agreement was known, indicated to Henderson that Tibet should not 'be compelled by duress to accept violations of its autonomy' and that the Tibet people 'should enjoy certain rights [of] self-determination'.[22]

In June the Dalai Lama was satisfied with the American answers, and was ready to go into exile through India. The Americans, unlike the British, indicated they were willing to suffer damaging relations with the government of India for the greater goal of suppressing Communist aggression. For its part, the United States hoped to see vigorous resistance to occupation by the Ganden Phodrang. Instead, the Dalai Lama indicated that he would hold talks with the Chinese in Yatung. The Dalai Lama's brother implored him to disavow the Seventeen Point Agreement and go into exile immediately. This was followed by another strong supporting letter from the United States government, again unsigned, promising to support a new appeal to the United Nations, arranging asylum for the Dalai Lama, and offering to embrace any denouncement of the Seventeen Point Agreement by the Tibetan government. The abbots of Drepung, Sera and Ganden, plus the state oracles, came to Yatung to dissuade the Tibetan leader from going into exile. The Dalai Lama changed his mind, and indicated that he was indeed returning to Lhasa.

In Washington, Taktser Rinpoche was informed that the U.S. government would recognize Tibetan self-determination and encouraged the Dalai Lama's ultimate return to Tibet as an autonomous but non-Communist state. On 23 July the Dalai Lama returned to Lhasa. The debate of the Tsongdu tilted towards believing that China would honour the status quo of the position of the Dalai Lama and the administration of the Ganden Phodrang. It also felt that the American offer was largely symbolic: they needed troops, supplies and ammunition to fight Communist China, as much as the South Koreans were given. Finally, Ambassador Henderson drafted an official letter outlining the offered support, showed it to a Tibetan messenger, locked up the letter, and sent the messenger off to Lhasa to report of America's sincerity. It is not known if he was ever able to deliver the message. The Tsongdu voted to accept the Seventeen Point Agreement. Although the Dalai Lama was opposed to giving up Tibetan independence, he found the pro-Chinese monastic faction too powerful to overcome. Making the best of it, the Dalai Lama sent a flattering telegram to Mao Zedong on 24 October 1951.

Tenzin Gyatso and his government would try to work with the Communists for the next eight years. It seemed to many as an appeasement, but the Fourteenth Dalai Lama was from the start able to apply the Buddhist concept of *ahimsa*, or non-violence, to the challenging situation. By offering practically no resistance to the entry of the People's Liberation Army and agreeing to the demands of the occupiers, he was on the higher moral ground. By trying to provide understanding to the Chinese, the Dalai Lama was practising compassion, his primary role. By facing evil and trying to transform it into good, he was applying tantric principles to the situation. But as non-violence may be good for making friends with hostile neighbours, it is not necessarily good

Chokyi Gyaltsen, the Tenth Panchen Lama (left), and the Dalai Lama (right), with Mao Zedong in Beijing, 1954. The Sixth Ling Rinpoche appears behind.

for the maintenance of national sovereignty. It did seem to work for Gandhi's India, but it was successful largely due to Britain's desire for dignified abandonment of their empire rather than expansion. China had a different idea.

Mao's honeymoon with Tenzin Gyatso resulted in the young man being invited to Beijing in the summer of 1954. Not much had changed since the Great Thirteenth visited the court of Cixi and Guangxu: with a caravan of five hundred retainers, the Dalai Lama travelled overland for 26 days before arriving at Chamdo, the former capital of his province of Kham. Here he encountered his first Chinese Communist city, with squawking loudspeakers set up to resolutely wake up the proletariat each morning and extol to them the virtues of socialism. At Xi'an, he was joined by the Tenth Panchen Lama, Chokyi Gyaltsen. Together the two teenagers eagerly sped off by private train to Beijing.[23] Arriving to a warm reception, they were hosted at the Hall of Purple Light, used since the days of Kangxi to welcome leaders of vassal states and heads of state.

Mao took a paternal bent to the two boys, teaching them fine points on governance and flattering the ideals of Buddhism. Dressed in the latest ancient Mongol and Manchu dragon robes, with turquoise-encrusted British pith helmets, the Dalai Lama was wholly seduced by the modernism of China and the forward thinking of the Communists. In Beijing the Dalai Lama met Nikita Khrushchev and, for the first time, Jawaharlal Nehru. After nearly a year in Beijing, the Dalai Lama returned to Lhasa on 29 June 1955.

Mao had initially decided to rule Tibet directly from Beijing, but was impressed with Tenzin Gyatso's intelligence and desire to work with the Chinese Communist Party. So, change would come slowly for central Tibet, and a Preparatory Committee for the Autonomous Region of Tibet (PCART) was established that included the Ganden Phodrang, the

The Dalai Lama is seen with members of a Chinese government delegation on their official visit to Lhasa on 17 April 1956 for the inauguration of the Preparatory Committee for the Autonomous Region of Tibet (PCART). From left: Phünwang (with fur hat), the Dalai Lama, Vice-Premier Chen Yi (saluting, second from right) and the Panchen Lama.

Tashilhumpo Labrang and the Chamdo Liberation Committee, with the Dalai Lama as chairman. It was evident that Mao's divide-and-rule strategy equalizing the Dalai and Panchen Lamas was reaching a formal stage. The Chamdo Liberation Committee was the government established after the initial invasion in 1950. Now having separated Tibet into thirds, the PCART would gradually take over its entire rule. The Tibetan army was also slowly disbanded, and the state currency was changed to the Chinese yuan (*renmenbi*).

A garland of cabbage leaves

While the Dalai and Panchen Lamas were being chauffeured about Beijing from the opera to the banqueting halls, 'ethnic' Tibetans in the provinces previously created out of Tibet – large areas of Amdo and Kham – first felt the sting of collectivization, since they were not considered a part of the jurisdiction of the PCART held back on social reform. Nomadic pastoralists were outraged that they were commanded to settle down. The monastic estates, the firmament upon which the theocratic state was built, suddenly belonged to the people, who were now being stripped of their enmeshed national and religious identity. And for the fierce Khampas, the Communist order to confiscate their personal guns was taken as an emasculation. Rather than rising up as emancipated 'serfs' to tear up the monastic estates, people began attacking the Chinese instead, much to the Communists' surprise.

The first major uprising against the Chinese was in 1955 at Sampheling monastery, a Gelug stronghold in Kham. Having taken potshots at Chinese officials, thousands of CIA-armed Khampas joined a myriad of monks at the *dzong*. The army laid siege, finally resorting to bombing the community out of existence. The scenario was repeated at Lithang, birthplace of the Sixth Dalai Lama. The great abbots who beseeched the Dalai Lama to sign the Seventeen Point Agreement were now silent, and possibly dead.

The cat was out of the bag. The fighting in eastern Tibet drove many disgruntled Khampa and Amdowa to central Tibet, and Lhasa in particular, where much of traditional society continued as it always had. Lhasans learned of China's ultimate intentions from these refugees. The Chinese Communist Party had shown it was not the perfect socialist patron the Dalai Lama was led to believe. For many Marxists, Engels's theory of nationalism was clear: modern nation states are artificial constructs designed to keep elites in power. The competition between elites on the world stage drags nations into war and causes undue suffering among the masses. This was first demonstrated when the new Bolshevist government pulled Russia out of the First World War in 1917. The real nexus of power should lie with the peasants and workers as a similar class everywhere. Marxism was, of course, initially an international movement; thus it was believed that national divisions would dissolve in time in the face of the organic unity of the masses. It was Mao's essential strategy in overthrowing the landowning class throughout China, and collectivizing all agricultural, animal husbandry and industrial production. Mao also continued the Nationalist line that the republic was the heir of the Qing Empire.[24]

In the autumn of 1956 Sikkimese Crown Prince Palden Thondup Namgyal, nephew of Sidkeong, visited Tenzin Gyatso in Lhasa. He was bearing an invitation from the government of India to attend the 2,500th anniversary of the birth of Shakyamuni Buddha. Initially, the Chinese leaders refused to let the Dalai Lama attend, citing security reasons. But after a direct appeal from Nehru, the Dalai and Panchen Lamas were

Changtreng Sampheling monastery in 2013, to which the PLA laid siege and bombed in early 1956, and where refugees had sought shelter after fighting in surrounding areas.

Chushi Gangdruk (Chu bzhisgang drug), the Kham Four Rivers, Six Ranges
Tibetan Defenders of the Faith Volunteer Army, resisting the Chinese army in 1958
in Tsethang (U-Tsang).

permitted to go. For the Dalai Lama, this would present an opportunity
to represent Tibetan Buddhism and Tibet in the land of its religious
foundations. It was a chance to build political networks with Gandhian
non-violence partisans which the Dalai Lama was dedicated to. The
Dalai Lama left in November. Driven to Yatung, the party climbed the
pass and arrived at Gangtok, where they were greeted by the Chogyal
Tashi Namgyal. The Dalai Lama met up with his brother, who again
insisted that he request exile. A special plane brought him to New Delhi.
The Panchen Lama also arrived. It was the first opportunity for the Dalai
Lama to talk privately with Nehru, and on their first meeting Tenzin
Gyatso asked for asylum. Conjuring up a vision of nuclear war, Nehru
told him to go back to Tibet and continue to try to work with the Chinese.
By this time, the Indian government had finally taken over the trade
agencies in Tibet that had previously been established by treaty with the
British. India did not, however, honour the other provisions of the Simla
Convention: namely, recognition of Tibet as an autonomous state under
suzerainty of China and the acknowledgement of the treaty-making
powers of Tibet with foreign states. This was due to the lofty ideals of
the Pancha–Sheela agreement India had made with China in 1954.

Firearms and ammunition of Tibetan guerrilla fighters were seized from the three major monasteries: Sera, Ganden and Drepung. Pictured are rebels surrendering their guns.

Importantly, it maintained an understanding that nations would not interfere in the internal affairs of others, and Tibet was considered an 'internal affair' by China. To Nehru, the peaceful, neighbourly coexistence of the world's two most populous nations was far more important than any archaic obligations it had inherited from its former colonial masters. 'Hindi–Chini bhai bhai' (Indian–Chinese brotherhood) became a slogan of the hour. But for the Dalai Lama, it was the first foray into the world beyond Tibet and China. He met Buddhist leaders and representatives of the United States, Britain and other countries.

The Dalai Lama returned to Lhasa. Although he tried to maintain outward forms, the Ganden Phodrang was becoming a shadow of what it had been prior to 1950. He became quite dependent upon Ngapo, who had developed a reputation for being a good negotiator in dealing with the Chinese overlords. Occupying much of his time, however, was his final course of Buddhist studies, which would provide him with the highest monastic title of *geshe lharampa*. A brilliant, insightful scholar,

overleaf: Tibetan women surround the Potala palace, the main residence of the Dalai Lama, to protest against Chinese rule and repression in Lhasa, Tibet, 12 March 1959.

Tenzin Gyatso spent many hours in analytic study, in meditation and in dialectic debate.

Tibetan New Year in 1959 rolled past, followed by the month-long Great Prayer Festival, Monlam, established centuries before by Tsongkhapa. Tenzin Gyatso's final examinations were held at this time, being proctored at the three great monasteries of Drepung, Ganden and Sera. The Dalai Lama passed each with great distinction, as was expected. In recognition of his graduation, the Lhasa-based Chinese army chief, General Tan, wished to honour his achievement with a theatrical show at headquarters. The Dalai Lama was invited. Tenzin Gyatso was delighted to accept the invitation, and a date was set: 10 March. The Dalai Lama had failed to advise his staff in advance, however, and they were suspicious of the Chinese request, especially with the provision of coming without a bodyguard. Rumour-sensitive Lhasa immediately sensed that something might be afoot. Throughout the day, city folk began to surround the Norbulingka where the Dalai Lama was in residence, until thousands of Tibetans, fearing their holy leader would be kidnapped, prevented his departure to the Chinese base. The Dalai

Several thousand Tibetans, fearing that the Chinese might abduct the Dalai Lama, gathered at the Norbulingka summer palace to protect the Tibetan spiritual leader, 10 March 1959.

Lama first ordered them to disburse, but they would not budge. Next, he allowed representatives to enter and talk with his aides. Trying to save face with the Chinese, he sent the Kashag ministers to attend the theatre instead, which infuriated General Tan. His Holiness, sensing it was the end, called for the Nechung Oracle to render his opinion. The Great Protector of the Tibetan State and the Dalai Lama unequivocally told him: 'Leave now!' On 12 March the women of Lhasa amassed in protest at the foot of the Potala, calling for independence. The crowds still clung to the walls around the Norbulingka. A few days later the army trained its heavy artillery upon the park. They had told the Dalai Lama to find a secure spot in the complex, and inform them so they would not commence firing upon him. On 17 March, while the Dalai Lama was meeting with his ministers, a mortar shell landed in a pond within the Norbulingka complex. Another exploded in a marsh just beyond the northern wall, spraying mud on the crowds. At that point, the Dalai Lama made the decision to leave.

Tenzin Gyatso wasted no time, sending his mother, sister and youngest brother Ngari Rinpoche out of the Norbulingka in disguise. The women were dressed as men, the young Ngari in civilian clothes. They were headed for the border at Yatung. The Dalai Lama's group followed at about ten o'clock. The Dalai Lama, a few aides and servants changed into ordinary civilian clothes. Tenzin Gyatso removed his glasses and asked to borrow a rifle from one of the guards. Carrying the seals of state and an ancient silk *thangka* of the Protectoress Palden Lhamo, they walked out of a quiet gate of the palace. A third party, consisting of the four Kashag ministers, the senior and junior tutors, and the Gadong Oracle, followed closely after.[25] Crossing the Kyichu River, they rode steadily in the dead of night to Chaksum Ferry on the road to Yatung. Here they were ferried across the Tsangpo in coracles to the territory held by Tibetan guerrillas. It seemed a repeat of the Thirteenth Dalai Lama's flight into India nearly fifty years before. Guarded by well-armed Khampas, the Dalai Lama felt his first sense of freedom in years.

The Dalai Lama's party established a defence at Lhuntse *dzong* 100 km (60 mi.) south of Lhasa. The army began shelling the Norbulingka and the Potala to scatter the crowds that still thought they were protecting the Dalai Lama. The episode had turned into a fully fledged uprising. The following morning, hundreds of Tibetans lay dead at the Norbulingka

Tibetans surrendered to the Chinese troops in Lhasa, in front of the Potala.
Tibetan rebels being trained by the CIA for a guerrilla campaign against the PLA,
c. 1960.

gardens. Chinese troops picked through the ruins of the palace, looking
for the body of the Dalai Lama and his family. When none of the government ministers were found either, they finally realized on 19 March
that the Dalai Lama had taken flight. Fighting raged for three days in
the city. The Potala and Sera monastery were shelled. The Chakpori
Medical College on the peak across from the Potala was levelled. On
22 March they attacked Tibet's holiest shrine, the Jokhang, which was

Part of the Dalai Lama's palace (above) and lake pavilion (below)
at the Norbulingka, Lhasa, 1936, photographed by Frederick Spencer Chapman.

then giving asylum to 10,000 Tibetans; thousands were killed. Perhaps 12,000 Tibetans died in Lhasa, a staggering half the population of the city.

On 28 March Zhou Enlai broadcast an announcement, heard at Lhuntse, that the Ganden Phodrang had been dissolved. Chinese troops rushed eastwards from Bhutan to try to seal the border. Once at Lhuntse *dzong*, the Dalai Lama immediately sent messengers ahead to ask Nehru for asylum in India. Meanwhile, they had a bit of unfinished business.

The Dalai Lama (centre, wearing spectacles) and his escape party is shown on the fourth day of their flight to freedom as they cross the Zsagola pass, in southern Tibet, 21 March 1959.

The small group of ministers wrote out a proclamation and stamped their black seals to it. The Dalai Lama had his servants fish out the great seal from the luggage still strapped to the horses. Dipping it in the vermilion ink that was his unique privilege, he pressed it hard on the document. The Seventeen Point Agreement with the People's Republic of China was repudiated, and the Ganden Phodrang was restored. China had broken its promise primarily by interfering with the government of the Ganden Phodrang, which by now had been reduced to a few members of the PCART, most of whom were heading off to an unknown life in exile.

Over two high passes in blinding snow, the party moved as swiftly as possible, the Chinese troops closing in. The Dalai Lama became ill but continued on. A large transport plane flew over, giving them a terrible fright.[26] The party had chosen a little-used route rather than the heavily travelled trail through Chumbi Valley. This brought them into the now disputed Tawang territory, the Khampa guards and heavyset Amdowas towering over the slightly built Monpas at the tiny border village of Mangmang. Weakened by dysentery, the Great Protector of Tibet, his family and his ministers crossed the border into India.

EIGHT

The Two Tibets

Following his exile, the Fourteenth Dalai Lama would spend at least 120 times his tenure as fully empowered spiritual and secular sovereign of Tibet as head of the Ganden Phodrang in Dharamsala, India. In fact, after sixty years, he is one of the longest surviving members of the Tibetan *ancien régime*. During this time, he has been transformed from a near-mythical god-king from a relatively unknown part of the world to one of the most familiar and admired world leaders.

The unity of the state created by the religious kings of the Yarlung dynasty was not driven into extinction by the armies of the People's Republic of China. Rather, it was split into two distinct Tibets, perhaps more. First is the 'legitimate' Tibet taken into exile by Tenzin Gyatso, his cabinet, the nobility and holders of important religious lineages, which has been recreated in India and abroad. The second, the territory and people of Tibet that were left behind, represents a new state of affairs that would suffer the uncomfortable weight of the radical social reforms of a new and foreign China.

Another possible Tibet is the vessel for the Bodhidharma, a supra-national and spiritual realm shorn of much parochial political tincture. It is the religious culture of millions of Tibetans, Mongols, Manchus, Sikkimese, Bhutanese, Nepalese and Western Buddhist practitioners, and it seems to be doing fine without the state of Tibet. To understand modern Tibet, one must grasp these divergent threads.

Exile of the Ganden Phodrang

Unbeknownst to his party, the flight of the Dalai Lama was the lead story in world news. When he finally arrived at the Monyul capital of

Tawang he was already a celebrity. The world stood by breathlessly as the Indian government desperately tried to hold back the phalanxes of fedora-clad reporters and photographers with popping flashbulbs. Local telephone exchanges close to the point of entry were completely besieged by reporters competing to scoop the story. The Dalai Lama plunged into a sea of microphones amid the loud clatter of hundreds of camera shutters. He would never escape this new world.

At Monyul the Dalai Lama and his family were quickly escorted into the local magistrate's guest house. A Tibetan official appeared and read a statement from their leader, indicating the repudiation of the Seventeen Point Agreement, which the Dalai Lama stated was signed under duress. It was tantamount to a renewed declaration of independence.

That China had to negotiate with Ganden Phodrang at all is indicative of the prior sovereignty of Tibet. If it was an integral part of China, it did not need to be liberated. At his arrival in India, the Dalai Lama made clear that he was now fully in charge of a restored Ganden Phodrang, and that he had left Tibet on his own initiative. The Chinese press, emboldened by the success of their previous propaganda on the status of Tibet, however, responded by reporting that the Dalai Lama had been abducted by aliens: that is, imperialist forces. Hearing some news themselves, the Dalai Lama and his party were relieved that the Potala and Norbulingka had not been levelled, as the rumours had suggested during his flight. But he learned, with great sadness, of the thousands of his subjects who had died in his defence.

The Dalai Lama was not alone – hundreds then thousands of Tibetan exiles followed in his footsteps. Within a short time, the leaders of the major schools of Tibetan Buddhism, the Karmapa, Sakya Trichen and Dujum Rimpoche, also crossed the border. Both of the state oracles, the entire cabinet and most of the Tsongdu members followed into exile. Many aristocratic families had left with their treasures even earlier.

Nehru, who had been so discouraging to the political aspirations of the Dalai Lama and his government, now threw open the door of humanitarian concern for the young man and his followers. Asylum would be granted, but only on the condition that the Dalai Lama refrain from any political activity. Nor would the Indian leader recognize a government-in-exile. The Indian government would support, instead, the settlement of tens of thousands of Tibetan refugees, providing land, jobs, healthcare and education. Switzerland, the United States and many NGOs followed soon afterward. Many Tibetans were provided with employment building roads, especially in northern India. Nehru would alienate friendly China–India relations, which he had carefully cultivated, by having to support the Dalai Lama after all.

Tenzin Gyatso and his family were moved to Bomdilla, then to the hill town of Mussoorie. In 1960 Nehru suggested the old hill station of McLeod Ganj in Dharamsala, Himachal Pradesh, as a more permanent settlement. The Indian government made a good deal with local land-owner Nauzeer Nowrojee for the establishment of a Tibetan community. Located along spurs and foothills of the Himalaya, the site offered good security as well as access to communications and transportation. India wanted the Dalai Lama to be close to the Tibetan border in case the political climate with China changed. In fact, the upper Dharamsala region was adjacent to the old Tibetan provinces of Lahul and Spiti, and thus part of cultural Tibet. Larger, agricultural settlements were established, mostly in south India.

The Dalai Lama wasted no time re-establishing the Ganden Phodrang (renamed the Central Tibetan Administration [CTA]), with a Kashag, a prime minster, a Tsongdu and a cabinet of ministers for the interior, education, religious and cultural affairs, information, international affairs and treasury. At one of his first press conferences, the Dalai Lama stated that he was the perpetual, legitimate ruler of Tibet: 'Wherever I am accompanied by my Government, the Tibetan people will recognize such as the Government of Tibet.'[1] Later cultural offices were established in major capitals around the world, which serve as unofficial embassies.

The new Ganden Phodrang continued the tradition of the ancient de facto state of Tibet. The Dalai Lama surrounded himself with the old aristocracy, those families that had served the Ganden Phodrang for centuries: the Namgyal of Sikkim, Tsarong, Tethong, Surkhang, Yutok, the junior and senior tutors, the Nechung and Gadong state oracles, the abbots of many of the Gelug colleges. A key supporter of the Dalai Lama was his brother Gyalo Thondup, who had direct contact with the United States. Gyalo was a strong facilitator of the persistent offers of assistance from the United States, official and clandestine through the CIA and its

overleaf: Map of Tibet created by the U.S. Central Intelligence Agency, October 1967.

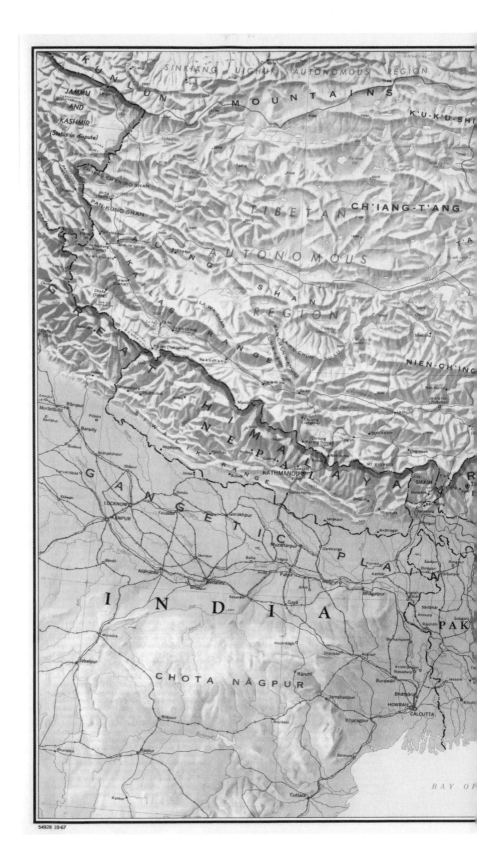

support of the guerrilla war of the Chu Shi Gang Druk in Kham. The Tibetan leader, however, refused direct American participation. Also supportive was Thupden Jigme Norbu, the Dalai Lama's eldest brother, who had been living in exile in the United States. Unlike their brother, Thupden and Gyalo were strong advocates of total independence for Tibet.

Refugees flowed in through Nepal, Bhutan and Sikkim, from Ngari and Tawang, until nearly 115,000 had arrived by the late 1970s. The microstate of Dharamsala was possible because nearly the entire treasury of Tibet had been moved to India in the years prior to the 1959 uprising. Like any state, Dharamsala is supported by voluntary 'taxation' of its population, the so-called Green Card scheme. Many of the ministries are also supported by grants from numerous NGOs throughout the world. Despite the rumours that Gyalo Thondup eroded much of these financial resources through bad investments,[2] the exiled government has always been well funded, internally and through NGO support.

Nehru did not allow the Dalai Lama at Mussoorie to have contact with foreign officials or the press. Nehru's first meeting with the Dalai Lama also did not go well; according to the latter, 'Nehru thought of me as a young person who needed to be scolded from time to time.'[3] Unfortunately, Nehru's fear of China's wrath pleased no one, least of all China, which condemned the government of India for interfering in the internal affairs of China. Nehru's position was attacked by the Indian opposition, who saw the Dalai Lama's plight as a failure of India to understand the strategic nature and cultural importance of Tibet to the region.

Although it was a strong Congress Party tenet not to support the stand for Tibetan independence, the Indian opposition was not so adamant. In fact, in May 1959 J. P. Narayan held a conference of Indian supporters of Tibetan independence.[4] Prime Minister Moraji Desi came close to recognizing Dharamsala in the 1970s.

One of the earliest political moves of the Dalai Lama in exile was to reignite the United Nations initiative. Tenzin Gyatso dispatched Gyalo Thondup, Shakabpa and Rinchen Sandutshang to argue the case. The Dalai Lama made a direct appeal to Secretary-General Dag Hammarskjöld, which was distributed among members.[5] As expected, the Tibetans were vehemently opposed by the Communist bloc nations. Finding support for sponsoring a discussion of the General Assembly from the small states of Malaysia, Ireland and Thailand, the Ganden Phodrang was encouraged by the resulting resolution that called for a basic respect for human rights in Tibet. This was among the first major challenges to absolute Westphalian sovereignty (see Article 2.7 of the UN Charter) in the face of human rights violations, and the beginning of member-state interventionism that would be seen in the Korean and Vietnamese civil wars. The 45 to 9 vote to support Tibetan human rights was an early exercise in 'contingent sovereignty',[6] although it had no practical effect on the People's Republic of China, not yet a member of the organization.

The United States managed to go one further and support the notion of self-determination for Tibet, and goaded its hapless ally Chiang Kai-shek to do the same, 'when the Communist regime on the mainland is overthrown'.[7] Understandably, declining imperial powers such as Britain and France found they could not encourage self-determination in Tibet without drawing unfavourable comparisons to their own former colonial policies.

The International Commission of Jurists ruled that Tibet was at least a de facto state prior to the signing of the Seventeen Point Agreement in 1951 and was in fact independent. As such Chinese activity in 1950 should be considered an act of international aggression rather than a domestic policing issue,[8] and that China had committed genocide. This had the effect of boosting Tibetan confidence and has served to maintain hopes of eventual freedom ever since.

Political activity aimed at the UN continued to be raised by the Tibetan government-in-exile. In September 1960 the Dalai Lama wrote a detailed account of Tibet's claim for independence based on historical precedence and had it sent to the secretary-general. In 1961 Thailand and Malaysia sponsored a resolution, based for the first time on the concept of Tibetan self-determination – it passed 48 to 14 with 35 abstentions.[9] India's abstention pleased no one.

Nehru's cafeteria style of treaty interpretation regarding Tibet backfired with the outbreak of military hostilities between India and China in October 1962. Advantageous to the government of India was the Simla Convention's border with Tibet at the McMahon Line, which included the former Tibetan dependency of Tawang on the Indian side. But acknowledging that territory also logically indicated that the British negotiations with Tibet were legal, and as such, Tibet was independent at that time since Britain had signed solely with Tibet. In fact, one of the first matters brought to the government of India after its independence was a demand from the Tibetan foreign bureau for the return of its Indian-occupied territories, including Dzayul, Walong, Pamkoe, Long, Lopa, Mon, Bhutan, Sikkim, Darjeeling, Lahul and Ladakh.[10] China, of course, claimed Tawang and these others through Tibet. Although a ceasefire was quickly reached, Tawang remains contested, as does the region of Aksai Chin in Ladakh. Nehru's miscalculation was a fatal blow to 'Hindi–Chini bhai bhai' (Indian and Chinese brotherhood). The unresolved border issue could at any time boil over to Bhutan, Sikkim, half of Nepal, large sections of Bengal, Bangladesh and the Dalai Lama's present neighbourhood of Dharamsala, all former tributaries of the state of Tibet, now subsumed into China.

China's Tibet

Whatever restraint Mao may have exercised initiating reform in Tibet following the initial occupation in 1950 evaporated with the uprising of 1959. It was dramatic evidence of the failure of the Seventeen Point Agreement of 1951. Tsering Shakya suggests that part of its failure was due to a systemic misunderstanding of the term 'autonomy', which was listed in the document in Tibetan as *rang skyong ljong* (self-rule): that is, continued control by the Dalai Lama.[11] Many Tibetans expected a continuation of the priest–patron system with China as a benevolent but passive partner. Centrist Beijing had different ideas. It was just a matter of time before the people realized that Mao was not like a sincere Buddhist Manchu emperor – he was not *nang pa*, an insider. He did not appear to understand that the Dalai Lama was the living incarnation of the protector deity of Tibet and its religious kings, not just another Gelug lama like the Panchen. Mao seemed not to grasp that the so-called superstitions held by the people for their Dalai Lama was the source of his authority. In Tibet, religion was not a Marxist superstructure but the core of their identity.

It is ironic that the period from the signing of the Seventeen Point Agreement in 1951 to the Tibetan uprising in 1959 was the era of greatest autonomy for the country under the People's Republic of China and the

Preparatory Committee for the Autonomous Region of Tibet (PCART). By the time of the actual formation of the Tibet Autonomous Region (TAR) in 1965, the region was fully under the direct control of Beijing. 'Autonomy' as a policy was carried forth only to the uprising of 1959. Social reforms had been consciously delayed in Tibet by Mao in order to help ingratiate China within traditional Tibetan society, using the Dalai Lama, the Panchen Lama and other elites as agents. The flight of the Dalai Lama in 1959 naturally signalled an end to that policy.

Despite an international show of studious indifference, the Tibetan uprising of 1959 was Communist China's first major setback. Communist allies had their eyes trained on the handling of this affair, and were critical of China not enforcing Marxist-Leninist principles of nationality among minorities. Self-determination had been a founding principle of the USSR, the union being a 'voluntary' association of various nationalities.

In an attempt to show control, the PCART met in Lhasa in early April 1959. The Panchen Rinpoche arrived from Tashilhumpo and pledged his support to the Chinese Communist Party. He was made acting chairman of the PCART. Ngapo was made vice-chairman. With the traditional hierarchy largely in exile, China made the decision to convert the masses into supporting their regime rather than simply relying on the traditional elites. Tibetan society was divided into those who participated in the revolt and those who abstained. The former were thrown into 'struggle sessions' (*'Thab 'dzing*) or prison; others were rewarded with positions. The lack of traditional leadership meant that Chinese forces could do much as they pleased. Prison labourers were sent to work at a hydroelectric dam or the borax works.[12]

The Great Leap Forward had been launched by Mao in an attempt to industrialize China, but the reforms for Tibet were to proceed slowly until the masses accepted that Tibet was part of the 'motherland'. Nevertheless, by June 1959 China was confident enough to announce the beginning of radical change. The flight of the Dalai Lama had ended adherence of the ideals of the Seventeenth Point Agreement from both sides.

For many Tibetans, the political reform of the masses was their first interaction with the Chinese. And it did not go well; many Tibetans were unjustly accused of taking part in the uprising, which was being described as the highest treason in trying to 'separate Tibet from the Motherland'. This was incomprehensible to many Tibetans, who never had looked upon China as a motherland.

The radical changes to traditional Tibetan land tenure would be the basis upon which the Chinese lost Tibet. While the seizure and redistribution of aristocratic estates was significant, as a class the secular nobility had been in decline for centuries. Throughout the 1950s their position was further eroded with the elimination of the Dalai Lama's traditional government. And in the years following the invasion, many of the old noble families escaped into exile, taking their gold and jewels with them. But it was the dismantling of the monastic system that was the greatest threat to Tibetan culture and identity. For 1,500 years Tibetan monasticism had been the foundation upon which the identity of the nation had been built. Tibet, as a land that justified itself as a place where the dharma flourished, was being told it could not continue. Monks and nuns were told to disband their estate and fend for themselves, as the lands were to be given to the peasants.

The Chinese Communists, like good Marxists everywhere, felt that religion, as a non-productive aspect of the social superstructure, merely justified the exploitation of the masses. Mao felt that the thousands of Tibetan monasteries had been a drag on the development of the region. He also felt that the common people, freed from centuries of this passive sort of exploitation, would revel in the change. He seriously miscalculated Tibetan motivation, the love of their traditional culture, and the depth to which Tibetan national identity is formulated on the responsibility of all Tibetans to provide for the abode of the Bodhidharma in their land.

The great miscalculation of China's leaders was based in a fundamental misunderstanding of Tibet's traditional relationship to China. So entrenched was the Confucian perspective that all revolved around the Central Kingdom that it was second nature to see Tibet as part of the Motherland. It was impossible to believe that there was a native nationalism that was not based in imperialistic coercion or selfish manipulation by local elites. The Chinese were dumbfounded that the Tibetan masses did not have a patriotic sentiment towards China, and were not united in overthrowing the landowning monastic and lay aristocracy. Unlike in China, where both the republican and Communist revolutions were born and sustained through deep-seated resentment towards the old ruling class, especially the 'foreign' Manchus, no such situation existed in Tibet. Unlike the popular Nationalist and grass-roots Communist revolutions in China, Tibet was invaded and annexed, its people never asked.

With a population largely illiterate and unsympathetic to their Chinese 'liberators', a priority in the administration of Tibet was to create a native cadre who could sustain the reform process. Selected Tibetans were taught and trained to serve in various lower levels in the local government. Many were taught the Chinese perspective that Tibet was historically a part of China.

With the Dalai Lama absent, the Panchen Rinpoche and his court in Shigatse sensed opportunity. The old animosity between Ü and Tsang was still evident. Shigatse had not taken part in the 1959 uprising, so it was expected that the Panchen's court would be treated most favourably in the new Tibet. This was not to be. The Tenth Panchen *tulku*, a Chinese creation, had been used by Mao primarily as a counterweight to the Dalai Lama to divide and rule Tibet. Once the Dalai Lama was out of the way, the political importance of the Panchen could be dramatically reduced.

Still the Panchen had symbolic value as a religious figure, especially since nearly all the other high *tulku*s had fled into exile. In his continuing capacity as the acting chair of PCART, the Panchen conscientiously toured Tibet and made a lengthy assessment of the conditions he found. Having been indulged all his young life by the supreme leaders of China, the Panchen felt emboldened to write a scathing, seventy-thousand-character report to the Communist leadership.[13] It was given directly to Zhou Enlai. The report criticized the handling of the post-uprising period, when many innocent people were arrested. The paper denounced the dissolution of monasteries and forcing monks to do manual labour. The Panchen insulted the cohort of sycophants who surrounded the party leaders, people who had shielded Mao and Zhou from the truth. In general, the report claimed that thus far the wished-for reforms in Tibet had been an utter failure. At a time when most young men his age are asking to borrow the family car, the Panchen Rinpoche was telling Mao Zedong how to run Tibet. Naturally, it did not prove acceptable to the Communist leadership. Eventually, the Panchen would be moved out of his lofty position, made to endure 'struggle sessions' (a form of public humiliation and torture that was used by the Communist Party in the Mao era),[14] and imprisoned for much of his adult life. Upon his 'reformation', he married a Chinese woman and had a child, now touted as the 'Yabshi' Pan Rinchinwangmo by post-reform propagandists.

Mao himself was going through a tough storm of protest from his external allies. The Soviet bloc had been upset at the Chinese minorities policy, which to them did not fit the ideals of the Marxist-Leninist system of self-determination. The Communists, of course, inherited much of their nationalistic fever from the Kuomingtang, who felt that a paternal, Han-based nation state was ideal for China. For the Soviets, clearly the Tibetan uprising had shown the failure of China's minorities policy. At home, the revolutionary fervour of the late 1940s was fading, and cadres were increasingly accused of living well off the masses; corruption was on the rise. And Mao's big idea, the Great Leap Forward, had been such a dismal failure that it called into question his continued leadership. Liu Shaoqi had become party chairman after 1959, and Deng Xiaoping was critical of Mao's economic policy. Something radical had

Statues destroyed at Tholing monastery, which was built in 996 by the second king of the Guge Kingdom.

Buddha statues being burned during the Cultural Revolution.

to be done to save the momentum of the revolution and purge Mao of his enemies.

In 1966 Mao launched the nationwide ideological street theatre known as the Great Proletariat Cultural Revolution. It was aimed at rooting out 'reactionary' forces that were mostly based in old ways of thinking over 3,000 years of Chinese and Tibetan history. Mao proclaimed that cadres and others who had gotten rich by property redistribution were threatening to lead China back into capitalism, and they needed to be forced back on the socialist path. To achieve this radical reform, Mao was turned into a god; his writings became dogma to be memorized and chanted. The younger generation, those born after the Second World War, were especially in need of experiencing revolutionary fervour. Gangs of youths were taught to disrespect everything old, from their parents to the thousand-year-old temples down the street.

The Cultural Revolution ignited the masses in an unstoppable chain reaction of violence and thoughtlessness throughout China. The Forbidden City itself was saved only when Zhou called out the army. The Red Guards, as they were called, were particularly vicious towards Tibet, which they saw as particularly backward, superstitious and

Jokhang Temple, 2014.
Photograph of Red Guards and secondary-school children in front of Jokhang
Temple, August 1966, with a portrait of Mao Zedong and a banner that reads:
'Completely destroy the old world! We shall be the master of the new world.'

subversive. While Mao disappeared in a cloud of grey serge and tobacco smoke, Zhou Enlai did his best to prevent the excesses of ravages against China's ancient cultural heritage. Mao's wife Jiang Qing caused widespread chaos in the party structure during her leadership of the Red Guards.

In Tibet General Xhang Guohua helped create a Tibetan Red Guard, partly to keep himself in power. Among the 'Four Olds' that were the target of the frenzy,[15] Tibet's religious base was foremost. All religious objects and practices were banned; monks and nuns were secularized, and photographs of the Dalai and Panchen Lamas were banned.

In the crosshairs of the Red Guards were the Norbulingka, which was largely destroyed, and the Jokhang Temple, which was turned into a pigsty and its ancient statue of Shakyamuni Buddha destroyed. In Shigatse, the townspeople were forced to tear down, brick by brick, the five-hundred-year-old *dzong*, the palace of the ancient kings of Tsang. Reminiscent of the attack on the royal tombs of Saint-Denis in Paris during the French Revolution, the tombs of the Panchen Lamas at Tashilhumpo were destroyed. Ganden monastery, severely damaged in the 1959 uprising, was completely destroyed during the Cultural Revolution. Among other blasphemies, Bomi Rinpoche was forced to

The reconstructed Shigatse *dzong*, 2014.

Ruins of Ganden monastery, 1985.
Ruins of Drepung monastery, 2006.

Burial chorten of the Tenth Panchen Lama at Tashilhumpoo monastery.

carry the mummified body of Tsongkhapa from its stupa to a bonfire.[16] Throughout Tibet thousands of monasteries were razed, their precious statues cut up and shipped off for scrap. Under threat of death, monks and nuns were forced to publicly fornicate, and sacred texts were used for toilet material or to line shoes. Children were made to ridicule or kill their parents. Even Ngapo was subject to a 'struggle session'. Ever the moderating force in the madness, Zhou Enlai is credited with saving the Potala itself, as well as the loyal Ngapo.

By 1968 Mao had achieved his objective to destroy Liu Shaoqi. He then ordered the Red Guards to cease fire. In Tibet the Red Guards were formed into Revolutionary Committees that replaced the local government they had eliminated.[17] In 1976 Mao and Zhou died, and Jiang Qing was arrested and later committed suicide. The terror of the Cultural Revolution came to an end.

Tibetan Bodhidharma in the West

As a universalistic religion, Buddhism has been remarkably resistant to nationalistic impulses. Quite the opposite, Buddhism has been the nexus of multi-ethnic unification since the times of Aśoka, and was a powerful force in the coalescing of the Mongol and Manchu empires. Through Tibetan exiles, it has firmly established itself in the West, but has not markedly furthered Tibetan nationalism.

'Entrepreneurial Buddhism' is a mode established by charismatic lamas who, lacking traditional monastic estates, have had to attract students and resources from the sheer popularity of their enthusiastic teachings. It is a subset of Buddhist Modernism that has successfully adapted Buddhist practices to a non-monastic following, largely in the West.[18]

Most of the important lineage holders from all four major schools of Tibetan Buddhism and Bon have escaped from occupied Tibet, and most have successfully re-established their institutions in exile. Many have been adept at building their establishments without the direct support of the exiled Ganden Phodrang of the Dalai Lama.

The number of arriving high lamas and Western academic programmes grew throughout the 1960s and '70s, and many 'secular' lineages of Tibetology were started. The Dalai Lama's own monastery, Namgyal, was re-established at Dharamsala, together with a central cathedral, the Tsulakhang, as it had been in Lhasa. Ganden monastery was inaugurated at Mundgod, Karnataka, under the leadership of the Trichen Rinpoche, technical head of the Gelug. Sera Je College, alma mater to Reting Rinpoche and many other famous lamas, was re-established at Bylakuppe, and Drepung Loseling also in Karnataka. These settlements have far more land than in the mountainous regions in north India like Dharamsala.

Generally, the re-establishment of Buddhist centres in the West has tended to create small dharma communities. Rented houses rather than vast monastic estates are the rule. Often these organizations consist of the teacher, perhaps accompanied by a novice or two, a secular house manager, perhaps a board of directors, and a congregation of lay devotees who may spend several hours a month cleaning, painting, cooking and writing cheques for the support of the centre. Such groups frequently invite prominent lamas and rare lineage holders to give teachings and empowerments. Centres hold frequent retreats, and often instruct lay practitioners in the basic practices, which may or may not lead to advanced practice.

Importantly, nearly all these Western centres operate independently of the Ganden Phodrang in Dharamsala. This is not an innovation due to exile in the West; rather it is typical of the centripetal nature of the Tibetan monastic system. In general, Tibetan monasteries were self-supporting and autonomous from the central government. Revenue flowed from the monastic estates to the abbot or *tulku* who made most of the decisions. The central government in Lhasa would then tax these monasteries to provide for the state apparatus, but it was difficult to enforce central authority upon monasteries, even Gelug ones. Similarly, dharma centres in the West do not directly support the administration of the Dalai Lama in Dharamsala; if they do, it is usually through an informal gift exchange or hosting of important personages from the exiled government. It is evident in the general lack of support by Western dharma centres towards Tibetan nationalism.

One of the early pioneers in the establishment of Tibetan Buddhism in the West was Geshe Ngawang Wangyal, a disciple of Agvan Dorjiev, the confidant of the Thirteenth Dalai Lama. Wangyal, like Dorjiev, was a Kalmyk Mongol. Having studied in Lhasa, Wangyal moved to Beijing in the 1930s. He also lived in India for a time, becoming associated with the British political agent Sir Charles Bell. Wangyal returned to Lhasa to finish his studies, earning the geshe degree. Very soon after China invaded Tibet, Geshe Wangyal escaped. In 1955 he found his way to the United States as lama to a community of Kalmyks settled in New Jersey. In 1958 the first Tibetan monastery was established in the USA, Labsum Shedrub Ling. A popular teacher, Geshe Wangyal taught many early Western students Buddhism, and taught many refugee lamas English and how to teach Tibetan Buddhism to Americans. He was given a teaching position at Columbia University. Geshe Wangyal could be considered the 'root guru' of several lineages of academic Tibetologists, having instructed 'hipsters' like Robert Thurman, Jeffrey Hopkins and Anne Klein. Geshe Wangyal was also the founder of the American Institute of Buddhist Studies.

The late 1960s saw the flowering of the counterculture in the West, with hippies experimenting with everything from drugs and communal living to Eastern religions. Tibetan lamas fleeing Chinese-occupied Tibet found an instant home in Western Europe and the United States. Beat philosophers Timothy Leary, Allen Ginsberg and Richard Alpert (Baba Ram Das) were philosophical descendants of Helena Blavatsky and Alexandra David-Neel. Incense, colourful mandala posters, meditation and tantric sex were all elements of Indo-Tibetan traditions that found their way into the flats of Haight-Ashbury in San Francisco and the college dorm rooms of a disaffected generation.

Chogyam Trungpa was one of the first lamas to introduce the esoteric Vajrayāna practices to lay students in the West. For this he received a certain amount of criticism, tantra being a higher practice that was largely the privilege and specialty of the monastic *sangha*. Chogyam founded Naropa University in Boulder, Colorado, and hired professors such as Ginsberg to teach there. Despite the lama's heavy drinking and general incontinence, he was able to establish over a hundred dharma centres worldwide.

THE COUNTERCULTURE'S INTRODUCTION to Tibetan Buddhism in the 1960s was sustained through the next generation of Western seekers, the New Age movement. Like the hippies before them, New Age was drawn to the Theosophists of the late nineteenth and early twentieth centuries and to the Vendanta movement in the West. To this were added interests in neo-pagan Wikka, Native American shamanism and other exotica. Like Buddhist Modernism, New Age is characterized by an individualistic approach to religion and a general abhorrence of dogma and rigid discipline.

These pioneering lamas, Western scholars and adventurers helped to establish, for the first time, a broad base of knowledge about Tibetan culture outside of Tibet. So many knowledge holders left Tibet in the 1950s and '60s that Tibetan Buddhist culture now exists transnationally.

The political shift in India and the success of the dharma centres abroad gave encouragement to the Dalai Lama that the West was interested in Tibet. And because of the combined religious and political nature of his position, he could travel as a relatively innocuous religious leader and still convey a subtle political message in those countries uneasy about their relationship with China. However, such interest has not crystallized as overwhelming political support for Tibetan self-determination.

The Dalai Lama's popularity has made him perhaps the most beloved 'Chinese' leader in history, rendering the chieftains of the Communist Party green with envy. But the Buddhist universalism that the Dalai Lama promotes does not encourage Tibetan nationalism. It has emptied the Ganden Phodrang of much of its *raison d'état*.

Reform in China's Tibet

While the world was beginning to embrace Tibetan Buddhism, Mao Zedong and Zhou Enlai both died in 1976. Qiang Jing and the rest of the 'Gang of Four' were quickly arrested for the crimes of the Cultural Revolution, and Hua Gufeng, Mao's chosen successor, was shunted aside. The pragmatist Deng Xiaoping emerged as the new leader, supported by liberal Hu Yaobang as party secretary. A rapprochement with the Dalai Lama was attempted; many political prisoners, including the Panchen Lama, were released. Gyalo Dhondup, brother of the Dalai Lama, was invited to Beijing to discuss Tibet with Deng Xiaoping. With Gyalo as go-between, the Dalai Lama asked to send fact-finding missions to Tibet to ascertain the situation prior to any visit by himself to Beijing. This was accepted by Deng, who suggested that anything was negotiable except independence.[19]

The Dalai Lama responded to Deng's invitation by sending three fact-finding missions to Tibet. All involved family members and close political aides. China had begun to believe their own propaganda that reforms in Tibet had pulled the region out of backwardness and that there was a strong sentiment of appreciation by the people and a growing pride in the Motherland. They were shocked to discover the first group being received jubilantly in Qinghai (formerly Tibetan Amdo). Ren Rong, the party secretary in Tibet, on being questioned whether the group should continue to Lhasa, assured central leadership that Lhasans were much more ideologically developed and there would be no problems. The local government was so ill-informed about the emotive nature of the people that they organized neighbourhood sessions to instruct the masses not to throw stones or spit at the Dalai Lama's delegates. The Tibetan people listened, then did the opposite, mobbing the delegation for a glimpse of the Dalai Lama's brother and officials, crying, presenting *khata*, prostrating, holding flowers and incense. Some dared to shout the dreaded 'Tibetan independence!' (*Bod rang btsan*). Each of the delegations was met with an adulation born of desperation. The Chinese leadership was taken totally by surprise. The policy of trying to incorporate Tibet within the ideology of the Chinese Motherland was a total failure, as the policy of appeasement between 1950 and 1959 had been for the Tibetan government.

The fact-finding missions to Tibet strongly buoyed up the moral and political standing of the Ganden Phodrang in Dharamsala. The outpourings of affection and tears shown by the people of Tibet were as a referendum on the future of that land. Clearly, the hearts and mind of the nation were still held by the Dalai Lama, regardless of his present exile. It was a crisis for the leadership, and resulted in many high-level investigations and meetings. In 1980 Party Secretary Hu and Vice-Premier Wan Li made their own fact-finding visit to Tibet. They were appalled at the conditions they found. Hu announced a six-point plan to overcome some of the biggest abuses that the thirty years of occupation had fostered. First, a more genuine autonomy was called for. Second, since Tibet was far behind economically compared with the rest of China, tax relief was in order. Third, economic reforms should be carried out that were compatible with traditional Tibetan practices. The fifth point advanced the idea that as long as socialist progress was made, Tibetan traditional culture, including religion and language, should be cultivated. Finally, Tibet cadres should form a two-thirds majority in the local government.[20] By the late 1980s Tibetans living in exile were even allowed to visit their homeland without the threat of refoulement.

Hu's rollback from Mao's hard-line policy of assimilation was surprisingly similar to Nixon's contemporaneous policy shift towards Native Americans. After centuries of forced assimilation on reservations, U.S. policy shifted towards pluralistic ideals, and with it the notion of federally recognized 'internal sovereignty' for Native Americans. Having been severely criticized by the Soviet Union and most of the rest of the world for China's minority policy, Hu became dedicated to reform. However, unlike the changing policy of the United States, there would be no internal sovereignty for Tibet – it would continue to be administered by the central government.

Monasteries were rebuilt, and in many cases temples were restored so carefully that the scars of the uprising and the Cultural Revolution were erased. The sacred statue of the Jowo in the Jokhang in Lhasa miraculously reappeared. The artillery holes and shattered walls of the Potala and Norbulingka were plastered over and repainted. Drepung, Sera, Nechung, Sakya, Yarlung castle and even Ganden monastery were slowly rebuilt. The Panchen Lama was allowed to sweep up the remains of the predecessors and house them in a new stupa at Tashilhumpo. It was all just in time for the opening of Tibet, for the first time, to foreign tourism.

State-supported restoration of minority architectural heritage is almost always a trope demonstrating the largesse of the conquering culture.[21] The restored Potala, for example, is offered today to tourists as an example of the close cooperation of the Chinese and Tibetan peoples. In fact, there is a new, improved replica on the other side of town.[22] More often than not, however, restoration in Tibet has proceeded to reconstruct temples, monasteries and monuments as if they never had been touched, or even hyper-real, better than the originals. While a testament to excellent restoration, one nevertheless ponders the political implications of erasing the mistakes and imperfections of the past, each shattered brick representing a historic event not necessarily supportive of official Chinese narratives. In the 1980s naive foreign tourists encountered state-supported explanations of Tibet's past, but to China's horror native interpretations of Tibetan history were also emboldened. Views tended to be diametrically opposite, and Tibetans became increasingly reassured that there was broad support for them abroad.[23]

Clare Harris has confronted the problem of authority and voice in the curation of Tibetan art. She examines how the British and Chinese interpretation of Tibetan material culture has conveniently divorced itself from the people who created it.[24] Museum collecting, until the post-colonial era, was a legitimate way by which an imperial power could appropriate booty and exhibit it as a trophy of conquest. Harris argues that this attitude has been particularly pernicious towards the people of Tibet, observing that nowadays more portable objects of traditional Tibetan material culture exist outside the country than within. This 'ownership' of Tibetan culture has been articulated by both Western agency since the early twentieth century and China since 1950. Rather than being a reflection of national genius, the commodification of

Tibetan art in both cases has become a reference for exotic Otherness. This was seen in particular in the West during the countercultural movement of the 1960s and the New Age revalidations a generation later. Tibetan art is seen in China either as a symbol of the primitiveness of pre-liberation Tibet, or as colourful souvenirs in which Chinese tourists can wallow as an aspect of holiday play. Chinese tourists dressing up in Khampa fur hats and posing before the Potala are identical to American boys and girls 'playing Indian' in their backyard. Appropriation of a vanquished people's culture is the choice game of the victors.

Throughout the 1980s, a dogged Dalai Lama continued to negotiate with Chinese officials, taking Deng's words seriously that the only matter not subject to negotiation was independence. However, Hu had also made it clear that Tibet was not to be governed as before 1959: that is, by the theocratic government of the Ganden Phodrang headed by the Dalai Lama. A 'one country, two systems' policy used in Hong Kong was not applicable to Tibet.

The Dalai Lama was in a dilemma. He could not appear to negotiate away the concept of Tibetan independence without losing many supporters in exile. He could not move away from the goal of restoring a 'Greater Tibet', the old parts of Amdo and Kham that had been annexed by China before the Communists came to power, as he had made heroic efforts to accommodate Amdowa and Khampa personnel in his own exile government. He himself was an Amdowa from Qinghai. Nor could he simply walk away from the negotiations when so much was at stake for the material benefit of Tibetans in the homeland. On the other hand, international support for the Dalai Lama as a peacemaker might evaporate if he seemed to take a hard line.

A second negotiating team arrived in Beijing in 1984. The Dalai Lama's representatives called for a Greater Tibet with complete autonomy.[25] On this occasion, it appears that Dharamsala overplayed their moral leverage. China, of course, refused to consider the idea. The planned tour of the Dalai Lama to China was shelved.

With the negotiations accomplishing nothing by the mid-1980s, Beijing decided to seduce the masses in Tibet by greatly increasing their material well-being. Religious institutions would be supported, educational and medical facilities would be built, roads, airports and communications would be greatly improved. Tibetans would then look to Beijing as the source of all their lifestyle improvements. But to many Tibetans, it was all so much bread and circuses.

By the 1980s, while the Dalai Lama was met with immutability from Beijing, he had found broad support in the West, so Dharamsala thought. Since so many of the foreign policies of Western nations had shown themselves hobbled by treaty obligations and new overtures of rapprochement with Communist China, the Ganden Phodrang struck at the soft underbelly of these democracies, their legislative bodies. Here the Dalai Lama could plead for sympathy and receive acknowledgement for the suffering of his subjects. With parliaments, he could continue to receive international media attention without being blocked by foreign ministries. Through the influence of such powerful u.s. senators as Daniel Inouye, the Dalai Lama was finally issued an American visa.[26] The Ganden Phodrang developed a focused policy for wooing both the United States and the European Union through their acknowledgement of human rights abuses in Tibet. The plan was remarkably successful. In June 1987 the House of Representatives passed a bill condemning China's human rights abuses in Tibet. This was followed by a major speech by the Dalai Lama before the u.s. Congressional Human Rights Caucus.

On these occasions, Tenzin Gyatso stated without equivocation that Tibet had been an independent country before the 1950 invasion, and was now a country under an illegal occupation by China. By these powerful speeches, he cleared the air of generations of misunderstanding about the status of Tibet, the smoke and mirrors set up by the British in their dealings with the country. Not that the Dalai Lama felt that it would change anything, but he wanted to go on record to state the baseline from which any negotiations with China would be established. On 6 October 1987, the Senate passed a bill corresponding to the earlier House initiative.[27] This was followed by an Act signed by President Reagan that denounced human rights abuses in Tibet. While the toothless denunciation was merely a slap on the wrist for Beijing, it was interpreted as a major political victory for the exile community and undoubtedly among the Tibetans in the homeland and raised unreasonable expectations.

Throughout the spring and summer of 1987, the streets of Lhasa were buzzing with anticipation that the Dalai Lama's new initiative was bearing fruit; the West did seem to care about political Tibet after apparent years of abandonment and betrayal by Britain, India and the United

Tibetans, including Buddhist monks, throw stones and demonstrate outside the public security office early in October 1987, Lhasa.

States. The Dalai Lama had shown true international leadership. The streets of Lhasa, and to some extent Shigatse and Gyantse, were a heady mix of visiting Tibetan refugees, who carried the latest word from friends and family in exile; Western Tibetologists, many like myself who had never been to Tibet before; dharma centre managers and lamas; tourists, who represented an interested and devoted outside world; anxious residents; and an army of foreign journalists. In that spring and summer, signs of nationalism began to sprout: small portraits of the Dalai Lama appeared everywhere. Recorded speeches given by the Dalai Lama were circulated, often disguised in pop music cassettes. Occasionally, the forbidden Tibetan national flag would be unfurled. Each small act of defiance towards Chinese officialdom was seen as a micro-victory in the war for the heart and soul of Tibet. Each act encouraged others in a chain reaction that was reaching critical mass. Local expectations

Tibetan monk Jampa Tenzin and protesters in Lhasa, 1987, photograph by John Ackerly. The photo became the emblem of the Free Tibet movement, and John Ackerly became an international Tibet advocate and eventually president of the International Campaign for Tibet (1999 to 2009).

were high; by the end of the summer 1987 it was clear that a massive uprising was fomenting.

Towards the end of September, a small group of Drepung monks decided to circumambulate the Barkor, the pilgrim's path around the central Lhasa cathedral of the Jokhang, shouting nationalistic slogans. Nothing happened. Then they marched down the main boulevard towards the offices of the TAR, where they promptly received the attention of public security forces and were arrested. In response, a larger group of monks took up the banner of protest in support of their imprisoned brethren. They were arrested by the police and beaten. Townsfolk then joined the protest, gathering at police headquarters and demanding that the monks be released. It developed into a full-scale riot as vehicles, shops and even the police headquarters were burned to the ground. The police reacted by shooting into the crowd, killing perhaps two dozen Tibetans and wounding many more. The rebellion was videotaped by journalists, including Americans John Ackerly and Blake Kerr. Elsewhere in the city, a Dharamsala refugee, a popular English-speaking tour guide, was detained by the police and forced to make a televised appeal to the foreigners in Lhasa to leave and not photograph the disturbances.[28] Ackerly and Kerr left Tibet and broke the story to the world.

The magnitude of the rebellion, the level of anger shown, and the reaction of the international media profoundly shocked the Chinese Communist Party, who thought their conciliatory reforms of the decade would build affection of Tibetans for the Motherland. Suddenly they found thousands of angry Tibetans to contend with, and the ire of the world. Beijing placed the blame primarily on outside agents: the Dalai Lama and his supporters. Certainly, the Dalai Lama's success in gaining international sympathy for Tibet through the U.S. Congress had indirectly raised expectations among everyday Tibetans, but he had hardly orchestrated the riots.

Throughout the rest of 1987 there were continual but generally small-scale demonstrations of nationalism in Lhasa. As such, the promotion of 'ethnic sensitivity' in Tibet by the central government came under increasing criticism by hardliners in Beijing. Hu Yaobang was forced to resign, replaced by Zhao Ziyang as party secretary. Beijing nevertheless decided to go ahead with the promotion of 'ethnic culture' in Tibet as the Monlam festival loomed forth in the early part of 1988. Here, thousands of monks would descend upon Lhasa to recite the great unifying prayer written by Tsongkhapa, which traditionally follows immediately after the New Year's festivities. The Panchen Lama was even sent in to help placate the monks prior to the start of the festival. Most of the prisoners arrested the year before were released, and the Panchen announced that Beijing was willing to spend about $500,000 in reparations to the three main Gelug monasteries.[29] But the monks were not convinced or tempted. The abbots, knowing the riotous tradition of the Monlam, recommended that the Great Prayer be held in the individual monasteries, rather than convene in mass in Lhasa. Party officials, not wishing to lose face with admitting they were not in control, insisted that the festival convene as planned in the city.

The Monlam proceeded in an orderly fashion until the very last day. One monk shouted at the officials in the grandstand to release a certain monk still being held. He was told to be silent. This was followed by others chanting for Tibetan independence. The streets of Lhasa erupted into another general rebellion, followed by the inevitable Chinese clampdown, all recorded by the world's media.

The cause of the rebellions in 1987–8, the worst since 1959, is simple: multiple generations of Tibetans were now harbouring a deep-seated resentment for the loss of their country to a foreign invader; they had lost their all-encompassing leader to exile; they had witnessed endless blasphemies enacted towards their religion in the name of socialist progress. Now the Tibetans saw that their Dalai Lama seemed to be making real progress with engaging the support of the world's superpower, the United States. Tibetans began fighting back.

A particularly sensitive issue for both Dharamsala and the people of Tibet was a perception that China was trying to swamp Tibet with Han Chinese settlers. With a population of less than six million confronting over a billion Chinese, it seemed that Chinese migration was the 'final solution' to the perceived genocide of the Tibetan people. Often quoted by Ganden Phodrang officials in exile was the example of Manchuria, where even despite anti-miscegenation laws, the local Manchus were eventually overwhelmed by Han settlers, with the resulting disappearance of Manchu language and identity.[30] Official Chinese histories are replete with the political dynamic of using assimilation as a tactic to quell the rebellious frontier regions. Goldstein, however, argues that Han Chinese were brought to the Tibetan cities largely because they needed educated, highly skilled workers to support all the infrastructural projects launched to ultimately boost the standard of living in Tibet.[31] Han received the good jobs, and of course this added to the resentment. The assault seems everywhere: urban planning to house all the new workers and the military-police system has ploughed under much of the ancient city of Lhasa, replacing centuries-old Tibetan buildings with cinderblock and concrete utilitarian edifices.

The year 1989 started ominously. The Panchen Lama returned to Tashilhumpo to reinter the remains of his predecessors. The grand event seemed to demonstrate that the reforms being initiated by Hu Yaobang were sincere, Tibet's history and religion were being respected. The party leader personally attended the ceremony, and the Panchen promptly died of a heart attack. China had lost a great ally in its attempted social- ist transformation of Tibet. It was not a good sign to welcome the new year: a year that saw the collapse of Communism throughout the world and China in revolt.

The Dalai Lama had indeed transformed the moral high road into political capital. In April Beijing made a small concession that offered the Dalai Lama the option of domicile in Tibet if he abandoned the demand for independence. Tenzin Gyatso responded with another important speech, given at a meeting of the European Parliament at Strasbourg on 15 June 1988. The proposal included the following terms:

1 A Greater Tibet would exercise genuine autonomy within a People's Republic of China.
2 China could be responsible for Tibet's foreign affairs. However, in non-political activities, Tibet would create its own depart- ment of foreign affairs.
3 The government of Tibet would be chosen democratically.
4 Tibet would follow the UN's Universal Declaration of Human Rights.
5 Tibet would constitute a zone of peace.

The plan was nothing new to the Chinese, as these points had been suggested by the Dalai Lama's representatives in secret talks in 1984. Ever consistent, the political arrangement of genuine autonomy under a loose suzerainty with China is the Simla Convention of 1914 all over again. However, it was rather shocking for the West and for many of the Dalai Lama's own people that Tenzin Gyatso could disassociate himself from the cherished goal of so many. Many felt then, as they do now, that the Dalai Lama overplayed his cards. Giving up the right to independ- ence seemed to be an appeasement to China and an acceptance of the occupation.

However, the Strasbourg proposal demonstrated to the outside world how much the Dalai Lama was ready to offer in his negotiations with the Chinese. It lofted the ball directly into Beijing's court, with everyone remembering Deng Xiaoping's message that everything was negotiable except independence. But Beijing found it could not accept the other points of the deal without destabilizing the party's grip on the monopoly of power throughout China. The UN Universal Declaration of Human Rights mentioned by the Dalai Lama also provides for self-determination, where each individual is 'entitled to a social and international order in which the rights and freedoms set forth in that Declaration can be fully realized'.[32] Many in China felt this was a veiled claim for independence. It had to refuse. Six months later another revolt erupted in Lhasa, followed by another on 5 March 1989. Martial law was declared, a public relations nightmare for the Communist Party.

In April the great reformer Hu Yaobang died. The event caused widespread demonstrations by students who supported his liberalizing policies. The protests in Beijing and many other cities escalated, discrediting moderates like Zhao Ziyang and bringing hardliners into the foreground. Finally, 300,000 troops were called out to maintain control under martial law in Beijing. The student uprising focused on the symbolic centre of China, Tiananmen Square. Between 3 and 4 June, the army cracked down and ended the uprising. It is estimated that up to 3,000 people were killed. As a result, Zhao was replaced with Jiang Zemin as party secretary, and reforms throughout China were halted.

The year 1989 would develop as the worst for Communism in history. Poland began by leaving the Warsaw Pact under the banner of Solidarity. Soviet President Gorbachev refused to intervene. The granite monolith known as the Soviet Union then began to fall apart in a flurry of local nationalisms; Yugoslavia also broke into its constituent states.

China's intransigence fed right into the Dalai Lama's rising star in international affairs. In October 1989 the Nobel Committee in Oslo announced that he had been awarded the Nobel Peace Prize. Tibetans were ecstatic around the world – it demonstrated that the outside world was finally getting the message about Tibet. A gift from the United States also appeared in late 1989. Representative Barney Frank introduced legislation to Congress to provide 1,000 residence visas to 'displaced Tibetans'. The bill was passed as the Immigration Act of 1990. The U.S. Tibet Resettlement Committee was established privately to help Tibetans find homes, jobs and general relocation services in over a dozen communities around the country. By allowing Tibetan refugees to settle in the United States and to work, it greatly increased the visibility of the Tibetan people to everyday citizens of the world's remaining superpower.

It too had a buoyant effect upon Tibetan nationalism within and without the homeland.

Seeing its once-great ally, the Soviet Union, break into its constituent republics was horrifying to China. It was interpreted as a mark of weakness in the reforms initiated by Gorbachev. Tibetan nationalism seemed to be at its all-time height, and Xinjiang and other outlying regions were beginning to be restive as well. China's approach was to clamp down hard on any liberalizing trend: Mao's soft approach on accommodating the Dalai Lama and the Ganden Phodrang led to the uprising of 1959; Hu's liberal 'ethnic' reforms in Tibet led to the revolts of 1987–8. Since these policies were failures, only firm, hardline socialist rule could restore stability in Tibet and the entire country.

China abandons the Dalai Lama

For its part during negotiations, China was content to treat the Dalai Lama like an ordinary citizen, an individual. He would be pensioned off and would have to live in Beijing or someplace outside of the TAR. He would have to recognize himself as a citizen of the People's Republic of China, and would have no part in the local government of Tibet, however it was reconstituted. China made it clear they would no longer support the institution of the Dalai Lamas, but only the man of the current incarnation. China had experience in 'rehabilitating' former rulers: notably with Xuantong (Puyi), their last emperor who ended his days as a librarian in Beijing. The Dalai Lama, however, continued to insist that he was concerned with the six million Tibetans inside the TAR, in Greater Tibet and in exile.

Despite the Dalai Lama's apparent moves to compromise with China, the leadership was convinced that his talk of a 'Greater Tibet' and 'genuine autonomy' was a veiled call for independence. The logic of these fears is based on the understanding, although hardly stated, that the people of Tibet, if given democracy and the right of self-determination, would opt out of China. Perhaps this was an implicit acknowledgement that the 1950 'liberation' of Tibet by the People's Liberation Army was indeed an occupation. The people had never asked to be liberated. Refulgent nationalism was evidently clear in the break-up of the Soviet Union. Continuing to negotiate with the Dalai Lama, clearly the world symbol of Tibetan independence, would be further destabilizing. Beijing decided to rule Tibet without him. Subsequently, photographs bearing the image of the Dalai Lama were banned. The Tibetan language liberalization policy of previous years was reversed. Monasteries came under increased regulations.

The first major opportunity to attempt to destroy the lingering authority of the Dalai Lama was to circumvent his traditional right to discern the reincarnation of the Panchen Lama. Centuries ago, the Qianlong emperor rightly recognized that one of the major sources of destabilization in theocratic Tibet was the reliance upon abbots and *tulkus* to determine the successor of a high incarnate lama. Although the spiritual qualifications of these discoverers were paramount, the system was naturally subject to political machinations. Young *tulkus* were often conveniently found in families and regions prefigured to be supportive of the institution, be it a small monastery or the Ganden Phodrang itself. Instead, the emperor developed a blind lottery of several promising candidates whose names would be thrown in a golden urn. The successful boy would be drawn, all supervised by the Manchu *ambasa*. Not only did this provide a mechanism for controlling the selection from Beijing, it diffused any favouritism or partisan influence while maintaining a degree of supernatural agency. The Manchu emperor had, of course, some credibility as a Buddhist leader in his own right, and so final authority for the selection of the highest *tulkus* was often credited by Chinese sources to the throne, especially during the Qianlong period and beyond. In reality, the lamas discerned candidates through spiritual means.

Twenty-first-century Tibet, like eleventh-century Tibet, is wracked by opposing forces of centralization and decentralization, sectarianism and ecclesiasticism. The Ganden Phodrang was designed to combine the authority of one of the highest religious lineages with the secular rule of the old kings to provide a universal government for all Tibet. Each of the religious lineages, however, derived its authority from its founding teacher, and passed its authority down through an unbroken chain of sacerdotal reincarnations, each in theory possessing the entire teachings of the founder. Most of these high lineages revert ultimately to the Buddha and the bodhisattvas. But like the papacy, the Tibetan theocracy has no patience for secular powers interfering with its spiritual authority.

The relational aspect of the teacher–student dyad seems to take precedence in operation over the theoretical hierarchy of the beings in the Buddhist pantheon. This is, of course, the primary component of the priest–patron relationship and why the patron or student cannot be superior to the teacher in the matter of religious authority (and the heart of the contention between modern China and the Ganden Phodrang). While most of this is designed to ensure the purity of teaching transmissions between teacher and student, the system becomes strained when the student is given secular power. Secular rulers need to make alliances with many groups of people, including their patrons, and this is naturally beyond the control of any particular teacher and lineage holder. This asymmetry is the core of the tendency for Tibet to resist centralization and place sectarian interests above national ones.

The atheistic Communist Party, believing itself to be the inheritor of the religious rights of the imperial throne as well, tried to establish precedence by recognizing Ogyen Trinley Dorje as the Seventeenth Karmapa in 1992. However, the party wished to roll out the golden urn for the selection of the next Panchen Lama. Beijing did not want to ignore the Dalai Lama, who would probably select his own Panchen if he was left out of the process, but they also did not want him to use the occasion to display his ancient authority either. The Dalai Lama notified the Chinese through their embassy in New Delhi and via brother Gyalo Dhondup that he was interested in participating in the selection. China responded by allowing the head of the search team, Chadrel Rimpoche of Tashilhumpo, to contact the Dalai Lama. The weeks went by and Chadrel and his team assembled a list of promising boys. The lama also suggested to the Dalai Lama that one, Gendun Choskyi Nyima, seemed to have all the signs of being the true reincarnation.

Back at Dharamsala in 1995, the Dalai Lama examined all the evidence and conducted a divination. It too suggested that Gendun was the right choice. Tashilhumpo was delighted that finally the Dalai Lama and the Chinese leadership through Chadrel had agreed on this important discovery. However, Beijing nevertheless asked Chadrel to submit a list of names for selection with the golden urn, and started making plans for an inauguration ceremony. Ignoring the possibility of unity, China continued its Tom-and-Jerry game to attempt to show superior authority. On 14 May 1995 the Dalai Lama pulled the rug out from under them and proclaimed to the world his choice of Gendun Choskyi Nyima. It was a major coup for the Dharamsala government.

The media did not record the exact shade of purple Party Secretary Jiang Zemin turned when he heard the news. The People's Republic of China had desperately groped for legitimacy in deciding Tibet's most sensitive affair. But the Dalai Lama had upstaged the party for its sin of hubris. He had demonstrated that the religious system of Tibet, indeed the Buddhist pontificate, was still very much intact, and he continued to reign over it. The hapless Chadrel was arrested and sent to prison for six years for national security breaches and sedition, accused of telling the Dalai Lama that Beijing had insisted on using the urn despite an agreement that Gendun had been chosen by Tashilhumpo lamas and the Dalai Lama.

Beijing was in a dilemma, but finally decided to disqualify Gendun Choskyi Nyima and select another from the golden urn. A boy named Chokyi Gyalpo appeared and Gendun Choskyi Nyima disappeared, presumably under arrest to prevent his escape into exile. The Dalai Lama immediately denounced Chokyi Gyalpo as a false incarnation, and told the world that the Chinese selection was an act of defilement against Tibetan religion and the people. He made clear that only the Dalai Lama has the authority for these decisions. The Dalai Lama only scored a pyrrhic victory, however, as the world is now lacking a credible Panchen Lama and the boy he chose will probably spend his life in detention. If he had simply been a secular politician, the Dalai Lama could have easily found a suitable bright boy in exile and socialized him to become a Panchen.[33] However, within the religious system itself, the 'selection' is really only a matter of the recognition of the appropriate *tulku*. The choice of where, when and to whom to be reborn is the exclusive prerogative of the previous incarnation by virtue of their spiritual merit. It was Chokyi Gyaltsen's decision to be reborn in the People's Republic of China, and Chadrel and the Dalai Lama discovered this in Gendun.

China, realizing that it had nothing to gain by working with a Dalai Lama it could not trust, has developed two strategies to deal with the Tibetan issue. First, Beijing believes that massive development and investment in Tibet will eventually shift people's loyalties from nationalism to a wish to be more fully integrated with the Motherland. Economic opportunities have fostered the migration of people, mostly Han, from other parts of China to Tibet. As a result, many Tibetans are anxious about becoming a minority in their own land. In recent years, the term 'ethnic Tibetan' has been seen in the world press, which is a sure sign that population transfer is further marginalizing Tibetans in their own homeland. Second, China has developed a tit-for-tat response to any pronouncements made by the Dalai Lama regarding conditions in Tibet, and most of the responses verge on insult. Firmly believing that religion is subordinate to the state, it also does not recognize bishops exclusively chosen by the pope in Rome.

Despite the abuse erupting out of Beijing, the Dalai Lama has stuck to his Strasbourg line, now referred to as the Middle Way approach to reconciliation with China. During his 1997 trip to Taiwan, the Dalai Lama stated that his trip clearly proved that he had abandoned the position of Tibet independence.[34] Many in the exile community feel this conciliatory approach has seen its day, and it is time to reconsider the higher goal of independence. Trying to drive a wedge into the exile community may be a Chinese strategy, however, which further destroys the Dalai Lama's credibility. But it would be hard to imagine that China would homeopathically use Tibetan nationalism to destroy the Dalai Lama's credibility. China is adamant in believing that creating a dominion status for Tibet, and a greater Tibet at that, will create a stem-state situation where nationalism will increase rather than decrease, eventually leading to armed conflict and secession. They need look no further than their fractured neighbour to the northwest, the former Soviet Union.

Shugden controversy

China increased its attacks on the Dalai Lama by promoting an old schism within the Gelugpa leadership. Some Gelug monks had worshipped the spirit Shugden, who in life had been the lama Drakpa Gyaltsen and a losing candidate for the position of Fifth Dalai Lama. The latter became the Third Panchen Lama. Gyaltsen died violently under mysterious circumstances – some blamed the Dalai Lama. The spirit of the lama was believed by some to have reincarnated as a *preta* (T., *yi dags*), an angry ghost, and by others as a powerful protector of the Gelug lineage. He was called Dorje Shugden, or Dolgyal. Pehar, the god behind the state oracle of Nechung, and the Fifth Dalai Lama disliked this spirit who seemed to act maliciously. Shugden was propitiated by many favouring a 'pure' Gelugpa heritage, as opposed to the non-sectarian interests of the Fifth (and Fourteenth) Dalai Lamas. This dissonance perpetuated into the exile of the Dalai Lama, becoming a fundamental problem by 1975. The Dalai Lama responded by declaring Shugden worship anathema. In 1996 he completely banned worshippers of the spirit from attending his own teachings, where a teacher–student relationship had been established. China seized on the controversy and began to fund Shugden followers, therefore demonstrating that the Dalai Lama did not tolerate religious freedom.

Where high-kicking Rockettes normally haunt, the Dalai Lama instead appeared in July 2008. Here at Radio City Music Hall in New York he was picketed by Shugden followers. Outside the hall, about five hundred audience members exchanged insults with about one hundred Shugden adherents in a scene that looked more like the streets of Lhasa during the Reting uprising than Sixth Avenue, New York.[35] Shugden followers filed suit against the Dalai Lama and the Central Tibetan Administration in Indian courts, and lodged protests with Amnesty International for infringement of religious freedom. By 2015 it was shown that China had funded the protests.[36]

Trains and games

On 1 July 2006 a long-term dream of party officials convinced that modernizing Tibet was the correct way of further integrating the region into China was realized. Party Secretary and President Hu Jintao welcomed the first train linking Tibet with China. The International Campaign for Tibet, an organization started by John Ackerly, a former journalist who helped document the 1987 revolts in Lhasa, claims that this measure will greatly increase migration of Chinese into Tibet, further exacerbating the population transfer issue for Tibetans.[37] China believes that the heavy infrastructural investment of the railway will be key in extracting the valuable mineral resources of Tibet.

China's frantic modernization was showcased in the run-up to the 2008 Summer Olympics. The country finally felt it had been accepted as an equal among highly developed countries, an economic giant facing the bright, new twenty-first century. Everything had to be perfect:

the most modern sports complexes, the best high-speed railways to whisk sports fans from around the world to their sparkling new hotels. China's young athletes trained endlessly to haul in the most gold metals.

Meanwhile, the 10 March Uprising day passed in Lhasa in 2008 with upwards of five hundred monks from Drepung demonstrating on the streets for their colleagues to be released from prison. By 14 March it had turned into a huge riot, with Tibetans attacking Chinese-owned businesses. Shops, vehicles and other property were burnt to the ground and people were killed. Police eventually fought the crowds back. It was the largest uprising since the 1959 event that had sent the Dalai Lama into exile. Around the world, eighteen Chinese embassies were attacked. Accused by the Chinese media of orchestration, the Dalai Lama denied any involvement, stating that the dissatisfaction of the Tibetan people themselves was the cause of the insurrection. The protest spread beyond Lhasa to other cities, and even beyond the TAR. James Miles, the only foreign correspondent allowed into Tibet during this time, remarked that it did not appear that the protest was organized – it was sponta-neous.[38] From this unfortunate baseline, the Olympic torch relay was launched.

In a crypto-pagan rite at the site of the Temple of Zeus at Olympia on 24 March 2008, actress Maria Nafpliotou ignited the torch that would travel the world and arrive at Beijing to symbolize the start of the games. Before it even left Greece, Free Tibet demonstrators began an interna-tional protest of China's human rights violations in Tibet. Major protests were held in London and Paris, with the torch actually being grabbed and extinguished at several points. The Tibetan national flag could be seen everywhere. Buses had to be called in to ferry the flame around the cities. In San Francisco, several hundred pro-Tibetan protesters were heckled, backed by several hundred long-time Chinese-American resi-dents and Chinese nationals who were bussed in for the counter-protest. This time the actual route of the torch was kept secret; nevertheless, protesters located the bus with the torch and tried to prevent it returning to the airport. Earlier San Francisco City Council passed a resolution that the torch would be received with 'alarm and protest at the failure of China to meet its past solemn promises to the international commu-nity, including the citizens of San Francisco, to cease the egregious and ongoing human rights abuses in China and occupied Tibet'.[39]

Tibetan Buddhist protesters and Dalai Lama supporters clash after a speech by the Dalai Lama at Radio City Music Hall in New York, 17 July 2008.

Protests continued around the world, including rallies in Nepal and India. The Ganden Phodrang issued a statement that it did not support the disruption of the torch procession. The bedraggled torch, incongruously referred to as 'holy' by the Communist state, finally arrived in Beijing in time for the August opening ceremony.

A different fire

As Chinese athletes hauled away their hoard of gold metals and the rising smoke from the extinguished Olympic torch merged with the choking brown smog of Beijing, Tibetans in the homeland began to express their hopelessness in another way; they began to set themselves on fire. As of December 2018 over 155 Tibetans have self-immolated to protest China's continuing occupation of Tibet.[40] Most have died. Almost all have occurred since 2011, and many suicides have taken place in Sichuan and other provinces outside of the TAR. This is surprising, because these older Tibetan regions were seen as being the most integrated with China. Other immolations have occurred in Kathmandu and New Delhi. Bhuchung D. Sonam quotes a poignant last communication from Phagmo Dhondup, a young Tibetan from Tsaphuk in eastern Tibet:

Over one hundred Tibetans from all parts of Tibet set themselves on fire. They were true heroes of the Tibetan people. If Tibet does not win independence and freedom, it is certain that China will eliminate Tibet's culture and traditional ways of life. This year the authorities have banned the teaching of Tibetan language in Bayan district. All the Tibetan teachers were expelled. It is out of sheer sadness that today, on the evening of the fifteenth day of the Tibetan New Year, I am setting myself on fire in front of the Jakhyung Monastery. Today is Tibetan Independence Day.[41]

While again China has accused the Dalai Lama of inciting the people to commit suicide, Tenzin Gyatso himself has vigorously denied this. The Dalai Lama is in a dilemma, for as a Buddhist he is bound to preserve life, but if he should call for an end to the practice, he is sure to alienate a sizeable portion of his followers, especially the more radical element of the Tibetan Youth Congress and other pro-independence organizations.[42]

Modernization in Tibet continues unabated, erasing difference between traditional Tibetan and modern Chinese cultures. The ancient city of Lhasa has been particularly impacted by culturally insensitive urban planning schemes. Thousand-year-old buildings have been razed to be replaced with concrete block houses. Some modern construction, such as the new Lhasa train station, bears a pastiche of Tibetan ornamentation. But one wonders if this is placed to satisfy tourists' expectations. The authentic, native-built capital city is being destroyed while a modern Chinese city takes its place. Remaining are a few temples, the Norbulingka and the Potala (and its replica) which intrude ever more hyper-realistically upon an otherwise nondescript western Chinese landscape.

Much of the recent frustration in Tibet and in the exile community is due to the apparent failure of dialogue between the Ganden Phodrang and the Chinese leadership. The continuing adherence to a Middle Way is seen by more and more as an appeasement that has failed. Many in the exile community, as well as those broad international supporters (the 'imperialist Dalai clique' referred to in the Chinese press), view renewed independence as a better goal. Many are convinced that this sort of nationalist stance does not have to equate with violence. In the face of an intransigent China and the underwhelming response to the

Middle Way, one can speculate: is the nation state the best vessel for achieving the goals of preserving Tibetan language, religion and culture? If the nation cannot be perpetuated in the homeland, can it continue beyond?

NINE

Charting a Tibet without Tibet

The liberation of all colonies, the liberation of all dependent, oppressed, and non-sovereign peoples [is necessary for the maintenance of international peace].

V. I. LENIN[1]

The ongoing debate as to the historical reality of Tibet as a state is subject to culture-specific paradigms of interpretation. Few argue that Tibet was not a de facto independent state between 1913 and 1950; some even suggest that Tibet was a *de jure* state as well under international law of the time. In the more distant past, Tibet also exhibited episodes of complete self-rule. But precedent only supports the argument secondarily. What is overriding in the contemporary Tibet issue is the right of self-determination, which is the one sustained, coherent message that is being generated in both exile and homeland Tibetan communities. And it is not dependent upon history, however strong the arguments may be.

While self-determination is enshrined in the United Nations charter, its universal application is problematic. Existing states generally are resistant to change: nationalism in a neighbouring state is potentially disrupting. In the case of Tibet, it is not just China that feels it would be destabilized by Tibetan independence; India, Bhutan and Nepal would all be impacted. This was certainly characteristic of Nehru's cold response to the political appeals of the Ganden Phodrang. The two main forces of modern nationalism – self-determination and the integrity of states – are diametrically opposed.

Working to maintain international equilibrium is the process whereby states and borders become 'essentialized' or enshrined as perpetual boundaries between polities. Similarly, erased boundaries are quickly forgotten; it is difficult to remember what any neighbourhood looked like before the high rises were built. This process fosters irredentist sentiments, a position most clearly seen in modern Chinese policy.

In the adjustments of empires following the end of the Great Game and the decolonialization of the British and Russian empires, Tibet no longer served as a buffer state of convenience. Rather than encourage self-determination, it was largely ignored. International law provides for the presumption of the continued existence of a state unless other states can provide rebuttable evidence under law that sovereignty was extinguished. The Ganden Phodrang's acceptance of the Seventeen Point Agreement is not legal evidence for China's annexation, as the 'treaty' was signed under duress. Michael van Walt van Praag states:

> The People's Republic of China could not have obtained a legal title of sovereignty over Tibet on the basis either of the military invasion of the State or of the subsequent exercise of a measure of effective control. The continued support of the Dalai Lama among the overwhelming majority of the population, the active resistance to Chinese rule in Tibet, the successful development of Tibetan polity in exile, and the functioning of a government in exile are all factors that contribute to the continuity of the Tibetan State. On the other hand, in view of the illegality of China's invasion of Tibet and the nullity of the Seventeen Point Agreement, neither the degree of control exercised by China through maintenance of a strong military presence in Tibet, nor the amount of time that has elapsed since the invasion has been sufficient to permit the conclusion that China has legally acquired the whole territory of Tibet. To the present time nothing has occurred that, according to generally accepted norms of international law, can justify the conclusion that the State of Tibet has been totally extinguished and legally incorporated to form an integral part of the People's Republic of China. The State of Tibet still exists ... as an independent legal entity, with a legitimate government, in exile in Dharamsala, to represent it. Accordingly, that government and the people of Tibet have the right to resume the exercise of sovereignty of their own territory, free from the interference of other States.[2]

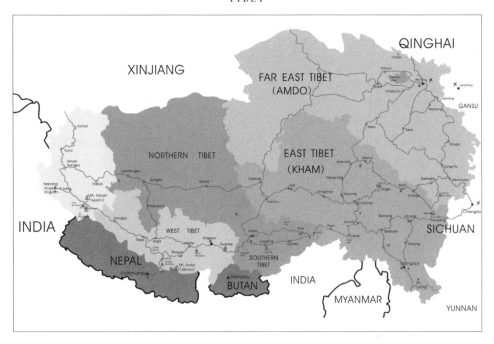

Administrative map of Tibet.

A prevailing notion in international law since the end of the Second World War is that states can no longer invade and annex other countries. But these events happen (such as Kuwait and the first Gulf War), and once one country is subsumed in another, they often become 'integral' parts of the succeeding state. However, as witnessed by the thousands of refugees and the worldwide spread of Tibetan culture, the idea of the state of Tibet still exists. There are two possible scenarios for its continuation: 1) China releases occupied Tibet; 2) Tibetans continue as a unified people and culture without the homeland territory, a 'Tibet without Tibet'. While seemingly unlikely, the first scenario has actually succeeded with another former component of the Chinese Empire: Mongolia.

The Mongolian candidate

Mongolia emerged from the same post-imperial hatchery as the modern state of Tibet. Mongolia has managed to free itself from the orbit of China, and later the Soviet Union, and its position vis-à-vis the empire was most similar to Tibet.

One of the chronic difficulties in modern Tibetan historiography is the tendency to concentrate on the political machinations between the Ganden Phodrang, China and Great Britain from the late nineteenth century to the mid-twentieth. Overlooked in this process is the attitude of the Republic of China towards its other former tributaries and neighbours in the transition between empire and secular state. There, parallels with Tibet in China's approaches to Mongolia, Manchuria, Korea, Annam (Vietnam), Myanmar and other states may shed light on the hardening concept of *Sinica irredenta* that developed with republican nationalism. One case, Mongolia, has significant implications for broadly understanding the current political situation of Tibet, and helps to explain the nature of the state envisioned by the Thirteenth Dalai Lama, now truncated and fractured in exile.

The position that China has taken towards Tibet since the formation of the republic in 1911 is based on conquest: since Genghis Khan's annexation of Tibet in 1206 and the formation of the Yuan dynasty under grandson Kublai, Tibet has been considered an integral part of the 'Chinese' realm. Under similar logic, Mongolia, Genghis's homeland, remained an essential component of this hypothetical 'Chinese' Empire, even after the Yuan dynasty was deposed and the Mongols retreated back to Inner Asia. But the Ming were not the successors of the empire created by Genghis, a position supported by the subsequent creation of states peripheral to China that were also once parts of the empire. Although Ming China patronized some Kagyupa lamas, they never succeeded in administering even a small part of Tibet through the priest–patron relationship.

Similarly, the alliance created by Manchu founder Nurhaci of Mongol, rebel Chinese, Tibetan and other groups was the force that took China proper from the Ming. The Qing had a relationship with the peripheral states that was more similar to Mongol-Yuan forms than to traditional Chinese ones. Like the empires of Genghis and Kublai, the Manchu Empire was a supranational one, and many Mongol and Tibetan rulers felt they had a personal and spiritual relationship with the emperor. The Qing emperor was the Great Khan of the Mongols and Manchus, and a bodhisattva in the Tibetan Buddhist system, in addition to being emperor of China and centre of the world in the Confucian system. Sun Yat-sen (Yixian), founder of the Nationalist movement (Kuomintang), envisioned his republic as the natural successor to the Celestial Empire, his 'Five Races under One Union' jingle. As summed up by Kuzmin, 'On April 8, 1912, the Chinese President Yuan Shikai issued a decree abolishing the status of Mongolia, Tibet and East Turkestan as vassal territories, and they became equated to ordinary provinces.'[3] There was a minority opinion among republican leaders to let the 'barbarian territories' go to create buffer states to secure China from the British and Russian empires.

The republican hubris led to several peripheral states unilaterally declaring their independence. Unlike under the Qing, neither Mongolia nor Tibet felt a natural affiliation with the secular Chinese Republic, either through elite kinship (Mongolia) or religion (Tibet). Kuzmin observes that with the signing of the Tibetan-Mongolian Treaty: 'The State of Mongolia became a legally capable subject in international law. The Tibetan-Mongolian Treaty did not require recognition by other States at that time. Hence, the recognition of Tibet by Mongolia made Tibet an international personality as well.'[4]

Earlier, the Manchurian homeland had been divided into a Russian Outer Manchuria and an Inner Manchuria under Japanese influence. The latter would become a Japanese-run state, Manchukuo, under the last Qing emperor, Puyi, as the Kang Teh emperor. Once dominated by China, Korea and Taiwan also became part of the extended Japanese realm.

As in Tibet, the collapse of the Qing dynasty renewed thoughts of a 'Greater Mongolia' to include all Mongol peoples. This state would form around the Khalkha-based monarchy of the Bogn Khan, the eighth Jebtsundampa Khutuktu, and would encompass the Buryiat region, Inner Mongolia, Tuva, the Altai Republic and Barga. In fact, it was not too much different from Lattimore's 'segmentary opposition' descent groupings that were so crucial in the formation of the empires of Genghis and Nurhaci. Here descent was reckoned further and further backwards in direct proportion to the military needs of the expansionist ruler. By all becoming relatives serving a common goal, the military might of both the Mongols and Manchus grew exponentially.[5] While the people of Inner Mongolia were largely content to accept the Republic of China, the elite of Outer Mongolia were wary of democracy and looked to Russia to help defend at most a concept of loose suzerainty and strong autonomy under China. Furthermore, Inner Mongolia was largely agrarian, Outer Mongolia mostly nomadic. They had been drifting apart for generations. Change was in the air: the Qing did much to prevent the unbridled expansion of the religious establishment in Mongolia, as it had in Tibet. It also prevented migration of the Chinese to Mongol lands, which may have affected traditional cultural ways. With the Manchus gone, both restraints evaporated.

Coming on the heels of the Simla accord between Tibet and Britain, Russia entered into bipartite negotiations with Yuan Shikai in 1915. In the Kyakhta Treaty Russia agreed to recognize China's suzerainty over Outer Mongolia, which would have autonomy under the Bogn Khan. It was almost exactly parallel to the provisions of the Simla agreement, with the exception that the Russo-Chinese accord did not include Mongolian negotiators. To counter this, Mongolian officials tried to contact foreign officials at every opportunity to press for their recognition of independence. They even sent a delegation to St Petersburg. Their requests were largely ignored.[6]

Unlike Tibet, which successfully fought off attempts by China to integrate them into the republic for the first half of the twentieth century, the Mongolian state experienced a revolving door of annexation and secession during the same period. This is primarily because imperial Russia and the succeeding Soviets sought the formation of a buffer state between them and China, something that Britain had not been interested in forming with Tibet. Britain was largely content with Bhutan, Nepal and Sikkim to serve as buffer states on the southern flanks of the Himalaya. Mongolia was close to Russia's Trans-Siberian Railway, and Urga was eventually connected; lacking railways, roads and airports, the costs to supply Tibet as a buffer state were prohibitive to a retrenching Britain. Russian influence in the region continued to decline with the outbreak of the First World War and the subsequent Russian Revolution.

With an exchange of gifts in 1915–16 between the Bogd Khan and Yuan Shikai, the latter rather preemptively proclaiming himself emperor of a new dynasty in China, many politicians in China interpreted this as the re-establishment of a tribute relationship. When titles were offered the Bogd, he responded by telling Yuan he was already khan by virtue of Qing recognition, and any further titles were unnecessary. This is similar to the rejection of Chinese titles by the Thirteenth Dalai Lama.

With the Bolshevik Revolution, fears arose in Mongolia of Russia's civil war spilling over into their land. The government of the Bogd Khan requested the Chinese high commissioner in Urga to send troops from China. The pan-Mongolian movement was also threatening the Khalkha government of the khan, and he requested even more soldiers from China. The Mongolian princes rebelled, wishing to be restored to the privileges they had enjoyed under the Qing. China took this as an opportunity to reinstate Chinese sovereignty. Chinese warlord Xu Shuzheng effectively deposed the Bogd Khan in 1919. The following year a White Russian mercenary, Baron Roman von Ungern-Sternberg, entered Mongolia and drove the Chinese away, but he kept the khan as a figurehead monarch. At that point, the new Soviet Union decided to intervene and helped establish a Communist Party under the leadership of Damdin Sükhbaatar. Mongolian independence was newly declared on 11 July 1921. With the death of the eighth Jebtsundampa Bogd Khan in 1924, the country became the People's Republic of Mongolia and a search for the reincarnation of the Jebtsundampa was forbidden.[7]

As in Tibet in the 1950–70s, the Communists began a systematic destruction of Buddhism in Mongolia. It began to destroy monks and monasteries. This caused great fear in Tibet, both during the 1920s and later with the rise of the Chinese Communists, as noted in the Thirteenth Dalai Lama's valedictory address.

Near the end of the Second World War, the Soviets invaded parts of Inner Mongolia and Manchukuo. Perceiving an imminent threat to China's territorial integrity, Chiang Kai-shek finally signed an agreement with the Soviets that gave Chinese recognition of Outer Mongolian independence, upon a successful referendum. It is reported that 100 per cent of the population opted for complete independence. In return for the fulfilment of this longtime Russian and Soviet foreign policy goal, the agreement stated that Mongolian independence would only be effective 'within [Outer Mongolia's] existing frontiers'. The Outer Mongolian troops subsequently withdrew from China.[8]

On 6 October 1949 Mongolia and the newly formed People's Republic of China recognized each other. Mao always wanted Mongolia back, but Stalin prevented it. In 1990 Mongolia was able to shake off the last vestiges of its Russian/Soviet satellite heritage. In 1994 the People's Republic of China and Mongolia signed an accord recognizing each other's territorial integrity. In 2002 the Republic of China on Taiwan recognized Mongolian independence.[9]

The existence of the state of Mongolia, formerly an 'integral part of China', as a completely independent state is a check against irredenta propaganda of both Communist China and the Kuomintang. It refutes the inviolate, essentialist 'sacred' nature of the Chinese Motherland. It also counters ill-informed British and American foreign policy statements that the state of Tibet was never recognized by other countries. This has enormous implications for sustaining the future of Tibetan aspirations.

A state without territory

The impasse between China and Tibet is not just about land and resources; it is over the hearts and souls of the Tibetan people. Can sovereignty, then, be acknowledged without possession of territory? Key to this notion is the right of Tibetan religious hierarchs to choose their own successors, wherever they may be. China views all Tibetan lamas as Chinese subjects and reincarnation as a process requiring regulation by the Communist Party.

It is vitally important for the legitimacy of the party to demonstrate to China and the world that the Tibetan people are solidly behind the building of the People's Republic. Without Tibet, they would stand to lose massive segments of the current territory, including Xinjiang, Inner Mongolia, large portions of Qinghai, Sichuan and even Manchuria, which were non-Chinese parts of the Qing Empire, some of which have strong nationalist ambitions. As such, the common response of party officials is to attempt to micromanage and plan even the most abstract worldview beliefs, notably *tulku* reincarnation. In August 2007 MSNBC noted:

> In one of history's more absurd acts of totalitarianism, China has banned Buddhist monks in Tibet from reincarnating without government permission. According to a statement issued by the State Administration for Religious Affairs, the law, which goes into effect next month and strictly stipulates the procedures by which one is to reincarnate, is 'an important move to institutionalize management of reincarnation'.[10]

This, of course, violates nearly every principle of the United Nations and the international community, including the rights of self-determination, freedom of conscience and religious conviction. The ability to direct one's stream of consciousness into a specific rebirth is a fundamental consequence of spiritual adeptness, a principal belief professed in Buddhism, and is an individual prerogative and aptitude. No secular power, much less an atheistic one, could possibly have the moral right, skill or authority to direct a transmigration of any high lama, much less a Dalai Lama. This is why Chokyi Gyalpo is generally not accepted as the true Panchen Lama. The Qing emperors of China claimed such authority, but it was almost always ignored. China has historically found it difficult to depose a living Dalai Lama, as was the case with the sixth, thirteenth and fourteenth incarnations, for the people would not permit it.

The precedent leading up to the party edict of 2007 was the contentious selection of the Eleventh Panchen Lama, one selected by the Dalai Lama, the other by the Communist Party. After this debacle, the Dalai Lama stated that he would not be reborn in an occupied Tibet; his next incarnation, should he decide to return, would be born in exile. He has also made it clear that his decision would be based on the wishes of the Tibetan people and their perceived usefulness of his position. As an emanation of the god Avalokiteśvara, and by the strictures of his bodhisattva vows, he is compelled to forego nirvana and continue to be reborn to be of benefit to all sentient beings. Transmigration, according to Buddhist belief, is bound only by the laws of karma and the spiritual adeptness of the being in question. It is beyond the capacity of any secular authority. At last look, China's boundaries only extend to the Himalaya in the south, not to the Pure Land heavens or the hot and cold hells.

In July 2011, feeling the weight of a lifetime of service to the Tibetan people, the Dalai Lama resigned from his secular post as head of the Ganden Phodrang. An election among the Tibetan diaspora placed a Harvard law fellow, Dr Lobsang Sangay, as the new prime minister in exile. In recognition of his enhanced position, he was titled *sikyong*, roughly translated as 'regent', but often referred to as president. The Dalai Lama assured his people that he was not relinquishing his spiritual authority, however. Although the exact division of labour is still in process, it appears that the Ganden Phodrang is moving away from theocracy and is becoming a secular democratic government.

In September 2011 the Dalai Lama further announced that he alone was in charge of his next incarnation. He prophesied at a meeting of the heads of four major schools of Vajrayāna Buddhism:

> When I am about ninety I will consult the high Lamas of the Tibetan Buddhist traditions, the Tibetan public, and other concerned people who follow Tibetan Buddhism, and re-evaluate whether the institution of the Dalai Lama should continue or not. On that basis we will take a decision. If it is decided that the reincarnation of the Dalai Lama should continue and there is a need for the Fifteenth Dalai Lama to be recognized, responsibility for doing so will primarily rest on the concerned officers of the Dalai Lama's Ganden Phodrang Trust. They should consult the various heads of the Tibetan Buddhist traditions and the reliable oath-bound Dharma Protectors who are linked inseparably to the lineage of the Dalai Lamas. They should seek advice and direction from these concerned beings and carry out the procedures of search and recognition in accordance with past tradition. I shall leave clear written instructions about this. Bear in mind that, apart from the reincarnation recognized through such legitimate methods, no recognition or acceptance should be given to a candidate chosen for political ends by anyone, including those in the People's Republic of China.[11]

In any case, he would be reborn in freedom. This statement of personal self-determination was immensely reassuring to his followers, considering widespread speculation that the political manoeuvrings in China would soon reach a crisis should Tenzin Gyatso die soon. The announcement also reaffirms that the idea of Tibet, the 'vessel holding the complete teachings of the Buddha', does not need the territory of Tibet, much less a meddling China, to continue.

Even a Chinese official as high as Hong Lei of the foreign ministry ventured to comment on the Dalai Lama's decision, stating that any attempt by the Dalai Lama to appoint a successor through traditional reincarnation would break Chinese law.[12] The statement is remarkable, for it posits that the People's Republic of China has decreed that even in death there is no freedom. It also suggests that the Communist state has extra-territorial powers over Tibetans in exile, not withstanding Chinese claims to realms beyond this world.

Such absurdity has called into place the essential question: is the state the best vessel for the reproduction and evolution of the cultural collective? Given modern technology's instantaneous transmission of information, the strong evidence of 'traditional' Tibetan culture thriving outside of Tibet for over sixty years, and that Tibet itself is rapidly being transformed into just another part of China, is the land of Tibet even needed for the maintenance of Tibetan identity and the continuation of Tibetan culture?

The state as defined by Max Weber is an institution with a legitimate monopoly on the use of physical force.[13] As such, the state may be construed as antithetical to Buddhist *ahimsa*. A state like Tibet, defined on the ethical principles of non-violence, needs some sort of subjective machinations to resolve the contradictions inherent in the Weberian definition of the state. In the last eight hundred years of Tibetan history, the ecclesiastic state has been supported through the priest–patron relationship. In the case of the Mongols and Manchus, the physical use of force to support the Tibetan state had been actually quite rare and always involved the Tibetan military in alliance with the patron's forces. We have seen, after the demise of the priest–patron relationship, how the Thirteenth Dalai Lama's attempt to significantly strengthen Tibet's military in opposition to increasing Chinese aggression was met with violent opposition from the monastic elites. For the Tibetan theocracy, having an outside defensive patron in the armies of the Mongols or Manchus was considered better for the karma of the state. The sins of warfare would devolve upon the patron rather than the priest. This is a characteristic feature of Tibetan political and even personal action. Tibetan society resolved long ago the contradictions inherent in the ecclesiastic state founded on Buddhist principles by enlisting mercenary agents and patrons. The same is occurring in exile: Tibetan nationalism is successful because it is non-violent.

Persistence

Hand in hand with nationalist essentialism in the modern Chinese state is the positivist Marxist notion that more 'primitive' cultures will inevitably disappear under the bright lights of modernism. Thus China is 'doing Tibet a favour' by fostering its rapid development, despite the alienation of the native people in the process. But the rhetoric of Marxist determinism fails when the people who are supposed to be subsumed into a broader identity persistently maintain their group loyalties. One hundred years ago the nationalistic republicans and foreign scholars of China ventured to predict that the Manchu people would soon be as extinct as their recently collapsed dynasty. Indeed, as recently as ten years ago the number of individuals who spoke native Manchu language was down to a few old ladies living in northeast China, particularly in Heilongjiang province. But then, it suddenly became fashionable again in the Chinese world to be Manchu. The current registration is over ten million, and the Manchus are the fastest growing minority as formerly Han people revert to a Manchu identity.[14] Manchu language can be heard on the nightly news from the Manchu-speaking Xibe people, and the native voice of Qing emperors is found in Korean movies.[15] Ethnic identities are far more persistent than most modernists would wish.

That cultural identity can be persistent, even when economic, social and coercive forces render the enterprise illogical, is a salient point in ethnographic studies around the world, and in particular among Tibetan refugees.[16] Comparisons are drawn between the Free Tibet movement and the Zionism of Herzl in the late nineteenth and early twentieth centuries. In the latter, the agenda was to convene a Jewish homeland in the divinely promised regions of Judaea and Israel after centuries of diaspora. Another Jewish movement, called autonomism, advocated Jewish autonomy within Europe. Still another, territorialism, sought a Jewish state anywhere it could be found. The last idea has been gaining some currency in discussions of Tibet's future, especially considering the power and expectations of the 'Tibetans and Friends' Free Tibet movement. Events have shown the Free Tibet movement not to have been merely a fad of the counterculture 1960s or New Age 1980s. And despite the Dalai Lama's Middle Way path, the passage of time has shown that rarely has legal autonomy of a minority within another state resulted in satisfaction for either the minority or the majority: the state is still an ideal.

The second European example is the society that grew up around the early Christians of the Roman Empire. Persecuted for centuries, the Christians of Rome were led by their bishop, the pope. Eventually, however, they came to dominate Roman society. With the fall of the empire, the pope filled in the leadership vacuum, and the old Roman Empire became the Christian Empire, mostly dominated by converted Germanic tribes. A long-enduring structural opposition between the Germanic emperor and the Roman pope erupted over the Investiture Controversy, which disputed who among the two rulers had the right to appoint local bishops. The pope, claiming the mystery of apostolic succession, said he did; the emperor, claiming the authority to rule over the empire, said he did. The emperor had the sword; the pope the authority to excommunicate, and thus damn the emperor and his followers. For generations, popes and emperors waged war and deposed one another, resulting in competing lineages of popes and anti-popes, emperors and anti-emperors. For a thousand years, secular powers

Three-dimensional view of Lhasa, showing how the city fills a flat river valley nestled in the ranges of the Himalaya Mountains, November 2005.

attempted to assimilate the Papal States, sending the pope into exile on several occasions. When Rome was finally annexed to the Kingdom of Italy in 1870, Pius IX went into internal exile, locking himself up in the Vatican. The pope had insisted the secular rulers had no authority to interfere in godly matters, especially apostolic succession, for it was guided by the Holy Spirit. The Italian state eventually backed away. In 1929 Mussolini worked out an agreement with papal successor Pius XI creating Vatican City as an independent city-state within Rome.

The current stand-off between the Dalai Lama and China has parallels with both examples: a vigorous diaspora, enhanced by native leadership, backed by numerous NGOs, private benefactors and a form of voluntary taxation, and a structural conflict between secular and religious authority. Unless compromise is reached, the future portends the existence of lineages of Dalai and anti-Dalai Lamas, like the two Panchens and two Karmapas of today. If legitimacy is held by the current Fourteenth Dalai Lama in exile, then the real Tibet will be the one enacted by Tibetans living abroad. And it will be vastly different from China's province of Xizang.

Tibet outside the walls

Like the lizard that drops its tail to escape a predator, it is entirely reasonable to suggest that the state of Tibet has left the land behind to save its business end. It can regenerate elsewhere. The establishment at Dharamsala in northern India functions pretty much as a transnational organization with very minimal 'territory'. It is, in fact, a de facto microstate. And as we have seen in Tibetan history, ambiguity has not been much of an impediment for the operation of the state of Tibet. There is an international organization at the cusp of statehood that could provide some insight to the possible future of the state of Tibet. Of all the current states of the world, the Sovereign Military Order of Malta (SMOM) is the smallest,[17] and is both a secular and a religious organization. It presents an example of a Tibetan sovereignty the world might live with. It would seem on the surface to be the most anachronistic and implausible of all tiny survivor states, were it not for a mission that was generally unassailable in the Western world: to defend Christendom and to succour the poor and the sick. Like the phoenix, it rose from the ashes of at least three annihilating defeats, moving, as a truly international body, from its origins in Jerusalem, through Cyprus, Rhodes, Malta and Russia to present-day Rome.

This sovereign nation of superlatives does have a territory: a whopping 1.6 acres but an independent territory nevertheless. In secular matters, the SMOM holds allegiance to no one. As an independent entity, secular SMOM is only subject to international law. It has a constitutional government headed by a prince-grand master, enjoys the status of Permanent Observer at the United Nations, and issues its own passports, stamps and coins. The grand master is assisted by an elected government, the Sovereign Council, which together provides for the day-to-day government and the executive capacity of the SMOM. The Sovereign Council consists of four Great Officers (the Grand Commander, Grand Chancellor, Grand Hospitaller and Receiver of the Common Treasure) and six other officers. The legislative duties are ensconced with the Chapter General, which represents the grand assembly of knights. Two dozen or so individuals comprise the permanent population. Most of them are dual citizens, and in keeping with nearly a thousand years of male monasticism, all leadership has been of males exercising the three monastic vows of obedience, poverty and chastity. This extraordinary polity has diplomatic relations with over 110 countries.[18]

The SMOM received its main properties in Rome with extraterritorial rights in the early nineteenth century from the pope. It was given this as a reward for defending Christianity over the previous eight hundred years. It had also been independent on Malta and Rhodes, and beholden only to the pope in religious matters. Its sovereignty has been justified and used as a tool to carry on its mission to care for the poor and the sick around the world without political hindrance. In this matter, it is similar in derivation as the Holy See ruled by the pope, with its sovereign territory, Vatican City. So under the usual definition of a state under international law, nearly a thousand years qualifies as much as the Vatican does.

A similar microstate could be established for the Dalai Lama and the Dalai Lama's Tibet, a state whose mission is to spread compassion and wisdom to all sentient beings. Like the SMOM and the Holy See, the cultural baggage of such a state and its territories is relatively inconsequential compared with the mission. The establishment of such a state should not, in theory, conflict with a pragmatic China, as the resources of the geographic entity of Tibet are not being repossessed. The envisioned state would also provide a certain stability in the transmission of leadership. Like the 12,500 knights and dames of the SMOM, one would not have to live there to maintain one's *communitas* and identity with the state. As mentioned before, it could be a way for sympathetic governments to recognize the universalistic work of the Dalai Lamas' Ganden Phodrang and their worldwide followers without antagonizing the People's Republic of China. Granted, this 'Vaticanization' of the institution of the Dalai Lama may not immediately solve the problems of the several million Tibetans left behind, but it may provide a structure of leverage to which China may eventually respond, as it did with Mongolia.

Greater Tibet gets bigger

A brief image of where this new Tibet may be going was seen in recent years. The massive Olympic protest, the failure of the eighth round of talks with China, and the occasion of the fiftieth anniversary of the Tibetan uprising and diaspora led to an urgent convening of two international conferences in India in November and December 2008. First, a Special General Meeting of the Tibetan People was held in Dharamsala, attended by 560 Tibetans living in ninety countries. From this, the Tibetan government-in-exile was able to collect opinions and suggestions from many Tibetans living in the occupied lands and in China. A week later over a hundred representatives of Tibet support groups from more than thirty countries were convened at the Special International Tibet Support Groups meeting in Delhi. Here the 'foreign' contingent of the Free Tibet movement was apprised of the results of the Dharamsala meeting. The Kalon Tripa (then prime minister of the Ganden Phodrang), Samdung Rinpoche, stated that 85 per cent of the participants of the Dharamsala conference supported the Middle Way approach of the Dalai Lama with its expressed conviction of genuine autonomy with a Chinese framework. Acknowledging the split in the Tibet movement, the prime minister said, 'Nevertheless, Tibet support groups should not be influenced by this outcome – His Holiness is open to any suggestions.'[19] In fact, one subgroup at the Delhi conference suggested that if China continues to stonewall the Middle Way, self-determination could be

President Barack Obama meeting with the Dalai Lama in the Map Room of the White House, 21 February 2014.

implemented with a call for full independence. That would raise the stakes tremendously for China, because while there has been no precedent for broad autonomy in Chinese regions other than Hong Kong, former tributary states to the empire have quite successfully broken away, the latest being Mongolia. Together with Taiwan and Xinjiang, a powerful call for Tibetan independence would have a devastating effect on the integrity and mandate of the People's Republic.

Furthermore, the Ganden Phodrang, for the first time, acknowledged the position of non-Tibetan individuals within the transnational, trans-ethnic Tibetan movement. At the inaugural session of the Special International Tibet Support Group meeting, a message from the Dalai Lama was read: 'The Tibetan issue is not merely the issue of the rights of the Tibetan people. It concerns not just the six million Tibetans, but the *over 13 million people in the world* who share this culture' (emphasis added). This is a culture Tenzin Gyatso defines as one sharing of the values of *ahimsa* (non-violence) and *karuṇā* (compassion). One subgroup of the Tibet Support Group conference echoed his remarks:

We as Tibetan supporters shall always support the Tibetan Government-in-Exile and never dictate any terms to it. But when it comes to the institution of His Holiness the Dalai Lama, we will also assert our right to say [that he] belongs not only to the Tibetan people, but also to the people of the Himalayas in India, Bhutan, and Nepal, the people of Mongolia, the people of the three Tibetan Buddhist regions of Russia and the millions of followers of His Holiness in the rest of the world.[20]

That is vastly different from the idea of a homeland-based nation state populated by Tibetans. It suggests that 'Free Tibet' is a transnational concept considerably larger than even so-called ethnic Tibet, the old boundaries of the Tibetan Empire.

In contrast, one would wonder where the non-Tibetans would fit in Tibet had the 'genuine autonomy' Middle Way proposed by the Dalai Lama succeeded. A transnational Tibet existing outside of the TAR

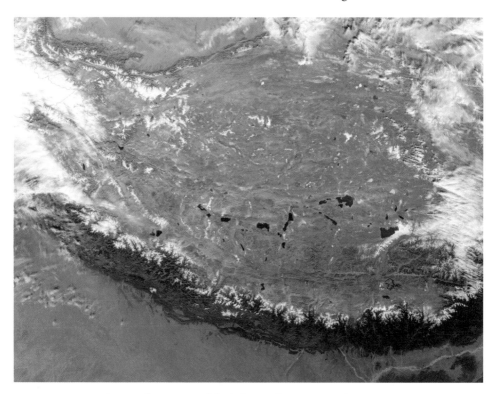

True-colour image of the Tibetan plateau, December 2002, from NASA's Terra satellite.

seems to appeal to the immigrants of Shangri-La, the Western wannabe Tibetans whose lifelong support of the cause of Tibet entertains a conceit that there is a place for them in the enchanted kingdom.

The Internet and social media have developed as a way of sharing opinions, thoughts and news throughout the world and directly to Tibetans in Tibet. It is perhaps too early to tell if this 'virtual democracy' will continue to develop in a relatively unrestricted manner, but it does represent a substantial portion of the 'Tibet without Tibet'.

The concept of monolithic Chinese nationalism is also changing. Propelled by the relative success of the Beijing Olympics and an increasingly globalized market, forms of transnationalism are appearing that seem to transcend the older, more rigid concept of the Chinese nation state. Shanshan Du suggests that a 'positive energy' (*zhengmengliang*) grassroots movement has been particularly transformative in the globalizing socio-political landscape of China.[21] She argues that traditional Kuomintang and Communist nationalism has been problematic due to its origin in the humiliations of the Opium Wars and the tearing apart of the empire by foreign extra-territorial demands. As such, perceived threats to China's sovereignty often generate fervent reactions. The Beijing Olympic torch fiasco is an example. However, since that time, the 'positive energy' movement has offered an alternative nationalism, highlighted by individualism and universalism, located more in an increasingly globalized space, which is the reality of modern China. In this sense it shares much with Buddhist modernism and is compatible with the Dalai Lama's globalism and Tibetan transnational self-determination.

While the Ganden Prodrang in exile maintains its official government websites from Dharamsala, Rang bstan Tibet is heavily represented by NGOs and many individual bloggers such as Jamyang Norbu ('Shadow Tibet') and Lhadon Tethong. China's Tibet is kept in the spotlight by bloggers such as Woeser, who works out of Beijing ('Invisible Tibet' in Chinese). Tibetan literature is supported with the blog 'Where Tibetans Write' on www.phayul.com, one of the more popular political news sites.

The people of the Tibet who live outside China are inventing novel ways to express their nationalism. 'Bringing Tibet Home' is a documentary film by Tenzin Tsetan Choklay that tells the story of Tibetan artist

Tenzing Rigdol as he sets out on a unique mission to bring Tibet closer to Tibetan exiles through an unprecedented art project – a site-specific art installation titled 'Our Land, Our People' that involved smuggling 20,000 kg (44,000 lb) of native Tibetan soil across the Himalaya. A small portion of China's 'unalienable' Tibet was appropriated and deposited in Dharamsala on 26 October 2011. The soil was spread out on a stage designed by the artist and people were invited to walk, sit and express their feelings through a standing microphone. The Dalai Lama was one of them. The installation was a metaphysical expression signifying that Tibet exists where the Tibetan people and the Dalai Lama are, not within the geographic coordinates of the plateau now ruled by China. Those Tibetans still inside are prisoners in their own homeland.

That a transnational mega-Tibet exists is not in doubt. Like an electron that is both a wave and a particle, this Tibet is both a movement and a political entity. Only a fraction of this Tibet is now administered by the Ganden Phodrang in Dharamsala. It is also comprised of many independence groups and avowedly non-political dharma centres around the world. To create something that foreign governments, sympathetic heads of state and NGOs can recognize as being valuable to the high moral responsibility of the global society is really the essence of this mega-Tibet. It is encouraging that the Fourteenth Dalai Lama has been given practically every major humanitarian award available, but it is another matter to transform those symbolic gestures to something sustainable. Currently, the present Dalai Lama and government-in-exile are not situated in a manner that countries may recognize. It is not so much the fear of China as that of embarrassing the host government of India, which could jeopardize the refugee status of His Holiness and his Tibetan followers. It is this reticence that prevents Dharamsala from official recognition by sympathetic states. A tiny segment of extraterritorial land could change everything, and Tibet could continue to exist without the threat of political machinations of India, China or any other state.

The Communist Party expects that with the death of this Dalai Lama the Tibet separatist idea will wither away too. On the contrary, the Dalai Lama's work is not done, since Avalokiteśvara has incarnated in every Tibetan head of state. The mantle will probably be picked up by a Fifteenth, then a Sixteenth. It is an institution and not a single man or his personality that is behind the support by and for the Tibetan people.

That the institution of the Dalai Lama and the state of Tibet need to be established in exile under international law, and recognized (much as the pope is) as a self-replicating, sovereign institution that governments and other international agencies may further accredit, are the hopes of many. Whereas the historical precedent for the existence of the state of Tibet is concrete, it is the acts of self-determination that effectively maintain the dream of Tibet in a changing world.

Afterword

Contested Histories:
The Presents and Futures of Tibet and Tibetans

Professor Dibyesh Anand, University of Westminster
Weaving together disparate narratives around the histories of Tibet and Tibetans, especially vis-à-vis old empires based in China as well as the contemporary colonial power of the People's Republic of China, Klieger provides hope. This hope is based on the myriad ways in which Tibetan cultures and polities have evolved and negotiated with much stronger, more powerful and bigger neighbours to the north and the south.

If we focus on the contemporary situation of Tibet under Chinese occupation and of Tibetans forced to live with severely limited cultural, religious or human rights within the PRC or to live with precarity in exile, hope comes across as a precious commodity. China is emerging rapidly as a major power with a footprint in different parts of the world. Even as the world undergoes one crisis after another, and democracies face severe challenges, the PRC seems to go from strength to strength. In the recent Covid-19 pandemic, China, the source of the virus, is the major country whose economy has bounced back the quickest. Several developing countries, and an increasing number of developed countries, are dependent on Chinese trade, investment and markets. Beijing is also weaponizing its economic power to get foreign countries to accept its sensitivities around contested issues including Tibet, Xinjiang, Hong Kong and democracy.

In this climate, support for Tibetans is decreasing in the West and in India. Academic study of Tibet often shies away from being what many see as 'political', owing partly to fear of losing access to Tibetan regions and partly to disciplinary conservatism. Academic production of knowledge around Tibet in the West and in India sees Tibetans as mere native informers or passive subjects of study and not as co-producers of knowledge about themselves. Unfortunately, the situation is not very different for numerous studies of Tibet within China whose sole purpose is reinforce the idea that Tibet is 'China's Tibet'. Even more than outside China, it is within the country that the inextricable link between knowledge and power is witnessed. Histories, ethnographies and testimonies of Tibetans are only allowed in public if they do not defy the Chinese image of Tibet as a place that was not, is not and never will be independent. Klieger's scholarship is instrumental in resisting this pressure to either conform to the Chinese view or eschew politics and exoticize Tibetans.

Not only is there a crisis in scholarship around Tibet, but even pro-Tibet activism is at a low point. The community in exile is spreading itself thin as very few Tibetans can manage to escape Tibet now, and more and more young Tibetans in exile are moving away from Nepal and India to different Western countries. The singular dependence of exiled Tibetans on their religious leader, the political symbol of Tibetan nation, the Fourteenth Dalai Lama, also makes their situation fragile as the venerable leader is getting old and there are no negotiations between him and Beijing to provide a solution to China–Tibet conflict that allows Tibetans to live with some semblance of dignity within China, let alone freedom.

Yet Klieger's work provides hope. He was a rare Tibetanist who was willing to be multi-disciplinary, not bound to academic conventions, and saw the arbitrariness of the divide between academia and activism. Though he did not use the term 'queer' in the same way I do, in his own way he queered the study of Tibetan and Tibetans in a radical manner. Through his work, he offered us new ways of being in solidarity.

This work reminds us that there is nothing constant in history. All empires come to an end. There is no reason to believe that the empire of modern colonizing PRC will be an exception. There is no reason not to hope that there will be a free Tibet in the future, living as a friendly neighbour of China and freed from authoritarianism.

WE MUST RESIST the temptation of worshipping power; we must continue to recognize Tibetans as real, living, breathing people who have the right to tell their own histories, to shape their own struggles, and most crucially, to determine their own futures.

REFERENCES

Introduction

1 Christine Sleeter, 'State Curriculum Standards and the Shaping of Student Consciousness', *Social Justice*, XXIX/4 (2002), pp. 8–25.

ONE Bedrock

1 Clare E. Harris, *The Museum on the Roof of the World* (Chicago, IL, 2012).
2 Stephen Oppenheimer, *Out of Eden* (London, 2003), p. 257.
3 Peter Clift and J. Blusztajn, 'Reorganization of the Western Himalayan River System after Five Million Years Ago', *Nature*, 438 (2005), pp. 1001–3.
4 Carole McGranahan, *Arrested Histories: Tibet, the CIA, and Memories of a Forgotten War* (Durham, NC, 2010).
5 John Bellezza, *Zhangzhung: Foundations of Civilization* (Vienna, 2008), p. 202.
6 Yungdrung Bon, www.yungdrungbon.com, accessed 6 January 2013.
7 Bellezza, *Zhangzhung*, p. 205.
8 John Bellezza, *Spirit Mediums, Sacred Mountains and Related Bon Textual Traditions in Upper Tibet: Calling Down the Gods* (Leiden, 2005), pp. 20–25.
9 For the Monpa, see Mark Aldenderfer, 'Defining Zhang Zhung Ethnicity', in *Discoveries in Western Tibet and the Western Himalayas*, ed. Amy Heller and Giacomella Orofino (Leiden, 2007), p. 14. The Rawang people's oral history suggests that they moved from the eastern Changtang about 2000 BCE, which would correspond to the entry of the Zhang Zhung people into the region. The Rawang, according to their accounts, headed southwards along the great river valleys to Southeast Asia, in pursuit of their herds of wild oxen. See P. Christiaan Klieger, 'A Tale of the Tibeto-Burman Pygmies', in *Tibetan Borderlands*, ed. P. Christiaan Klieger (Leiden, 2006), p. 245.
10 Aldenderfer, 'Zhang Zhung Ethnicity', p. 2.
11 Bellezza, *Zhangzhung*, p. 218.
12 Ibid., p. 221.
13 In an environmentally supportive statement, the Fourteenth Dalai Lama recently forbade the use of rare animal skins in the crafting of traditional robes and hats.
14 A reference to the king being carried on the shoulders of those proclaiming him.
15 Namkhai Norbu, *Drung, Deu and Bön* (Dharamsala, India, 1995), p. 209.
16 Robert Paul, *The Tibetan Symbolic World* (Chicago, IL, 1982), p. 263.

17 Norbu, *Drung*, p. 209.
18 Ibid., p. 215.
19 Paul, *Tibetan Symbolic World*, p. 265.
20 From the *rGyal rabs gsal ba'i me long* by Sonam Gyaltsen (1312–1375), cited in Norbu, *Drung*, p. 75.
21 Tsepon W. D. Shakabpa, *Tibet: A Political History* (New York, 1984), p. 24.
22 Shakabpa, *Tibet*, p. 24 n. 3.
23 Pasang Wandu and Hildegard Diemberger, *dBa' bzhed: The Royal Narrative concerning the Bringing of the Buddha's Doctrine to Tibet* (Vienna, 2000), p. 26 n. 15.
24 Shakabpa, *Tibet*, p. 27.
25 Ibid.
26 Ibid., p. 26.
27 In recent times, the Gyasa has emerged as a cultural heroine for nationalist Chinese propagandists, as embodying the 'civilizing mission' of China towards Tibet.
28 Christopher I. Beckwith, *The Tibetan Empire in Central Asia: A History of the Struggle for Great Power among Tibetans, Turks, Arabs, and Chinese during the Early Middle Ages* (Princeton, NJ, 1987).
29 Shakabpa, *Tibet*, p. 41.
30 So familiar is Padmasambhava in the iconography of Tibet that it is difficult to believe he was most likely a historical figure. In fact, it is said that he invented beer. See Paul, *Tibetan Symbolic World*, p. 152.
31 Ellen Pearlman, *Tibetan Sacred Dance: A Journey into the Religious and Folk Traditions* (Rochester, VT, 2002), p. 94.
33 See Donald S. Lopez, Jr, *The Heart Sutra Explained: Indian and Tibetan Commentaries* (Albany, NY, 1988), p. 21.
33 Sam Van Schaik, *Tibet: A History* (New Haven, CT, 2011), p. 37.
34 Ibid., p. 39.
35 David A. Scott, 'Buddhism and Islam: Past to Present Encounters and Interfaith Lessons', *Numen*, XLII/2 (1995), p. 141.
36 Mostly Buddhist hybrid Sanskrit, a somewhat simplified version ultimately derived from Vedic Sanskrit.
37 As this great religious empire was being consolidated, another universal religion was being utilized for the maintenance of empire: on Christmas Day 800, Charlemagne was crowned Roman emperor by the pope in Rome. The diarchy of the Holy Roman Empire would function very similarly to the priest–patron relationship later established between Tibet and secular powers in Inner Asia. And the Investiture Controversy, the right to choose bishops, contested between the emperor and pope for generations, is parallel to one of the principal battles between the current Chinese government and the Dalai Lama. It is doubtful that Trisong Detsun and Charlemagne ever knew of one another's existence, but it is remarkable that history possesses numerous examples of exactly this type of synchronicity and parallel structural development.
38 Shakabpa, *Tibet*, p. 51.
39 Paul, *Tibetan Symbolic World*, p. 288.

40 According to Shakabpa, 'Od Sung was legitimate in the patriline, while Yum Tan was not. See Shakabpa, *Tibet*, p. 53.

41 Paul, *Tibetan Symbolic World*, pp. 288–92.

TWO The Rise of Theocracy

1 Sam Van Schaik, *Tibet: A History* (New Haven, CT, 2011), pp. 62–3.

2 John Brough, 'Thus Have I Heard . . ', *Bulletin of the School of Oriental and African Studies*, XIII/2 (1950), pp. 416–26.

3 See 'Kagyu Lineage: The Second Karmapa, Karma Phakshi (1205–1283)', www.kagyuoffice.org, accessed 2 February 2013.

4 See 'Sakya Tradition', www.hhthesakyatrizin.org, accessed 14 February 2013.

5 Ibid.

6 Used in reference to the Manchu establishment of the priest–patron relationship with Tibet. See legal codes of rDzong gsang sngags bde chen, *c.* 1653–8. Cited in P. Christiaan Klieger, *Tibetan Nationalism* (Berkeley, CA, 1992), p. 45.

7 'Sakya Tradition'.

8 Van Schaik, *Tibet*, p. 82.

9 Manuel Komroff, 'The Journal of Friar Odoric', in *Contemporaries of Marco Polo* (New York, 1928), p. 244.

10 During this bleak time, the worst epidemic in world history was raging in Western Europe, the Great Plague.

11 'Yuan Dynasty', www.wikipedia.org, accessed 6 February 2013.

12 Tsepon W. D. Shakabpa, *Tibet: A Political History* (New York, 1984), p. 71.

13 'Ukhaatu Khan', www.wikipedia.org, accessed 6 February 2013.

14 Shakabpa is perhaps the most transparent in this regard.

15 Georges Dreyfus, 'Cherished Memories, Cherished Communities: Proto-nationalism in Tibet', in *The History of Tibet*, vol. II: *The Medieval Period: c. AD 850–1895, the Development of Buddhist Paramountcy* (New York, 2003).

16 The Koko Nor district, in the borderlands between Mongol, Tibetan and Chinese cultures, would figure largely in the history of the Tibetan state, providing not only Tsongkhapa but Mongol armies and Dalai Lamas.

17 Van Schaik, *Tibet*, pp. 103–4.

THREE Ganden Phodrang

1 Mark Elliott, *The Manchu Way* (Palo Alto, CA, 2001), p. 56.

2 See Pamela Kyle Crossley, *The Manchus* (Oxford, 1997), p. 8.

3 Patricia Berger, *Empire of Emptiness* (Honolulu, HI, 2003), p. 25.

4 S. Grupper, 'Review of Hans-Rainer Kampfe, "Ni ma'i od zer/Naranu gerel: Die Biographie des 2. Pekinger, Lchan skya-Qutuqtu Rol pa'I rdo rje (1717–1789)"', *Journal of the Tibet Society*, IV (1984), p. 51.

5 From the *Manbun rōtō*, quoted in Elliott, *Manchu Way*, p. 69.

6 Crossley, *Manchus*, p. 112.

7 Berger, *Empire*, p. 25.

8 Elliott, *Manchu Way*, p. 63.

9 Ibid., p. 85. This rather nebulous concept of a Manchu homeland –
   'Manchuria' – was supported throughout the Qing, and was prevalent in
   Asian consciousness throughout the twentieth century with the semi-legal
   existence of the Japanese colony of Manchukuo, even though there were
   very few professed 'Manchus' at the time in Manchukuo.
10 Crossley, *Manchus*, p. 113.
11 With the title applied retroactively to three previous incarnations of the
   Fifth Dalai Lama's teacher, Lobsang Chokyi Gyaltsen is often listed as the
   Fourth Panchen Lama.
12 Sam Van Schaik, *Tibet: A History* (New Haven, CT, 2011), p. 117.
13 'Teacher: Fifth Dalai Lama', Himalayan Art, www.himalayan art, accessed
   23 December 2012.
14 Giuseppe Tucci, *Tibetan Painted Scrolls* (Rome, 1949), p. 58.
15 Ibid., p. 64. Shigatse *dzong*, built in 1621, was completely destroyed, stone
   by stone, in the Cultural Revolution. In 2007 it was rebuilt, albeit to a
   more modest plan.
16 'Teacher: Fifth Dalai Lama'.
17 Tsepon W. D. Shakabpa, *Tibet: A Political History* (New York, 1984),
   pp. 106–9.
18 Ibid., p. 111.
19 Andreas Gruschke, 'Der Jonang-Orden: Gründe für seinen Niedergang,
   Voraussetzungen für das Überdauern und aktuell Lage', in *Tibet, Past and
   Present*, ed. Henk Blezer (Leiden, 2000), pp. 183–214.
20 P. Christiaan Klieger, *Tibetan Nationalism* (Berkeley, CA, 1992), p. 41.
21 Ibid., p. 41.
22 Shakabpa, *Tibet*, p. 114.
23 Ibid., p. 114.
24 Susan Naquin, *Peking: Temples and City Life, 1400–1900* (Berkeley, CA,
   2000), p. 311.
25 Ngag dbang blo bzang rgyatsho, *Du ku la'i gos bzang* (Autobiography of
   the Fifth Dalai Lama), in *The Illusive Play*, ed. Samden Karmey, vols I–III
   (Chicago, IL, 2014).
26 For the seating arrangement, see Zaharuddin Ahmad, *Sino-Tibetan
   Relations in the Seventeenth Century* (Rome, 1970), pp. 166–91. William
   Rockhill, *The Dalai Lamas of Tibet and their Relationship with the Manchu
   Emperors of China* ([Leiden, 1910], Dharamsala, 1998), p. 14.
28 The disparity between records is based on political differences in
   memorializing the event for later generations. Both the official Qing court
   records and the Tibetan ones are based in a subjective interpretation of
   the meetings. The Tibetan accounts are a basis for the claim that Tibet
   operated as an independent state at the time. Where records diverge
   significantly, I try to apply common sense to maintain a cogent narrative.
   For example, the young Shinzhi emperor most likely acted more like a
   Manchu khan than a Confucian emperor during these early years of the
   Qing in Beijing, and thus could receive the Dalai Lama as someone other
   than a subordinate. This was perhaps necessary for the still-consolidating
   Qing, but would be ignored later under the Kangxi and Qianlong.
28 Van Schaik, *Tibet*, p. 126.

29 Rockhill, *Dalai Lamas*, p. 14.

30 Ibid., p. 14. Note that Rockhill's Chin wang shuo sai is Heshuo qinwang, a 'Prince of the First Rank'.

31 Ibid., p. 80.

33 Shakabpa, *Tibet*, p. 116.

33 Samden Karmey, 'The Gold Seal: The Fifth Dalai Lama and the Emperor Shun-chih', in *The Arrow and the Spindle: Studies in History, Myths, Rituals and Beliefs in Tibet* (Kathmandu, 1998), vol. I, pp. 518–31.

34 Gray Tuttle, citing Gest Library's *Qingliang shan xinzhi* [1701], vol. III, 17a, and Yen-ching Library's edition, Wang Benzhi, *Qingliang shan jiyao* [Summary of Clear and Cool Mountain] [post-1780], vol. I, 63a, in 'Tibetan Buddhism at Wutai Shan in the Qing', *Journal of the International Association for Tibet Studies*, no. 6 (December 2011), pp. 168–74.

35 Alexander Gardner, 'The Fifth Dalai Lama', www.treasuryoflives.org, 2009, accessed 29 December 2012.

36 Robert Barnett, 'The Dalai Lama's "Deception": Why a Seventeenth-century Decree Matters to Beijing', *New York Review of Books*, www.nybooks.com, April 2011.

FOUR Qing Consolidation

1   See 'Some Poems of the Sixth Dalai Lama', Tibet Writes, www.tibetwrites.org, accessed 1 March 2013.

2   See Sam Van Shaik, *Tibet: A History* (New Haven, CT, 2011).

3   Ibid., p. 134.

4   Tsepon W. D. Shakabpa, *Tibet: A Political History* (New York, 1984), pp. 132–3.

5   'Cha de jung jung kar po / nga la shog tsel yar dang / thak ring gyang ne min dro / li thang gor ne leb yong.'

6   Shakabpa, *Tibet*, p. 134.

7   Jonathan Spence, *Emperor of China* (New York, 1974), p. 31.

8   Pamela Kyle Crossley, *The Manchus* (Oxford, 1997), p. 100.

9   Luciano Petech, *China and Tibet in the Early 18th Century* (Leiden, 1950), p. 100.

10 *Amban* in the singular.

11 Chu Wen-djang, *The Moslem Rebellion in North-west China, 1862–1878* (The Hague, 1966), p. 1.

12 Mark Elliott, *The Manchu Way* (Palo Alto, CA, 2001), p. 503.

13 See 'Battle of Qurman', www.battle-of-qurman.com, accessed 5 March 2013.

14 Shakabpa, *Tibet*, p. 153.

15 See Toni Huber, *The Holy Land Reborn: Pilgrimage and Tibetan Reinvention of Buddhism in India* (Chicago, IL, 2008). See also Shakabpa, *Tibet*, pp. 154–5.

16 Crossley, *The Manchus*, pp. 112–17.

17 Ibid., p. 115.

18 Ibid., p. 113.

19 Dkong chog' jigs me dbang po, the Second Jamchang Zhapa of Labdrang Trashikhil, *Sa skya'i gdung rab rin chen bang mdzod* ([late eighteenth

century] New Delhi, 1971). Cited in P. Christiaan Klieger, *Tibetan Nationalism* (Berkeley, CA, 1992), pp. 47–8.

20 Raoul Birnbaum, *Studies on the Mysteries of Mañjuśrī* (Charlottesville, VA, 1983). 'An ideal ruler in ancient Indian mythology who governs with justice rather than force and brings tranquillity and comfort to the people.' See 'Wheel-turning King', Nichiren Buddhism Library, www.nichirenlibrary.org, 3 February 2020.

21 David Farquhar, 'Emperor as Bodhisattva in the Governance of the Ch'ing Empire', *Harvard Journal of the Asia Society*, XXXVIII (1975), pp. 11–12.

22 Ibid., p. 9.

23 The legal ban by the Tibetan government on further Shamarpa incarnations remained in place until 1963, after the Dalai Lama had gone into exile. In the meantime, the Karmapa had been secretly recognizing the *tulku*.

24 Nik Douglas and Meryl White, *Karmapa: The Black Hat Lama of Tibet* (London, 1976), pp. 150–51.

25 Shakabpa, *Tibet*, p. 169. The Dingri base still exists, guarding now, as it did then, the road to Kathmandu.

26 Max Oidtmann, *Forging the Golden Urn* (New York, 2018). Warren W. Smith, Jr, *Tibetan Nation: A History of Tibetan Nationalism and Sino-Tibetan Relations* (New York, 1997).

27 Fourteenth Dalai Lama, 'Reincarnation', www.dalailama.com, 24 September 2011.

FIVE **Independence**

1 Abbé E. Huc, *Travels in Tartary, Thibet, and China [1844–1846]* ([1851] London, 1928), vol. II, p. 198.

2 Ibid., p. 203.

3 A second war with Nepal was fought in 1855–6. No Manchu troops were involved.

4 Tsepon W. D. Shakabpa, *Tibet: A Political History* (New York, 1984), p. 192.

5 Tibetan activist Jamyang Norbu commented in 2008, 'There has never been a study of the origins of modern Tibetan nationalism or national identity stemming from this period [1876–1912], nor a review of the factors that could have caused or influenced it.' Jamyang Norbu, Shadow Tibet, www.jamyangnorbu.com, 2008. This point, of course, is contested.

6 Shakabpa, *Tibet*, p. 198.

7 A dak bungalow was a government guest house. Many still exist in the Himalayan foothills, even in Upper Burma. Shakabpa, *Tibet*, p. 199.

8 Ibid., pp. 195–6.

9 L. A. Waddell, *Lhasa and its Mysteries* ([1905] New York, 1972).

10 Shakabpa, *Tibet*, p. 203.

11 Cited in Glenn Mullin, *Path of the Bodhisattva Warrior* (Ithaca, NY, 1988), pp. 109–10.

12 John Snelling. *Buddhism in Russia: The Story of Agvan Dorzhiev, Lhasa's Emissary to the Tsar* (Shaftesbury, 1993).

13 Shakabpa, *Tibet*, p. 209.

14 F. Spencer Chapman, *Lhasa: The Holy City* (London, 1938), p. 137.

15 Shakabpa, *Tibet*, p. 217.

16 Clare E. Harris, *The Museum on the Roof of the World* (Chicago, IL, 2012), pp. 52–78.

17 N. N. Knyazev, *Legendarnyi Baron: Neizvestnye Stranitsy Grazhdanskoi Voiny* (Moscow, 2004), p. 67.

18 See 'Khalkha Jetsun Dampa', www.wikipedia.org, accessed 3 February 2013.

19 Charles Bell, *Portrait of a Dalai Lama* (London, 1946), p. 77.

20 Ibid., p. 78.

21 S. L. Kuzmin, *Hidden Tibet: History of Independence and Occupation* (St Petersburg, 2010), p. 128.

22 Ibid., p. 129.

23 Sam Van Shaik, *Tibet: A History* (New Haven, CT, 2011), pp. 183–4.

24 Snelling, *Buddhism in Russia*.

25 This was not the only time that the Dalai Lama would encounter emanations of himself while on this extended exile. The tsar in St Petersburg was also considered a male White Tara in the Tibetan pantheon. Later the Dalai Lama would encounter Empress Dowager Cixi, a Kuan Yin, a female Avalokiteśvara. In general Buddhist practice, however, gender does not matter so much since the highly realized have transcended most earthly classifications. Multiple emanations are also no problem metaphysically, but discouraged due to the confusion it would cause in the earthly realms.

26 Van Schaik, *Tibet*, p. 182.

27 Shakabpa, *Tibet*, p. 220.

28 Bell, *Portrait*, p. 80.

29 Shakabpa, *Tibet*, p. 221.

30 Bell, *Portrait*, p. 80.

31 Cited in Elliot Sperling, 'The Thirteenth Dalai Lama at Wu Tai Shan', *Journal of the International Association of Tibetan Studies*, 6 (December 2011), pp. 394–402.

33 Ibid.

33 Ibid.

34 W. Rockhill, *The Dalai Lamas of Tibet and their Relationship with the Manchu Emperors of China* ([Leiden, 1910] Dharamsala, 1998), p. 64.

35 An 'Iron Cap' prince of the first degree was hereditary. Normally, Manchu titles would diminish by one degree with each succeeding generation. An 'Iron Cap' was immune from this diminution.

36 From Reginald Johnston, *Twilight in the Forbidden City* (London, 1934). Manchu language usage had been declining at court since the move to Beijing, despite numerous measures to keep it alive. In his coerced autobiography, Puyi stated that during his studies, he only managed to remember a single word of Manchu, *ili* ('arise'), for use at audiences. This is a statement his anti-Manchu jailers would have liked to have read, and thus is suspicious. Countering this was the Manchu language fluency of his uncle Prince Zaifeng, for example. Several members in succeeding generations became professional linguists in Jurchen and Manchu languages, notably university professors Jin Guangping, Jin Qizong

and Aisin-Gioro Ulhicun. See 'Aisin-Gioro', www.wikipedia.com, accessed 12 April 2012.

37 Shakabpa, *Tibet*, p. 222.

38 The western temple had a counterpart with the eastern temple, which was officiated by the resident Gelugpa *tulku* of Beijing. It was destroyed during the Cultural Revolution.

39 Guangxu was confined here by Cixi after the failure of his attempted reforms of 1898.

40 Years later when Puyi, then emperor of Manchukuo, met the Showa emperor of Japan in Tokyo, they shook hands and each displayed just the slightest of bows, according to newsreel footage of the event. It was the first and only time that the emperors of Japan and China met.

41 He confided this to Sir Charles Bell during his exile in India: Bell, *Portrait*, p. 85. Tsepon Shakapba suggests that Guangxu was drugged: *Tibet*, p. 222.

42 A reference to the Lode Star, Polaris, the axis upon which the universe turned.

43 Evelyn Rawski, *The Last Emperors* (Berkeley, CA, 1998), p. 46.

44 Ibid., p. 48.

45 'Obituary – Empress Dowager of China', *New York Times*, 20 November 1908.

46 Rockhill, *The Dalai Lamas*, p. 70.

47 Bell, *Portrait*, pp. 84–5.

48 The official accounts again differ. Rockhill cites the official court records that suggest the Dalai Lama performed the kowtow, with three prostrations and nine head knockings, in appreciation of the title and gifts bestowed. Nothing of the sort is suggested in the Tibetan accounts, and it is highly doubtful that the Dalai Lama would have consented, considering his obstinacy at the first audience.

49 Eric Teichman, *Travels of a Consular Officer in Eastern Tibet* (Cambridge, 1922), pp. 14–15. Translated from the Imperial Edict of 3 November 1908, *Chinese Government Gazette*.

50 Frederic Wakeman, *Fall of Imperial China* (New York, 1975).

51 Der Ling, a lady at the court of Cixi, made it a point to emphasize that, as an intimate, she knew the truth about the demise of the Guangxu emperor. Der Ling, *Old Buddha* (New York, 1929), p. 311.

52 Ibid., p. 312.

53 This was confessed by Der Ling. Forensic researchers confirmed that Guangxu's exhumed body contained about 187 times the amount of arsenic as other members of his court buried with him. See 'Arsenic Killed Qing Emperor, Experts Find', *New York Times*, 4 October 2008.

54 Der Ling wrote that she was present during this first meeting with the child. The empress dowager oddly showed studious disinterest in Puyi, except for the mere fact he was being presented to her. A calculated drama may have subtly suggested her choice of succession, and that she wished to continue her rule as regent during the infancy of the boy.

55 Rawski, *The Last Emperors*, p. 293.

56 It is possible he used the telephone, as he was among the first in Beijing to possess the device.

57 Cited in Van Schaik, *Tibet*, p. 181.

58 Shakabpa, *Tibet*, p. 223.

59 Dong Lin translated these throne screens, personal communication.
60 Isaac Taylor Headland, *Court Life in China: The Capital, its Officials, and People* (New York, 1909).
61 Der Ling, *Old Buddha*, p. 333. Her informant was the eunuch who succeeded Li Lien Ying under Puyi.
62 Headland, *Court Life in China*.
63 John O. P. Bland and Edmund Backhouse, *China under the Empress Dowager* (Philadelphia, PA, and London, 1914), pp. 468–9.
64 Headland, *Court Life in China*.
65 Rawski, *The Last Emperors*, p. 277.
66 Rockhill, *The Dalai Lamas*, p. 72.
67 Memorials to the Throne of December 1908, in Rawski, *The Last Emperors*, p. 387 nn. 53–4.
68 It was an article of the terms of 'Favourable Treatment' signed between the Republic of China and Empress Dowager Regent Longyu that the Guangxu emperor's entombment be taken care of by the succeeding regime. It may have been the cardinal point for securing the cooperative abdication of the emperor. Consistently the Aisin-Gioro had showed extreme filial piety towards their departed ancestors. In fact, Puyi's acceptance of the throne of Manchukuo in 1936 was largely motivated by revenge against the Republic of China for their desecration of Cixi's and Kangxi's graves by the Kuomingtang forces.
69 Parshotam Mehra, *Tibetan Polity, 1904–37: The Conflict between the 13th Dalai Lama and the 9th Panchen: A Case Study* (Wiesbaden, 1976), p. 19.
70 Bell, *Portrait*, p. 86.
71 Mullin, *Path of the Bodhisattva Warrior*, p. 73.
72 Berry Scott, *Monks, Spies and a Soldier of Fortune: The Japanese in Tibet* (New York, 1995).
73 Ibid., p. 88.
74 Ibid., p. 89.
75 Thubten Gyatso, *The Prophecies of the Great Thirteenth*, cited in Mullin, *Path of the Bodhisattva Warrior*, p. 110.
76 Santiago Lazcano Nebreda, 'Apuntes Ethno-Históricos Sobre el entiguo Reino Tibetano de Powo (sPo-bo) y su Ifluencia en el Himalaya Oriental' (unpublished manuscript, courtesy of author, 2003), p. 16.
77 Shakabpa, *Tibet*, p. 226.
78 Bell, *Portrait*, p. 95.
79 Ibid., p. 96.
80 Usually performed by casting dice. The deity behind the divination is believed to be Mañjuśrī.
81 Shakabpa, *Tibet*, p. 230.
82 Ibid., p. 101.
83 The crown prince was a scion of the Namgyal, the ancient royal family that also ruled the kingdom of Ladakh, also a former feudatory of Tibet.
84 Imperial decree of 25 February 1910. In Teichman, *Travels*, pp. 16–17.
85 Alastair Lamb, 'The McMahon Line: A Study in the Relations between India, China and Tibet, 1904 to 1914', in *The McMahon Line*, vol. II: *Hardinge, McMahon and the Simla Conference* (London, 1966), p. 277.

86 Shakabpa, *Tibet*, pp. 234–7.
87 Longyu was appointed regent with the resignation of Zaifeng after Yuan became prime minister.
88 On the war department, see Shakabpa, *Tibet*, p. 239. Alex McKay, *Tibet and the British Raj* (Richmond, 1997), p. 53.
89 Shakabpa, *Tibet*, p. 242.
90 McKay, *Tibet and the British Raj*, p. 54.
91 Hildegard Diemberger, *When a Woman Becomes a Religious Dynasty* (New York, 2007).
92 Bell, *Portrait*, p. 400.
93 Michael C. van Walt van Praag, 'A Legal Examination of the 1913 Mongolia–Tibet Treaty of Friendship and Alliance' (Ulaan Baator, manuscript courtesy of author, 2011).
94 Ibid., p.23.
95 International Court of Justice Advisory Opinion, 'Accordance with International Law of the Unilateral Declaration of Independence in respect of Kosovo, 22 July 2010', Para. 84, www.wikipedia.org, accessed 22 July 2010.
96 This phrase paraphrases the seal given to the Dalai Lama by the people of Tibet when he returned from Beijing.
97 Shakabpa, *Tibet*, pp. 246–8.
98 Van Walt van Praag, 'A Legal Examination', p. 24.
99 The year 1913 marked the tercentenary of the Romanov dynasty. While the tsar continued his pursuits in mysticism, it would be Rasputin rather than the Dalai Lama who would further titillate the tsar's spiritual interests, ultimately contributing to the continued downfall of the Russian Empire.
100 Van Schaik, *Tibet*, pp. 192–3.
101 Melvyn C. Goldstein, *A History of Modern Tibet, 1913–1951: The Demise of the Lamaist State* (Berkeley, CA, 1989), pp. 69–70.
102 Ibid., pp. 71, 73.
103 Comparison to the protectorate over the kingdom of Tonga by Britain is also relevant. Never technically a colony of the UK, Tonga has retained its autochthonous monarchy right through to the current Commonwealth.
104 Shakabpa, *Tibet*, p. 255.
105 King Sidkeong died a few months after the Simla Convention. Alexandra David-Neel was devastated but did not attend the cremation. Sidkeong had been pushing radical reforms that alienated the conservative clergy, aristocracy and even the British. Hope Cooke, the last *gyalmo* of Sikkim, says that her uncle had been poisoned by aconitum (wolf's bane) by his stepmother. Indeed, the queen mother's son Tashi immediately succeeded to the Sikkimese throne. See Barbara and Michael Foster, *The Secret Lives of Alexandra David-Neel: A Biography of the Explorer of Tibet and its Forbidden Practices* (Woodstock, NY, 1998), p. 113. The Namgyals continued their influence in Tibet, with Sidkeong's nephew Jigme Taring marrying Tsarong's daughter Mary and becoming a general in the Tibetan army and, later, a leading figure in the exiled Tibetan settlements in India.
106 Shakabpa, *Tibet*, p. 259.
107 Ibid., p. 260.
108 Van Shaik, *Tibet*, pp. 1997–8.

109 Goldstein, *A History of Modern Tibet*, pp. 111–12.

110 Letter from British trade agent in Gyantse to the political officer in Sikkim, 18 November 1922 (ibid., p. 133).

111 Van Shaik, *Tibet*, p. 199. Goldstein translates 'moth' as 'butterfly' (Goldstein, *A History of Modern Tibet*, p. 117).

112 Shakabpa, *Tibet*, p. 250.

113 K. Dhondup, *The Water-bird and Other Years* (New Delhi, 1986), pp. 57–78.

114 Transformed into a prison after the 1959 uprising.

115 Dhondup, *Water-bird*, p. 80.

116 Ibid., p. 81.

117 Ibid., pp. 59–60.

118 Bell, *Portrait*, p. 430. This is Bell's translation of the document.

119 The homeland of the Manchus is an invention, just like the autonym 'Manchu'. During late Qing times, the three provinces of this area were usually referred to as the Northeast (东北三省, Dōngběi Sānshěng). This label has stuck, making the region seem like an integral part of China. Manchuria was claimed by the Ming from 1380, when it was taken from the Mongol Northern Yuan dynasty. But the Ming were confronted by Jurchen leaders, who remained effectively independent. This eventually led to the creation of a state under Nurhaci. This state was, of course, independent of China by the end of the Ming.

120 Goldstein, *A History of Modern Tibet*, p. 233.

six A Bright and Sparkling Lama

1 See Melvyn Goldstein, *A History of Modern Tibet, 1913–1951: The Demise of the Lamaist State* (Berkeley, CA, 1989), vol. I: *A History of Modern Tibet, 1951–1955: The Calm Before the Storm* (Berkeley, 2009), vol. II: *A History of Modern Tibet, 1955–1957: The Storm Clouds Descend* (Berkeley, 2014), vol. III. Goldstein presents an almost day-by-day account of the last days of independent Tibet. Tsering Shakya also provides an enhanced account of modern Tibet's final expressions. See Tsering W. Shakya, *The Dragon in the Land of Snows: A History of Modern Tibet since 1947* (London, 1999).

2 'Fifth Reting Rinpoche', www.reting.org, accessed 6 November 2012.

3 Charles Bell, *Portrait of a Dalai Lama* (London, 1946), pp. 221–2.

4 Goldstein, *A History of Modern Tibet*, vol. I, p. 188.

5 Ibid., p. 186.

6 Ibid., p. 189.

7 Notably by Goldstein and the Fourteenth Dalai Lama.

8 The stupa of the Fifth Dalai Lama is even larger. The sandalwood structure is covered in nearly four metric tonnes of gold and 20,000 jewels. *Potala Palace* (New Delhi, n.d.), p. 92.

9 K. Dhondup, *The Water-bird and Other Years* (New Delhi, 1986), p. 100.

10 Witness accounts in Goldstein, *A History of Modern Tibet*, vol. I, p. 315.

11 Thupten Jigme Norbu, or Taktser Rinpoche.

12 H. E. Richardson of the British mission noted in a report that 'nothing was said about the selection being approved by the Chinese Government as had been done for every Dalai Lama since the Seventh. Thus the Tibetan

Government appears to have asserted their independence in a most important manner.' In Goldstein, *A History of Modern Tibet*, vol. I, p 324.

13 Ibid., p 328.
14 Tsepon W. D. Shakhabpa, *Tibet: A Political History* (New York, 1984), p. 285.
15 Ibid.
16 Yeshe Thaye and Pema Lhadren, 'The Life Story of the Lord of Refuge, Chadral Sangye Dorje Rinpoche', *Light of Lotus*, III (June 2000), pp. 7–43.
17 Clare E. Harris and Tsering Shakya, *Seeing Lhasa* (Chicago, IL, 2003), p. 107.
18 'Basil Gould', www.wikipedia.org, accessed 11 November 2012.
19 Ldab ldob. These monk bodyguards were selected for their size, which was made more pronounced by padding their shoulders and darkening their faces. Their ferocious reputation was fuelled by the allegations that they preyed upon handsome younger monks for sexual purposes, and did not hesitate to resort to kidnapping.
20 Christopher Hale, *Himmler's Crusade* (Hoboken, NJ, 2003).
21 Ibid.
22 Attributed to Namgyal Tsedron, Dzapon Choktray's wife. See Isrun Engelhardt, 'Tibet in 1938–1939: The Ernst Schäfer Expedition to Tibet', *Tibetan Buddhism in the West*, www.info-buddhism.com, accessed 24 May 2013.
23 Hale, *Himmler's Crusade*, p. 270.
24 Beger continued his profession as a physical anthropologist upon return to Germany. In fact, he worked with the ss during the war and was directly responsible for selecting at least 83 living people at Auschwitz to become part of a skeleton collection. He was charged with war crimes after the Second World War. Ibid., pp. 362–4.
25 Sambo, interview, cited in Goldstein, *A History of Modern Tibet*, vol. I, p. 357.
26 Fourteenth Dalai Lama, *The Heart of the Buddha's Path* (London, 1999), pp. 100–101.
27 Melvyn Goldstein, 'A Study of the *Ldab Ldob*', *Central Asiatic Journal*, IX/2 (1964), pp. 123–41.
28 Goldstein, *A History of Tibet*, vol. I, pp. 347–8.
29 *Ri bo bzas nas mi 'grangs / rgya mtsho 'thung nas mi ngom*. Quoted ibid., p. 344.
30 'Account of the Relationship between the Fifth Reting Rinpoche and Chatrul Sangye Dorje Rinpoche as related by one of Chatrul Rinpoche's Students', www.reting.org, accessed 22 November 2012.
31 Goldstein, *A History of Tibet*, vol. I, p. 378.
33 Ibid., pp. 434–5.
33 Ibid., p. 445.
34 Ibid., pp. 447–9.
35 Shakabpa, *Tibet*, p. 293.
36 Goldstein, *A History of Tibet*, vol. I, p. 473.
37 Recollection of Tsedrung Shartse Yeshe Thubten, prison guard, in Dhondup, *Water-bird*, pp. 201–2.
38 Ibid., p. 199.
39 Tsarong interview, cited in Goldstein, *A History of Tibet*, vol. I, p. 483.

40 Gyeten Namgyal, 'A Tailor's Tale, as recounted to Kim Yeshi', *Chö Yang*, 6 (1994), pp. 28–67.

41 Pebola (one of Reting's guards), interview. Cited in Goldstein, *A History of Modern Tibet*, vol. I, pp. 510–11.

42 Diki Tsering, *Dalai Lama, My Son: A Mother's Story*, ed. Khedroob Thondup (Harmondsworth, 2000), pp. 132–6.

43 Fourteenth Dalai Lama, *Freedom in Exile: The Autobiography of His Holiness the Dalai Lama of Tibet* (London, 1998), p. 32.

44 Fourteenth Dalai Lama, 'Concerning Dolgyal [Dorje Shungden] with Reference to Past Masters and Other Related Matters', www.dalailama.com, accessed 9 November 2012.

45 See 'Reting Rinpoche's Dating Sim', www.kongregate.com, accessed 25 February 2015.

SEVEN **Conquest**

1 Jamyang Norbu, 'Shadow Tibet', www.jamyangnorbu.com, 19 July 2008.

2 Tsepon W. D. Shakabpa, *Tibet: A Political History* (New York, 1984), pp. 294–5.

3 These were not the first Tibet passports. Goldstein cites the British commissioner's report to London, dated 1 June 1950 (FO371/84468) that the British government previously recognized four Tibetan passports in 1914, and one in 1920 on the recommendation of Charles Bell. See Melvyn Goldstein, *A Modern History of Tibet, 1913–1951: The Demise of the Lamaist State* (Berkeley, CA, 1989), vol. I, p. 654.

4 Shakabpa, *Tibet*, pp. 294–7.

5 Goldstein, *A History of Modern Tibet*, vol. I, pp. 576–8.

6 Ibid., p. 580.

7 Ibid., p. 581

8 Ibid., p. 603.

9 Ibid., p. 628.

10 J. Russell Morse and his family of the United Christian Missionary Society of USA fled into Upper Burma. They were successful in converting many eastern Tibeto-Burman speakers such as the Rawang and the Lisu to Pentecostal Christianity.

11 Jawaharlal Nehru, 'Declaration of Independence', www.constitutionofindia.net, accessed 9 March 2013.

12 Sam Van Shaik, *Tibet: A History* (New Haven, CT, 2011), p. 210.

13 Tsepon W. D. Shakabpa, *Bod kyi srid don rgyal rabs* (Kalimpong, 1976), vol. II, p. 4.

14 Goldstein, *A History of Modern Tibet*, vol. I, p. 676.

15 Ibid., p. 692.

16 Ibid., pp. 705–7.

17 Ibid., p. 686.

18 Telegram from British Foreign Office to the United Kingdom high commissioner in India (FO371/84454), dated 9 November 1950. Cited ibid., pp. 715–16.

19 Telegram from UK delegation to UN to British Foreign Office (FO371/84454), dated 14 November 1950. Cited ibid., p. 718.

20 Ibid., pp. 666–7.
21 'Domino Theory', www.wikipedia.org, accessed 5 April 2013.
22 Telegram from Secretary of State to U.S. Embassy in India (USFR, 793B00/5-2951), 2 June 1951. Cited in Goldstein, *A History of Modern Tibet*, vol. I, p. 780.
23 John Avedon, *In Exile from the Land of Snows* (New York, 1986), p. 39.
24 Kuzmin notes, 'In the first months of the Republic of China, among the Han establishment, debates about "five nationalities" took place. Differences related to the principles of the Great China (Da Zhongguo zhuyi) and Native China (Benbu Zhongguo). In early 1912, an article appeared with their summary. Proponents of the first principle recognized the Han as the only people capable of nation-building, denying that trait to the other four nations. Proponents of the second principle were in favour of granting independence to the "border" peoples, so as to secure the external borders. The latter remained in the minority. The first principle proponents triumphed, and the Mongols, Tibetans and the Turkic people were to be included in the republic to protect inner China, but to stop them from establishing their own states that could be used by foreign forces. This was how the concept of a "one Chinese nation" evolved. It was born only in the early 20th century under the influence from Western ideas of nationalism and the Han people's understanding of their Huaxia ancestors and their range.' Sergius Kuzmin, *Hidden Tibet: History of Independence and Occupation* (St Petersburg, 2010), p. 474.
25 Avedon, *In Exile from the Land of Snows*, p. 56.
26 Ibid., p. 58.

EIGHT The Two Tibets

1 'Protest and Uprisings in Tibet since 1950', www.wikipedia.com, accessed 19 April 2013.
2 Sam Van Schaik, *Tibet: A History* (New Haven, CT, 2011), pp. 239–40.
3 Fourteenth Dalai Lama, *Freedom in Exile* (London, 1998), p. 161.
4 Tsepon W. D. Shakabpa, *Tibet: A Political History* (New York, 1984), p. 320.
5 Tsering Shakya, *The Dragon in the Land of Snows: A History of Modern Tibet since 1947* (London, 1999), p. 225.
6 A challenge to the old norm of non-intervention in the internal affairs of other states.
7 Shakya, *Dragon*, p. 231.
8 Shakabpa, *Tibet*, p. 323.
9 Shakya, *Dragon*, p. 234.
10 Ibid., p. 280.
11 Ibid., p. 209.
12 Ibid., p. 246.
13 Tenth Panchen Lama, *A Poisoned Arrow: The Secret Report of the 10th Panchen Lama* (London, 1998).
14 Anne F. Thurston, 'Urban Violence during the Cultural Revolution: Who Is to Blame?', in *Violence in China: Essays in Culture and Counterculture*, ed. Jonathan N. Lipman and Stevan Harrell (Albany, NY, 1990), pp. 154–7.
15 Old ideas, old culture, old customs and old habits.

16 Thomas Laird, *The Story of Tibet: Conversations with the Dalai Lama* (New York, 2006), p. 126.

17 Van Shaik, *Tibet*, p. 247.

18 David L. McMahan, *The Making of Buddhist Modernism* (Oxford, 2008), p. 320.

19 Melvyn Goldstein, *The Snow Lion and the Dragon* (Berkeley, CA, 1997), p. 61.

20 Ibid., pp. 64–5. Curiously, Goldstein does not mention the fourth point.

21 P. Christiaan Klieger, 'Shangri-La and the Politicization of Tourism in Tibet', *Annals of Tourism Research*, XIX/1 (1992), pp. 122–5.

22 Gabrielle Lafitte, personal communication, 2014.

23 Klieger, 'Tourism in Tibet'.

24 Clare E. Harris, *Museum on the Roof of the World: Art, Politics, and the Representation of Tibet* (Chicago, IL, 2012).

26 Goldstein, *The Snow Lion*, pp. 73–4.

25 Senator Daniel Inouye, personal communication, 1978.

28 Goldstein, *The Snow Lion*, pp. 76–7.

27 The appeal was misinterpreted in Dharamsala as a denouncement of the Dalai Lama. When the man finally returned to McLeod Ganj, he and his family were subject to street gossip and derision. The guide eventually emigrated to Germany. See P. Christiaan Klieger, *Tibet-o-Rama: Self and Other in a Tale from the Edge of Tibet* (San Francisco, CA, 2002).

29 Goldstein, *The Snow Lion*, p. 82.

30 As noted previously, Manchu identity simply went underground, vigorously reappearing when it was again fashionable to be a Manchu.

31 Goldstein, *The Snow Lion*, pp. 84–5.

33 'UN Universal Declaration of Human Rights', Article 28, www.un.org, accessed 31 May 2013.

33 See Goldstein, *The Snow Lion*, p. 110.

34 'Taiwan: Spiritual Leader of Tibet Dalai Lama Press Conference', AP Archive, www.aparchive.com, 24 March 1997.

35 David Van Biema, 'The Dalai Lama's Buddhist Foes', *Time*, www.time.com, appended version 22 July 2008.

36 David Lague, Paul Mooney and Benjamin Kang Lim, 'China Co-opts a Buddhist Sect in Global Effort To Smear Dalai Lama', www.reuters.com, 21 December 2015.

37 International Campaign for Tibet, 'Tracking the Steel Dragon: How China's Economic Policies and the Railroad Are Transforming Tibet', www.savetibet.org, 28 February 2008.

38 See 'Transcript: James Miles interview on Tibet', CNN, www.cnn.com, 20 March 2008.

39 See '2008 Summer Olympics Torch Relay', www.wikipedia.org, accessed 12 March 2013.

40 See 'Self-immolation', www.savetibet.org, accessed 13 March 2019.

41 Bhuchung D. Sonam, 'We Must Love the Party', Tibet Writes, www.tibetwrites.org, 13 May 2013.

42 Huang Yanzhong, 'The Dalai Lama's Self-immolation Dilemma', Asia Unbound, www.cfr.org, accessed 13 May 2013.

NINE Charting a Tibet without Tibet

1 See Vladimir Lenin's 'Fourth Letter from Afar', 25 March 1917, quoted in Antonio Cassese, *International Law* (Oxford, 2004), p. 131.
2 Michael van Walt van Praag, *The Status of Tibet* (Boulder, CO, 1987), p. 87.
3 Sergius Kuzmin, *Hidden Tibet: History of Independence and Occupation* (St Petersburg, 2010), p. 500.
4 Ibid., p. 503.
5 Owen Lattimore, *Inner Asian Frontiers of China* (New York, 1940), p. 381.
6 Thomas E. Ewing, *Between the Hammer and the Anvil: Chinese and Russian Policies in Outer Mongolia, 1911–1921* (Bloomington, IN, 1980), pp. 49–50.
7 Thomas E. Ewing, 'Russia, China, and the Origins of the Mongolian People's Republic, 1911–1921: A Reappraisal', *Slavonic and East European Review*, LVIII/3 (July 1980), pp. 399, 414–15, 417, 421.
8 Walter Heissig, *The Lost Civilization: The Mongols Rediscovered* (New York, 1966), pp. 186, 193, 202–3.
9 See 'Pan-Mongolism', www.wikipedia.com, accessed 27 November 2012.
10 See 'China Bans Reincarnation without Government Permission', MSNBC, archived at www.huffingtonpost.com, 22 August 2007.
11 Fourteenth Dalai Lama, 'Statement of His Holiness the Fourteenth Dalai Lama, Tenzin Gyatso, on the Issue of His Reincarnation', www.dalailama. com, 24 September 2011.
12 See 'China Warns Dalai Lama About Choosing Successor', Voice of America, www.voanew.com, 25 September 2011.
13 Max Weber, 'Politics as Vocation', in *Economy and Society: An Outline of Interpretive Sociology*, ed. Guenther Roth and Claus Wittich ([1911] New York, 1968), p. 29.
14 Edward Rhoads, *Manchus and Han: Ethnic Relations and Political Power in Late Qing and Early Republican China, 1861–1928* (Seattle, WA, 2000), p. 282.
15 For example, see Victor Mair, 'Manchu Film', Language Log, www. languagelog.idc.upenn.edu, 31 December 2012.
16 Examples include Margaret Nowak, *Tibetan Refugees* (New Brunswick, NJ, 1984); Ann Forbes, *Settlements of Hope* (Cambridge, MA, 1989); P. Christiaan Klieger, *Accomplishing Tibetan Identity: The Constitution of a National Consciousness* (Honolulu, HI, 1989); Thomas Methfessel, '35 Jahre Tibeter im Exil', PhD thesis, Philipps-Universität Marburg, 1994.
17 P. Christiaan Klieger, *The Microstates of Europe: Designer Nations in a Post-modern World* (Lanham, MD, 2013).
18 Ibid.
19 Cited in P. Christiaan Klieger, 'Free Tibet, Ready or Not', paper read at International Studies Association conference, New York City, February 2009, panel 'Who's Afraid of China's Tibet?'
20 Cited ibid.
21 Shanshan Du, 'Social Media and the Transformation of Chinese Nationalism', *Anthropology Today*, XXX/1 (February 2014), pp. 5–8.

BIBLIOGRAPHY

Ahmad, Zaharuddin, *Sino-Tibetan Relations in the Seventeenth Century* (Rome, 1970)

Aldenderfer, Mark, 'Defining Zhang Zhung Ethnicity', in *Discoveries in Western Tibet and the Western Himalayas*, ed. Amy Heller and Giacomella Orofino (Leiden, 2007)

'Autobiography of the Fifth Dalai Lama', www.dalailama.com, accessed 17 November 2012

Avedon, John, *In Exile from the Land of Snows* (New York, 1986)

Barnett, Robert, 'The Dalai Lama's "Deception": Why a Seventeenth-century Decree Matters to Beijing', *New York Review of Books*, www.nybooks.com, April 2011

Beckwith, Christopher I., *The Tibetan Empire in Central Asia: A History of the Struggle for Great Power among Tibetans, Turks, Arabs, and Chinese during the Early Middle Ages* (Princeton, NJ. 1987)

Bell, Charles, *Portrait of a Dalai Lama* (London, 1946)

Bellezza, John, *Spirit Mediums, Sacred Mountains and Related Bon Textual Traditions in Upper Tibet: Calling Down the Gods* (Leiden, 2005)

—, *Zhangzhung: Foundations of Civilization in Tibet* (Vienna, 2008)

Berger, Patricia, *Empire of Emptiness* (Honolulu, HI, 2003)

Birnbaum, Raoul, *Studies on the Mysteries of Mañjuśrī* (Charlottesville, VA, 1983)

Bland, John O. P., and Edmund Backhouse, *China under the Empress Dowager* (Philadelphia, PA, and London, 1914)

Cassese, Antonio, *International Law in a Divided World* (New York, 1986)

Chapman, F. Spencer, *Lhasa: The Holy City* (London, 1938)

—, *Rebellion in Northwest China 1862–1878* ([1940] The Hague, 1966)

Chhaya, Mayank, *Dalai Lama: Man, Monk, Mystic* (New York, 2007)

Chu Wen-djang, *The Moslem Rebellion in North-west China, 1862–1878* (The Hague, 1966)

Clift, Peter, and J. Blusztajn, 'Reorganization of the Western Himalayan River System after Five Million Years Ago', *Nature*, 438 (2005), pp. 1001–3

Committee of 100 for Tibet and the Dalai Lama Foundation, *The Missing Peace* (San Rafael, CA, 2005)

Crossley, Pamela Kyle, *The Manchus* (Oxford, 1997)

Dalai Lama, Fourteenth, 'A Talk on Dolgyal by H.H. the Dalai Lama during the Course of Religious Teachings in Dharamsala', www.dalailama.com, April 1997

Freedom in Exile: The Autobiography of His Holiness the Dalai Lama of Tibet
 (London, 1998)
—, *The Heart of the Buddha's Path* (London, 1999)
Der Ling, *Old Buddha* (New York, 1929)
Dhondup, K., *The Water-bird and Other Years* (New Delhi, 1986)
Diemberger, Hildegard, *When a Woman Becomes a Religious Dynasty*
 (New York, 2007)
Dkong chog' jigs me dbang po, the Second Jamchang Zhapa of Labdrang
 Trashikhil, *Sa skya'i gdung rab rin chen bang mdzod* ([late eighteenth
 century] New Delhi, 1971)
Douglas, Nik, and Meryl White, *Karmapa: The Black Hat Lama of Tibet*
 (London, 1976)
Dreyfus, Georges, 'Cherished Memories, Cherished Communities:
 Proto-Nationalism in Tibet', in *The History of Tibet*, vol. II: *The Medieval
 Period; c. AD 850–1895, the Development of Buddhist Paramountcy*
 (New York, 2003)
—, 'The Shugden Affair: Origins of a Controversy (Part I)', Office of H.H. the
 Dalai Lama, www.dalailama.com, accessed 16 November 2012
Dutt, Ramesh, *Buddhism and Buddhist Civilisation in India* (Delhi, 1983)
Elliott, Mark, *The Manchu Way* (Palo Alto, CA, 2001)
Engelhardt, Isrun, 'Tibet in 1938–1939: The Ernst Schäfer Expedition to Tibet',
 Tibetan Buddhism in the West, www.info-buddhism.com, accessed
 24 May 2013
Ewing, Thomas E., *Between the Hammer and the Anvil: Chinese and Russian
 Policies in Outer Mongolia, 1911–1921* (Bloomington, IN, 1980)
—, 'Russia, China, and the Origins of the Mongolian People's Republic,
 1911–1921: A Reappraisal', *Slavonic and East European Review*, LVIII/3
 (July 1980)
Falk, Richard, 'Self-determination under International Law', in *The
 Self-determination of Peoples*, ed. Wolfgang Danspeckgruber
 (Boulder, CO, 2002)
Farquhar, David, 'Emperor as Bodhisattva in the Governance of the Ch'ing
 Empire', *Harvard Journal of the Asia Society*, XXXVIII (1975)
Forbes, Ann Armbrecht, *Settlements of Hope* (Cambridge, MA, 1989)
Foster, Barbara and Michael, *The Secret Lives of Alexandra David-Neel:
 A Biography of the Explorer of Tibet and Its Forbidden Practices*
 (Woodstock, NY, 1998)
Gardner, Alexander, 'The Fifth Dalai Lama', www.treasuryoflives.org, 2009,
 accessed 29 December 2012
Goldstein, Melvyn, 'Study of the *Ldab Ldob*', *Central Asiatic Journal*, I/2
 (1964)
—, *A History of Modern Tibet, 1913–1951: The Demise of the Lamaist State*
 (Berkeley, CA, 1989), vol. I
—, *The Snow Lion and the Dragon* (Berkeley, CA, 1997)
—, *A History of Modern Tibet, 1951–1955: The Calm Before the Storm*
 (Berkeley, CA, 2009), vol. II
—, *A History of Modern Tibet, 1955–1957: The Storm Clouds Descend*
 (Berkeley, CA, 2014), vol. III

Grupper, S., 'Review of Hans-Rainer Kampfe, "Ni ma'i od zer/Naranu gerel: Die Biographie des 2. Pekinger, Lchan skya-Qutuqtu Rol pa'I rdo rje (1717–1789)"', *Journal of the Tibet Society*, IV (1984)

Gruschke, Andreas, 'Der Jonang-Orden: Gründe für seinen Niedergang, Voraussetzungen für das Überdauern und aktuell Lage', in *Tibet, Past and Present*, ed. Henk Blezer (Leiden, 2000)

Hale, Christopher, *Himmler's Crusade* (Hoboken, NJ, 2003)

Hannum, Hurst, 'Self-determination, Yugoslavia, and Europe: Old Wine in New Bottles?', *Transnational Law and Contemporary Problems*, III (1993)

Harris, Clare E., *The Museum on the Roof of the World: Art, Politics and the Representation of Tibet* (Chicago, IL, 2012)

—, and Tsering Shakya, *Seeing Lhasa* (Chicago, IL, 2003)

Headland, Isaac Taylor, *Court Life in China: The Capital, its Officials, and People* (New York, 1909)

Heissig, Walter, *The Lost Civilization: The Mongols Rediscovered* (New York, 1966)

Huang Yanzhong, 'The Dalai Lama's Self-immolation Dilemma', Asia Unbound, www.cfr.org, accessed 13 May 2013

Huber, Toni, *The Holy Land Reborn: Pilgrimage and Tibetan Reinvention of Buddhism in India* (Chicago, IL, 2008)

Huc, Abbé Évariste, *Travels in Tartary, Thibet and China [1844–1846]*, vol. II (London, 1928) [*Souvenirs d'un voyage dans la Tartarie, le Thibet, et la Chine pendant les années 1844, 1845 et 1846* (Paris, 1851)]

International Campaign for Tibet, 'Tracking the Steel Dragon: How China's Economic Policies and the Railroad Are Transforming Tibet', www.savetibet.org, 28 February 2008

International Court of Justice Advisory Opinion, 'Accordance with International Law of the Unilateral Declaration of Independence in respect of Kosovo', Para. 84, www.wikipedia.org, 22 July 2010

Johnston, Reginald, *Twilight in the Forbidden City* (London, 1934)

'Kagyu Lineage: The Second Karmapa, Karma Phakshi (1205–1283)', www.kagyuoffice.org, accessed 2 February 2013

Kane, Stephanie, *Aids Alibis: Sex, Drugs, and Crime in the Americas* (Philadelphia, PA, 1998)

Karmey, Samten G., 'The Gold Seal: The Fifth Dalai Lama and Emperor Shun-chih', in *The Arrow and the Spindle: Studies in History, Myths, Rituals and Beliefs in Tibet* (Kathmandu, 1998), vol. I, pp. 518–31

Klieger, P. Christiaan, 'Tourism in Tibet and the Role of Tibetan Refugees', *Tibetan Review*, XXIII/2 (1988)

—, 'Accomplishing Tibetan Identity: The Constitution of a National Consciousness', PhD thesis, University of Hawaii, 1989

—, 'Shangri-La and the Politicization of Tourism in Tibet', *Annals of Tourism Research*, XIX/1 (1992)

—, *Tibetan Nationalism* (Berkeley, CA, 1992)

—, *Tibet-o-Rama: Self and Other in a Tale from the Edge of Tibet* (San Francisco, CA, 2002)

—, 'A Tale of the Tibeto-Burman Pygmies', in *Tibetan Borderlands*, ed. P. Christiaan Klieger (Leiden, 2006)

—, 'Free Tibet, Ready or Not', paper read at International Studies Association Conference, New York City, panel 'Who's Afraid of China's Tibet?', February 2009

—, *The Microstates of Europe: Designer Nations in a Post-modern World* (Lanham, MD, 2013)

Knyazev, N. N., *Legendarnyi Baron: Neizvestnye Stranitsy Grazhdanskoi Voiny* (Moscow, 2004)

Komroff, Manuel, 'The Journal of Friar Odoric', in *Contemporaries of Marco Polo* (New York, 1928)

Kuzmin, S. L, *Hidden Tibet: History of Independence and Occupation* (St Petersburg, 2010)

Laird, Thomas, *The Story of Tibet: Conversations with the Dalai Lama* (New York, 2006)

Lamb, Alastair, 'The McMahon Line: A Study in the Relations between India, China and Tibet, 1904 to 1914', in *The McMahon Line*, vol. II: *Hardinge, McMahon and the Simla Conference* (London, 1966)

Lattimore, Owen, *Manchuria: Cradle of Conflict* (New York, 1935)

—, *Inner Asian Frontiers of China* (New York, 1940)

Lazcano Nebreda, Santiago, 'Apuntes Ethno-Históricos Sobre el entiguo Reino Tibetano de Powo (sPo-bo) y su Ifluencia en el Himalaya Oriental' (unpublished manuscript courtesy of author, n.d.)

Lin, Shen-Yu, 'Pehar: A Historic Survey', *Revue d'Etudes Tibétaines* (19 October 2010)

Lipman, Jonathan N., and Stevan Harrell, eds, *Violence in China: Essays in Culture and Counterculture* (Albany, NY, 1990)

Lopez, Donald S., Jr, *The Heart Sutra Explained: Indian and Tibetan Commentaries* (Albany, NY, 1988)

McGranahan, Carole, *Arrested Histories: Tibet, the CIA, and Memories of a Forgotten War* (Durham, NC, 2010)

McKay, Alex, *Tibet and the British Raj* (Richmond, 1997)

McMahan, David L., *The Making of Buddhist Modernism* (Oxford, 2008)

Mehra, Parshotam, *Tibetan Polity, 1904–37: The Conflict between the 13th Dalai Lama and the 9th Panchen: A Case Study* (Wiesbaden, 1976)

Methfessel, Thomas, '35 Jahre Tibeter im Exil', PhD thesis, Philipps-Universität Marburg, 1994

Mullin, Glenn, *Path of the Bodhisattva Warrior* (Ithaca, NY, 1988)

Namgyal, Gyeten, 'A Tailor's Tale, as recounted to Kim Yeshi', *Chö Yang*, 6 (1994), pp. 28–67

Naquin, Susan, *Peking: Temples and City Life, 1400–1900* (Berkeley, CA, 2000)

Nehru, Jawaharlal, 'Declaration of Independence', www.cs.nyu.edu, accessed 9 March 2013

Ngag dbang blo bzang rgyatsho, *Du ku la'i gos bzang* (Autobiography of the Fifth Dalai Lama), in *The Illusive Play*, vols I–III, ed. Samden Karmey (Chicago, IL, 2014)

Norbu, Jamyang, 'Shadow Tibet', www.jamyangnorbu.com, 19 July 2008

Norbu, Namkhai, *Drung, Deu and Bön* (Dharamsala, 1995)

Nowak, Margaret, *Tibetan Refugees: A New Generation of Meaning* (New Brunswick, NJ, 1984)

Oidtmann, Max, *Forging the Golden Urn* (New York, 2018)

Oppenheimer, Stephen, *Out of Eden* (London, 2003)

Panchen Lama, Tenth, *A Poisoned Arrow: The Secret Report of the 10th Panchen Lama* (London, 1998)

Paul, Robert, *The Tibetan Symbolic World* (Chicago, IL, 1982)

Pearlman, Ellen, *Tibetan Sacred Dance: A Journey into the Religious and Folk Traditions* (Rochester, VT, 2002)

Petech, Luciano, *China and Tibet in the Early 18th Century* (Leiden, 1950)

Potala Palace (New Delhi, n.d.)

Prasse-Freeman, Elliott, 'Scapegoating in Burma', *Anthropology Today*, XXIX/4 (August 2013)

Rawski, Evelyn S., *The Last Emperors* (Berkeley, CA, 1998)

Rhoads, Edward J. M., *Manchus and Han: Ethnic Relations and Political Power in Late Qing and Early Republican China, 1861–1928* (Seattle, WA, 2000)

Ringu Tulku, 'The Rimé (Ris-med) Movement of Jamgon Kontrul the Great', paper read at the 7th Conference of the International Association for Tibetan Studies, June 1995, www.abuddhistlibrary.com, accessed 17 November 2012

Rockhill, W., *The Dalai Lamas of Tibet and their Relationship with the Manchu Emperors of China* ([Leiden, 1910] Dharamsala, 1998)

Sahlins, Marshall, *Historical Metaphors and Mythical Realities* (Ann Arbor, MI, 1981)

Scott, Berry, *Monks, Spies and a Soldier of Fortune: The Japanese in Tibet* (New York, 1995)

Scott, David A., 'Buddhism and Islam: Past to Present Encounters and Interfaith Lessons', *Numen,* XLII/2 (May 1995), pp. 141–55

Shakabpa, Tsepon W. D. (Dbang phyug bde ldan Zhwa sgab pa), *Bod kyi srid don rgyal rabs*, vol. II (Kalimpong, 1976)

—, *Tibet: A Political History* (New York, 1984)

Shakya, Tsering, *The Dragon in the Land of Snows: A History of Modern Tibet since 1947* (New York, 1999)

Sleeter, Christine, 'State Curriculum Standards and the Shaping of Student Consciousness', *Social Justice*, XXIX/4 (2002), pp 8–25

Smith, Warren W., Jr, *Tibetan Nation: A History of Tibetan Nationalism and Sino-Tibetan Relations* (New York, 1997)

Snelling, John, *Buddhism in Russia: The Story of Agvan Dorzhiev, Lhasa's Emissary to the Tsar* (Shaftesbury, 1993)

'Some Poems of the Sixth Dalai Lama', Tibet Writes, www.tibetwrites.org, accessed 1 March 2013

Sonam, Bhuchung D., 'We Must Love the Party', Tibet Writes, www.tibetwrites. org, 13 May 2013

Spence, Jonathan, *Emperor of China* (New York, 1974)

Sperling, Elliott, 'The Thirteenth Dalai Lama at Wu Tai Shan', *Journal of the International Association of Tibetan Studies*, 6 (December 2011), pp. 394–402

Teichman, Eric, *Travels of a Consular Officer in Eastern Tibet* (Cambridge, 1922)

Thaye, Yeshe, and Pema Lhadren, 'The Life Story of the Lord of Refuge, Chadral Sangye Dorje Rinpoche', *Light of Lotus*, III (June 2000), pp. 7–43

Thurston, Anne F., 'Urban Violence during the Cultural Revolution: Who Is to Blame?', in *Violence in China: Essays in Culture and Counterculture*, ed. Jonathan N. Lipman and Stevan Harrell (Albany, NY, 1990)

Tsering, Diki, *Dalai Lama, My Son: A Mother's Story*, ed. Khedroob Thondup (Harmondsworth, 2000)

Tucci, Giuseppe, *Tibetan Painted Scrolls* (Rome, 1949)

Tuttle, Grey, 'Tibetan Buddhism at Wutai Shan in the Qing', *Journal of the International Association of Tibetan Studies*, 6 (December 2011), pp. 163–214

Van Shaik, Sam, *Tibet: A History* (New Haven, CT, 2011)

Van Walt van Praag, Michael C., 'A Legal Examination of the 1913 Mongolia–Tibet Treaty of Friendship and Alliance' (manuscript courtesy of author, Ulaan Baator, 2011)

Waddell, L. A., *Lhasa and its Mysteries* ([1905] New York, 1972).

Wakeman, Frederic, *Fall of Imperial China* (New York, 1975)

Wandu, Pasang, and Hildegard Diemberger, *dBa' bzhed: The Royal Narrative concerning the Bringing of the Buddha's Doctrine to Tibet* (Vienna, 2000)

Weber, Max, 'Politics as Vocation', in *Wirtschaft und Gesellschaft* ([1911] Tübingen, 1921)

Zemay Rinpoche, *The Yellow Book* (*Thunder of the Stirring Black Cloud: The Oral Transmission of the Intelligent Father*), www.holybooks.com [1973], accessed 19 November 2012

ACKNOWLEDGEMENTS

For a book like this, which attempts to paint the entire history of the Tibetan state in broad strokes, the litany of preceptors, mentors, colleagues, friends, lamas, officials and maybe a few antagonists who have in some way contributed to its production can be extensive. There are a few who deserve special consideration. First, it is a pleasure to acknowledge the inspirational roots of this book. The idea hatched back in 2008 at a panel at a meeting of the Association of Asian Studies in Atlanta, Georgia, USA, organized by Dibyesh Anand, and evocatively entitled 'Who's Afraid of China's Tibet?' At that time, it was close to the fiftieth anniversary of the Tibetan uprising that sent the Fourteenth Dalai Lama into exile. My colleagues were thinking about the future of the institution of the Dalai Lama, Tenzin Gyatso's impasse in negotiating with China, the Dalai Lama's age, the Free Tibet movement, and the momentum of rapid development in China's Tibet. I am perhaps most inspired by discussions with archaeologist John Bellezza, whose pioneering work in Tibetan prehistory will take lifetimes to fully appreciate. I am also humbled by the powerful support of the Tibetological community, who have had the grace and patience to get through my hallucinatory memoir, *Tibet-o-Rama* (2002), and nevertheless encourage a more continent description of Tibetan history.

I am appreciative to my fellow board members of the Committee of 100 for Tibet who patiently listened to my ideas and interpretations of Tibetan political history, and who offered many useful suggestions and provided me with many opportunities to continue to engage with 'Tibet abroad'. In particular, Kazur Tenzin N. Tethong, former prime minister of the Ganden Phodrang-in-exile and a respected and veteran voice in the Tibetan world, has always been available and generous in his comments. Thanks also to the support of Darlene Markowitz, formerly of the Dalai Lama Foundation. I am inspired by the academic and political career of colleague Lobsang Sangay, who is now the *sikyong* or president of the Tibetan government-in-exile. Acknowledgements are respectfully given to His Serene Highness Prince Hans-Adam II of Liechtenstein and his Institute for Self-determination at Princeton, NJ, who helped me develop an understanding of nationalism among microstates. I am indebted to the late sovereign of the Order of Malta, Prince-Grand Master Frà Andrew Bertie. I have been inspired by discussions with Michael van Walt van Praag and Sergius Kuzmin regarding the status of Tibet under international law. Thanks to the great icons of modern Tibetan studies, Robbie Barnett, Melvyn Goldstein and Donald Lopez, Jr, for tolerating a litany of pesky questions. Thanks to Clare Harris at the Pitt Rivers Museum and Magdalen College at Oxford University for her ideas on Tibetan imagery.

Thanks also to my skilled research assistant and friend, Jamyang Lhawang, for spell-checking my Tibetan transliterations. The useful comments of editor Michael Leaman, and other editors and readers, have helped me polish an often unwieldy manuscript.

PHOTO ACKNOWLEDGEMENTS

The author and publishers wish to express their thanks to the below sources of illustrative material and/or permission to reproduce it. Every effort has been made to contact copyright holders; should there be any we have been unable to reach or to whom inaccurate acknowledgements have been made please contact the publishers, and full adjustments will be made to any subsequent printings. Some locations of artworks are also given below, in the interest of brevity:

Photo John Ackerly, reproduced with permission: p. 283; American Geographical Society Library, University of Wisconsin-Milwaukee: pp. 89, 93; photo Anonymous/AP/Shutterstock: p. 282; The Art Museum Riga Bourse: p. 172; from Charles Bell, *Tibet Past and Present* (Oxford, 1924): p. 180; photo John V. Bellezza, reproduced with permission: pp. 20–21; Bibliothèque de l'Arsenal, Paris: p. 56; Bibliothèque nationale de France, Paris: p. 124; Bodleian Libraries, University of Oxford: p. 46; The British Museum, London: pp. 71, 205, 206, 209, 255; Das Bundesarchiv, Koblenz (Bild 135-S-13-11-15): p. 215; from Edmund Candler, *The Unveiling of Lhasa* (London, 1905): p. 131; iStock.com/mamahoohooba: pp. 182–3; Landesarchiv Saarbrücken, Staatskanzlei des Saarlandes Open Gallery: p. 148; Library of Congress, Prints and Photographs Division, Washington, DC: pp. 117, 174; photo Curtis Means/NBC NewsWire via Getty Images: p. 295; Mitchell Library, State Library of New South Wales, Sydney: pp. 119, 181; Museo Civico d'Arte, Pordenone: p. 57; Museum aan de Stroom, Antwerp: pp. 134–5; Museum für Völkerkunde, Hamburg: p. 97 (foot); NASA image created by Jesse Allen, using data provided courtesy of NASA/GSFC/METI/ERSDAC/JAROS, and U.S./Japan ASTER Science Team: p. 310; Norbulingka Palace, Lhasa: p. 81; Official White House Photo by Pete Souza: p. 314; The Palace Museum, Beijing: pp. 66, 100, 143; courtesy Perry-Castañeda Library, The University of Texas at Austin: pp. 260–61; © Pitt Rivers Museum, University of Oxford (PRM 1998_285_136-P): p. 184; Potala Palace, Lhasa: p. 92; © President and Fellows of Harvard College, Harvard Art Museums/ Fogg Museum, Cambridge, MA: p. 145; private collection: pp. 18 (foot), 19, 24, 33, 68–9, 77, 97 (top), 114–15, 122–3, 130, 142, 167, 219, 237, 242, 244, 245, 248, 249, 250–51, 252, 254, 256; from Ferdinand Freiherr von Richthofen, *China: Ergebnisse eigener Reisen und darauf gegründeter Studien*, vol. I (Berlin, 1877), photo courtesy National Institute of Informatics, 'Digital Silk Road'/Toyo Bunko, Tokyo: pp. 8–9; Royal Collection Trust/© Her Majesty Queen Elizabeth II 2021: p. 121; The Rubin Museum of Art, New York: pp. 30–31, 40, 49, 53, 74, 88; Jeff Schmaltz, MODIS Rapid Response Team, NASA/GSFC: p. 315; courtesy TibetDiscovery.com: p. 300; photo Gary Lee Todd: p. 34.

INDEX

Illustration page numbers are in *italics*